Chapter 8

Crater Lake and the Rustless Iron and Steel Company: 1935-1938

By the spring of 1935, I had not yet completed the comprehensive examination at Berkeley for my dissertation, my three years as teaching assistant had run out, and, being married, I had to get a job. Dr. Warren D. Smith at Oregon, who always kept track of his former graduates, wrote that he was to be Ranger Naturalist at Crater Lake National Park that summer and that there were several similar positions open.

Although I had already applied for a job with the Soil Conservation Service on the Navajo Reservation in New Mexico (where, 18 years later, I was to spend two years), I also applied at Crater Lake. The SCS job disappeared when the agency was shifted from Interior to Agriculture, so I arrived at Crater Lake early in June, among ten-foot high snow drifts. I had spent my last penny for a $150 Ranger Naturalist's uniform, complete with choke-bore britches, leather puttees, and Smoky Bear hat!

Peggy and I set up housekeeping on the rim a few hundred yards south of the Lodge in a double tent upon a wooden platform. One tent was the bedroom, the other (facing it) was the living room, dining room, and kitchen. A wood stove (chop your own!), table, shelving, two chairs, and a bed were supplied. All other facilities (restrooms, washrooms, showers, and water) were 50 yards away. It was not easy for Peggy to have a freshly ironed shirt ready for me each morning, and to do all the cooking!

Besides Dr. Smith and myself on the Ranger Naturalist staff, there were two other geologists: Carl Swartzlow, Carl Dutton, a botanist, Elmer Applegate, an artist, Howard Crawford, and a poet, Ernest Moll. We were on duty from eight in the morning to five in the afternoon, six days a week, and gave lectures in the Lodge two or three times a week. The "free day" was for research, which we really did!

I wrote articles for "Nature Notes" on the caves and waterfalls around the lake, and did a detailed study of the dacite domes, which came out in the *Journal of Geology* as my very first published article, resulting in a full membership in Sigma Xi. One of the diagrams was reprinted in

65

Cotton's *Geomorphology of New Zealand*, the only time I have been cited in a textbook.

Our duties were varied enough so that the experience was interesting and stimulating. Besides the "Head of the Lake Trail" duty (which was to answer visitor questions like: "Why is the lake so blue?" "How deep is the lake?" "How far across is it?" "How far is it down to the water?" "How long is the trail?"), we took turns conducting a caravan around the rim drive and giving boating rides both to Wizard Island and around the shore of the lake.

We also gave lectures and answered questions at the newly built Sinnott Memorial viewpoint and museum. John C. Merriam had designed this structure, and he visited us several times that summer. Another visitor was David Griggs, who amazed us by his traverse from the lake over the face of Llao Rock and his climbing of Mount Scott on his motorcycle!

Our experiences with the wildlife were eventful, too. Besides the golden-mantled ground squirrels and the Canada jays, who frequently invaded our tent to sample peanut butter and jam, we were constantly harassed by the brown bears, who, after dining at the Lodge garbage dump each evening, always made the rounds of the campgrounds, knocking over all our garbage cans. Even though we kept a pile of rocks ready on the steps of our platform to throw at them, they could not be discouraged. We even tried setting a can on a low stump and wiring it to the 110 volt electric system. No bother to bears!

One night Peggy had cooked a small roast, and had set it overnight in a pot on the table in the corner of the cook tent. We were awakened in the dead of night by the sound of ripping canvas. Grabbing a small 22-caliber target pistol, I dashed outside just in time to see Mr. Bear scooping the pot off the table onto the ground through the ripped corner of the tent. He took off without the roast, and I let him have it in the rear. He went over the horizon so fast that he was only putting a foot down now and then to steady himself!

But that was *not* the end of the story. The very next night we were awakened by a terrific crash. Going into the other tent, we found that the six-foot high set of shelves, containing all our dishes, coffee, syrup, flour and other supplies, was flat on the floor in one large mess. Going outside we found that opposite the place where the shelves had been there was one large dirty paw print on the canvas. Mr. Bear had gotten his revenge!

Most visitors to Crater Lake spent only a few hours at the rim. I well remember one portly Californian who drove up in a Cadillac, got out, walked the few steps to the rim, took one look, announced "Humpf!" got back into his car and drove back down the hill. Such a tourist can have no idea of the hourly, daily, and seasonal variations in the color, light, clouds, and wind which make a fascinating panorama of changes in the aspect of the lake. We were there from early June to early October, when the first snows drove us out and really obtained a lasting appreciation of the lake's variable beauties.

For the entire summer, floating in the lake, was the dried up and debarked snag of a great tree. We kept track of its movement with the wind and waves, locating its position on a map each day that we could find it. This "Old Man of the Lake" as we called it, moved 26 miles around the lake during the 28 times we saw it. Some days it moved as much as two miles in one day.

During the summer, Dr. Smith was approached by C.E. Tuttle, then president of the Rustless Iron and Steel Company, a subsidiary of American Rolling Mills. He had received a letter from Walter Dorn, of Agness, located 35 miles above the mouth of the Rogue River, to the effect that there were large deposits of high-grade chromite in Curry County. Samples submitted had assayed 52% with very low iron content. He wanted Dr. Smith to recommend a geologist to make a survey of these purported deposits. I was hired to begin in October, 1935, as soon as the Crater Lake job was over, at $150 per month, plus all expenses, an excellent salary for those days!

At that time, the only winter access to Agness, located at the junction of the Rogue and Illinois Rivers, was by boat. One round trip from Gold Beach a week brought supplies, mail, and passengers to the community. Agness consisted of a store/post-office run by the Rileas, a fishing lodge operated by Mr. and Mrs. Larry Lucas, and about 15 to 20 pioneer-type cabins (mostly log) scattered over two or three miles of river bank and valley wall.

There were probably no more than 50 permanent inhabitants within five miles, including a tribe of displaced Klamath Indians, headed by Walter Fry, who supported most of them by working for the Forest Service. During two or three months of the summer, Agness was also accessible by a dirt road from Powers, 50 miles to the north, which had been built by the boys in a civilian conservation corps (CCC) camp nearby, who had also built a suspension bridge across the Rogue River a mile above Agness.

Arthur Dorn, a disbarred lawyer from San Diego, had, we suspected, been involved in drugs, and, like many others in Agness, had gone into the backwoods with his wife (whom we also suspected was a retired lady of the night) to get away from the temptations of civilization. They had originally built a large, comfortable log cabin 50 feet above the Illinois River on the south side, just above its junction with the Rogue. During the summer of 1935 they had built a second cabin higher up the hill. The lower cabin had floated away during the 1929 flood, and had been towed back into place. We rented the lower cabin, well furnished, for $40 per month.

Dorn was a character, like so many of the inhabitants of Agness. He was reading east Indian philosophy, and trying to write a book interpreting it. He had delusions of grandeur of trying to make a fortune from the chromite deposits, and had persuaded Tuttle to make him a vice president of a Rustless Mining Company to develop them. His wife was completely outspoken and quite rough-tongued, but she catered to his every whim.

When, at the end of the winter, I was finally able to show that the deposits were not economic, Dorn tried to bribe me to give a favorable report, and later attempted to prove to Tuttle that I was a communist and a spy, and should be discredited.

Starting in October, I hired local help, mostly Indians at $3 per day, to locate the deposits, which I would then examine, and if they showed potential value they would stake the claims. Each Monday, I would carry supplies and payroll out to the spike camp, which might be from 7 to 15 miles out on the trails south of Agness. I would saddle and load up two or three horses, mules, or burros rented from the Indian tribe, and if we were lucky we would get them on the trail before noon.

Upon arrival at the spike camp, I would spend three or four days mapping and measuring the deposits the crew had turned up, and then return to Agness to write up the payrolls, make out weekly reports for Tuttle, order new supplies, and split wood for Peggy's stove. During the eight months from October 25 to June 2, I covered 630 miles of trail.

If a camp was going to be occupied for more than a week or so, the crew would build a small shake cabin for shelter. They would cut down several Port Orford cedar trees, cut them to shake length, split out the shakes with a "froe," frame the house, line it with tar paper and shake the sides and roof in less than two days! We built three of these shelters during the winter. But even with these shelters I could not get the crew to work during heavy rains and snowstorms. During the entire month of February, I only got nine man-days of work from a crew which was nine men at maximum!

68

I really couldn't blame them too much. During one of the heaviest storms, the river rose 35 feet to within 15 feet of our house. A little stream which flowed down the hill next to the house, and which contained a 200-foot water pipe that gave us our water supply, filled up ten feet deep, and we were awakened one night by the grumble and roar of the boulders being washed down. The pipe was coiled up and broken and we could salvage only a part of it.

Bob Owens was my crew boss, assisted by the Indian Walter Fry. Both these men knew the country like a book. Bob once took me out on an eight-mile trip in six to ten inches of snow, where I couldn't even follow the trail. Then he kicked around in the snow and uncovered a 500-pound hunk of high-grade chromite!

Walter was always pointing out trees where he had treed a cougar 15 or 20 years before! He was chunkily built, and I could keep up with him on level ground, but when we climbed a hill, he just kept going, and I would arrive panting at the top of the hill to find him sitting and smoking a Bull Durham cigarette.

Bob Owens was a great story teller and at night amused us around the campfire with the stories of the "Baron Munchausen of the Rogue River," Hathaway Jones. I later wrote many of these out (see Concentrate 8a), and when a book of them had been published, I found that I had some not in the book.

Early in June I wrote a 30-page final report for Tuttle. This was my very first professional report and it detailed the location, tonnage, and grade of some 67 small (less than 150 tons) chromite deposits. The crew had staked and filed 92 claims, dug location pits, and had done some development work on the better deposits. It resulted, a week later, in a return telegram: "Fine work, but what the hell shall I DO?" I learned the hard way to put conclusions and recommendations first in all subsequent reports!

Since, in spite of the high grade of the ore, the deposits were too small and too scattered to be economic. Tuttle then expanded the program to include all the deposits on the Pacific Coast and, in the summer of 1936, we moved to Grants Pass as a base of operations. After living in a motel for several weeks, we moved into a little house on M Street, at the mouth of Skunk Creek.

For two years I examined properties ranging from the Twin Sisters, in northern Washington to sites around San Luis Obispo, California. In addition to nearly 50 chromite deposits, I even reported on a nickel deposit near Sedro Woolley, Washington, (my surface sampling agreed

BIN ROCK AND DUMP ROCK

almost exactly with that from a drilling program of the Bureau of Mines years later) and several tungsten deposits in Nevada.

The cost of shipping samples back to Baltimore for analysis became excessive, so we established an analytical laboratory in Grants Pass, with Howard Stafford as chemist and Ralph Mason as engineer to direct the prospecting crews. We also made magnetic and resistivity surveys (probably the first for chromite), of deposits at Sourdough in southern Curry County, Red Hill in northern California, and at San Luis Obispo.

We bought a Model A Ford Coupe for a company field car, and I took Dr. Smith on a trip to visit High Plateau. He never forgot how we could cross streams, jump logs, climb steep mining roads and generally get along on mountain roads. On another trip in to Sourdough, we had a heavy rainstorm when we started out and the river came up so high that it covered the road for half a mile, and we had to wait for several hours before we could "ford" the flood.

Our own crew learned how to run the Askania magnetometer, but for the resistivity surveys, Tuttle sent out a crew of physicists who presented me with a bunch of curves and profiles which I had to try to interpret. Needless to say, they were of questionable value. I reported on a total of 102 deposits during this period which I hoped to be able to write up as a dissertation later.

When I was ready to sign a contract to purchase Gene Brown's rich High Plateau Mine in northern Del Norte County in July, 1936, Tuttle decided he needed an experienced mining engineer to make contracts and supervise production and hired Herbert F. Byram.

I had a verbal agreement with Brown to purchase the mine for $8,000 (I had measured the ore, and knew there was at least 200 tons of 52% grade chromite), but Byram tried to negotiate a lower price and in the process so antagonized Brown that he refused to sell at all. The mine later produced over a million dollars' worth of ore! Because of this, I decided to leave Rustless at the first opportunity, which came ten months later, when I was asked to join the brand new Oregon Department of Geology and Mineral Industries.

Concentrate 8a

Tall Tales from the Red River Valley

Hathaway Jones, the "Baron Munchausen" of the lower Rogue

River Country during the early part of the century, has long been assigned a permanent place in Oregon legend. During the winter months he met the mail boat at Agness and was the only means of communication for all those living along the river for thirty miles upstream.

His mule train carried the mail through mud and flood, through slide and downed timber, along the narrow and treacherous Rogue River trail. He died with his boots on around 1934, when the cinch on his horse's saddle gave way and plunged him over a cliff high up on the wall of the Rogue River Gorge.

His narrative genius, lit by tangy backwoods idiom and imagination, resulted in scores of tall tales which for years were still being repeated around campfires and local post office gatherings. In 1935-36, when I was there, most of them were still extant in the memories of the inhabitants from Gold Beach to Agness to Illahe and Marial. I heard them from the lips of Robert Owen, who was the foreman of my mostly Indian prospecting crew.

Too Far from the Railroad

"Yup, there's a heap of mineral in the back country in Curry County," said Hathaway Jones, who had just entered the store/post-office/community meeting place, and had overheard a spirited discussion of the value of reported mineral occurrences.

"But ye cain't get it out over them trails the Forest Service builds—and when you pack it out over thutty ar forty mile of rough trail, no one wants ta buy it. The Guggenheims don't want this part of the country developed, 'cause it would make their big mines wuthless." The ten or 15 citizens of Agness, gathered at the store to await the mail boat, leaned forward, all at attention, for when Hathaway told a story, it was worth all ears.

"I recollect when I was a boy," continued Hathaway, "my pop and two brothers and I went huntin' one summer in the Tincup Creek country. We found some deer-sign along the big creek where we was camped, and Pop and the boys got busy trackin' em down.

"I allus was an in-di-vid-oo-list...so I moseyed off up a side branch; I figgered I'd see if'n I couldn't get me a towhead up the ridge. It was pretty late in the mornin' for huntin', though, and it got later and later and I got further and further from camp without no luck.

"Late in the afternoon, I commenced thinkin' about gettin' back,

71

and had just started down the ridge towards camp, when I near stumbled over the purtiest big crop of rusty quartz-vein you ever seen. It was 'bout three feet through and ran up over the ridge and through the country as far as I could see. An' when I looked close, there a-stickin' out of the comb-quartz was the biggest gold nugget you ever seen.

"It was all jagged and splintery, but was thick as the palm of your hand and twice as large. I kicked it loose and picked it up (it hefted nigh onto thutty pound) and put it in my pack and went a-kyhootin' down that mountain side like a bar with a forest fire on his tail, twenty feet to the jump, with the nugget poundin' agin my backbone at every jump.

"I tore into camp jus' as she was getting dark, plumb winded… took the nugget outta my pack and plumped it down on the duffle-box in front of Pop and the boys. Pop looks at it, turns it over, hefts it and looks at me, shakes his head, slow. I was too blowed over to say a word. 'Son,' say Pop, 'that's a mighty fine gold nugget you got there. A mighty fine nugget. But it's no use to us,' he says. 'It's too far from the railroad.'"

The Fastest Animal

"Nope, cougar and deer move right spry when there's a need, but for real speed I'll lay my bets on a bar, every time. I've seen 'em move so fast…wa-al, I was back south of Collier's Bar just March last. The snow was goin' off pretty fast an' the water was up. I aimed to get in a little ground-sluicin' on a right nice high bar up that way, but first I had to get some camp-meat, and was prowlin' along through a prairie when I ran into the durndest sight.

"A cougar musta killed during the night, an' the towhead carcass lay at the other end of the clearin'. A big bar was gnawin' on it when another bar came out of the buck-brush an' started in on the other end of the deer. Well! An argyment developed pretty quick; the first bar took a swipe at the second, and pretty soon they was really mixin' it up.

"One bar would get knocked sideways like, and then he would dash in and jump on t'other and tie into him, and then t'other would jump on the first, an' then the first onto t'other…they got to movin' so fast, one on top of t'other, that they naturally went straight up and outta sight…all you could see afterwards was little bits of fur floating down and a splatter of blood now and then. Never did know which

72

one won."

Erosion

"The gol-darned deepest and steepest canyon in Curry County lies back-country jes' south of the Craggies," announced Hathaway Jones as he leaned forward to send a brown jet of tobacco juice hissing into the heart of the campfire coals. "The walls run up well nigh three thousand feet on both sides of the leetle creek which empties into Tincup Creek a mile or so down-canyon." He settled himself against a stump, and we knew we were in for another of "Hathaway's stories."

"Ten-fifteen years ago, I was a-prospectin' down thataway, and happened to come along the ridge north of that particular canyon... it's a knife-edge ridge, and I was a-pickin' my way mighty slow, when I came upon one of them big round boulders a-roostin' on the narrow ridge-top, like a fool-hen on a log. It was balanced there so I could jiggle it with one hand, even tho' it was nigh ten feet high and musta weighed twenty ton.

"Yep....I did just what you'd a done...I put my back to it and heaved, and it teetered, and with another heave, it started to roll over, slow. But it sure picked up speed fast and before it had gone a hunderd yard 'twas a-tearin' down the canyon side bitin' out chunks of rock at ev'ry jump.

"By the time it reached the bottom it was hittin' up such a clip it only made one splash in the creek and then bounded right up the other side of the canyon, almost to the top of the ridge before it slowed and started to roll back. Them canyon walls was so steep and smooth that the blamed boulder just kept on a-rollin' back and forth, back and forth, not quite reachin' the top of the ridge on the either side. I watched it for nigh on half an hour before I reckoned it was gettin' late an I'd better hit for camp."

Hathaway took time out to replenish his quid, and after a moment, during which we all thought "Well, here it comes!" he remarked, with a twinkle in his eye, "Ye know, I was down that same place late last fall, just after the big fire, and durned it if that boulder wasn't a-rollin' yet...only it had wore itself down so 'twern't no bigger'n your head."

Penetrating!

"Did j'ever try out these new-fangled army-issue steel-jacket ca'triges in your thutty-ought-six? Talk about penetratin'! I used 'em

73

once last year, but never agin'. I was out to pick up some camp meat with a new gun I'd just got from Monkeys, but was havin' rotten luck. Five shots that day, all of them not more than three hunnerd yards, but every one a miss.

"It was latenin', and I was fair disgusted, when a leetle towhead jumps up only fifty feet away, and I sez to myself, wa-al, youngster, here's where I get my pot meat! That little feller was right spry, scooting away like lightenin' with those sideways hops of his, lickety-cut, but I ups and whangs away. He finally dropped, rollin' head over heels to a stop near a hunderd yards away. Wa-al, I sez to myself, that deer was sure travelin'!

"I was feelin' pretty good to have stopped him when I came up and looked him over, but durned it if he didn't seem to be full of bullet holes! He musta been jumpin' back and forth so fast that the durned steel jacket bullet went clean through him seven times, by my reckonin', before he keeled over."

Closest Shave

"The closest shave I ever had? Wa-al, I reckon a grizzly bar musta come as near to puttin' an end t'me as any other critter in these hills. It was fifteen-twenty years ago, where there were still a few roamin' about in the Craggies country up the Illinois.

"I'd been workin' on a prospect I'd located high above the river…good ore, too, the assayer over to Grants Pass gave me sixty dollars in gold, thutty dollars in platinum, and two ounces silver. It was a right hard place to get to, in a cliff at the top of a big rock slide, oh, mebbe a quarter a mile high—well, a good few hunderd yards, anyway.

"I'd shaked up a leetle cabin near the creek just below the slide, and had brushed out a trail that cut back up one side of the slide and zig-zagged up 'bout a mile to the drift just above the cabin. I had a hollowed-out log by the cabin to catch rainwater so I didn't have to climb down to the creek everytime I wanted a drink.

"The drift was only ten feet in, but the ore was gettin' better all the time and I figgered I was gettin' pretty close to the lode. One mornin' as usual, I was shovelin' out the rock left from the last night's blast, when I heared some rocks rattlin' outside, and wonderin' who had the nerve to come on my claim thataway, I backs out, my shovel still in my hand.

"My gosh almighty if it wasn't the biggest grizzly I ever seen in

74

these parts, and only about ten feet away! He was just as surprised to see me as I was to see him, but not as scared, for he let out a roar that sounded like an August thunderclap, and made a swipe for me. I was still pretty spry in those days, and I managed to dodge him and, grabbin' the shovel with both hands, made a dive down the slide.

"As I started slidin', I managed to get the shovel between my legs under me, and there I was, a-rip-snortin' down the mountain in a cloud of dust and rocks, with my back-hair a-risin' at the thought of how near that bar might be behind me. I couln't look back 'cause that shovel was the orneriest nag I ever tried to ride (I ain't never let on to be a cowboy), but I kept on board though I could feel the iron gettin' hotter and hotter as we slid faster and faster and the leetle cabin got bigger and bigger.

"Wa-al, by time I hit the level my pants was on fire for certain, and the only thought I had was to cool off my ass in the rainwater trough. I made one leap and hit it sittin' down, and man, that water felt better'n warm dry socks after a day's placerin'! I'd forgotten Mr. Grizzly complete, till I heared some more boulders dribblin' down, and jumped to my feet ready to make some real tracks.

"By golly, there in front of the cabin sat the biggest bar head a-grinnin' up at me! The ol' feller hadn't no shovel protectin' his fanny as he slid down, and he'd been worn off clear up to the neck. An' I've got the skull tacked up above the cabin door if yah want proof of it!"

Cutting Firewood

"One chore I allus hated was gettin' in the winter firewood. I useta be pretty fast on my feet, and one summer I figgered out a way to cut an' rick up the whole years stack in a few days. My cabin was at the foot of a steep clear slope, the timber was high above near the top of the ridge. I'd down a tree, lop the branches, and saw it up into ten-foot lengths. I'd take one length an' start it a-rollin' down the slope towards the cabin.

"Then I'd run along behind the log, holding my crosscut against it as it rolled, an' by the time we got to the cabin, it would be cut into two-foot lengths, just right for the fireplace. Worked real fine until one day I tripped on a boulder and the log got away from me and smashed the cabin to smithereens."

75

Tin Pants

"Back when I were a youngster, all we had for our old Sharps were ca'triges loaded with black powder. They sure didn't pack the same punch as the new smokeless ones which came out when I was about fifteen, and I never realized how slow they were until I went huntin' with Pop that fall.

"Pop had just bought me a box of the new ones, but had a lot of the old ones left over. He never took more ca'triges than'd be in the repeater, figgerin' that he could always bag a deer with six shots. This time he put a couple of smokeless ca'triges in his pocket, aimin' to try them out sometime.

"The weather was rainin' buckets, and I had my old tin pants on to try to keep dry. It was misty and dark by late afternoon, we'd had terrible luck; what deer we had seen were in the thick brush and our shots got turned off or missed until Pop only had one shot left in the magazine.

"He finally got a good chance at a doe across a clearin' about a hunderd yards away, an' Pop whispered to me, 'Son, the minute I fire, run over towards her as quick as you can to be ready to cut her throat; if I miss the first time, I'll reload as fast as I can with a shell from my pocket.'

"Wa-al, when Pop fired I took off liked a scalded cat, even though the deer didn't drop; I heared another shot when I was half-way there, and by the time I got there, she was on the ground. And when I leaned over to finish her off, that dad-gummed slow black powder bullet hit me spang in the middle of my ass! It sure was a good thing I'd wore my tin pants!"

Chapter 9

Oregon Department of Geology & Mineral Industries: 1938-1947

When Earl K. Nixon, director of the newly established Oregon Department of Geology and Mineral Industries asked me in June, 1938, to join his staff as field geologist for the Baker office in eastern Oregon, it was with great relief that I said good-bye to Rustless. Nixon, with years of experience in the Minnesota iron ranges and in South America as a consultant for major iron mining companies, was a dynamo of energy, an idea man, and he recognized that geology had an important role to play in the development of the mineral industries.

When Nixon first hired me, he said "John, I am putting you over in eastern Oregon to compile a *Mines Handbook* of all the mines and prospects in that part of the state. I may get over to see you once every five or six months. I am paying you ($4,250 per year) for your eight-hour-days work, *but* all your advancement and promotion will depend upon two things: 1) the number of new ideas you come with, and 2) the amount of overtime you put in." This is the best simple formula for success I have ever heard, and I have tried to follow it throughout my career.

The Baker office was located in a small one-story building on Court Street and consisted of a small front office, two cubby-holes for the assayer and chemist, Leslie Motz, and myself, and a slightly larger room for the assay laboratory. Albert Quine, whom I succeeded, had left to take charge of the Cornucopia Mine operations. I spent much of my time in the field, coming in for weekends and a day or so for report-writing. During my two years in Baker, I visited and wrote reports on 335 mines and prospects east of the Cascade Range in Oregon.

Most of these reports were published (without the maps) in 1939 as *Bulletin 14-A, Oregon Metal Mines Handbook, Northeastern Oregon - East Half*. Later I assisted in compiling *Bulletin 14-B, Northeastern Oregon - West Half*, which came out in 1940.

My reputation as the new young geologist at the Baker office was established on a visit to the Buffalo Mine, north of Granite, which was

77

one of the last profitable gold mines to close down many years later. It was located on a high ridge. Two veins about 300 feet apart cut across the ridge, both dipping steeply into the mountain. The lower vein was intersected by a 400-foot adit and had been mined to the surface from drifts in both directions from the adit. The adit had then been driven another 300 feet to intersect the upper vein, without finding it, so the management had decided to ask the "new geologist" to look at it.

I paced the distance into the first vein and then farther to the face of the exploratory crosscut; then, standing on the dump, I took a Brunton angle to the outcrop of the first vein on the surface up the ridge, and paced the distance up to it, and farther up the ridge to the second vein. Then I constructed a simple cross-section showing the adit and the veins, which on the top of the ridge were parallel. On the sides of the ridge, however, I found that the second vein flattened out a bit downward!

The cross-section told me that they should hit the vein in another 25 feet, so I told them so and packed up and went home. A week later, the manager burst into my office and announced to me that I was only six inches off in my estimate. Talk about compensating errors! At any rate, the news got around fast, and from then on I was swamped with requests for mine examinations, which really speeded up the survey.

During the summer of 1939, Dr. Smith led a party of eight geologists in making a reconnaissance map of the northern Wallowa Mountains. Although the base map had 500-foot contour intervals, by fall we had produced a pretty fair map covering over 250 square miles of country which had a relief of nearly a mile. Dr. Smith was assisted by myself, Ray Treasher, Lloyd Ruff, Wayne Lowell, Herb Harper and Wilbur Greenup.

Our main camp was at Aneroid Lake, and we put three to 5-day spike camps out with small parties who took their equipment in with pack horses. It took until noon each day to climb to the top of the ridges! On one trip Wayne and I took a horse south from Aneroid and then crossed over a high divide down into the Lakes Basin. We had to cross several snow drifts on the steep slopes, which we did by digging a trail for the horse in the packed snow. If the horse had slipped he would have gone over a 200-foot cliff.

Another important trip was to the top of Lookout Peak, west of the Lostine River, which was capped by Columbia River basalt. Beneath the basalt we found a 30-foot bed of giant quartzite conglomerate resting on the granite, obviously an ancient course of a large river from the Canadian Rockies.

Upon returning to Portland late in August, we drafted the map, made

78

three color plates, wrote a 16-page summary, and had it printed in 90 days, possibly a record for quick publication.

As homework I wrote the third of eight bulletins for the Department, the first being *Bulletin 9, Chromite in Oregon*, which I had abstracted from my work with Rustless. *Bulletin 18, First Aid to Fossils* was reprinted three times and used as a textbook at Vassar College!

I coordinated my field trips to various parts of eastern Oregon with evening courses taught for the Oregon Extension Division in Burns and Bend so I could teach in the evenings, once a week, in those towns. This was my first teaching experience since leaving school, and it firmed up my decision to eventually get into full-time teaching.

On one trip to Bend, I had to visit some prospects east of Lakeview first, so I took the long way around by driving south to Jordan Valley, and then west across the Alvord Desert through Whitehorse Ranch, Andrews, Fields, across Hart Mountain to Plush, Adel, and west to Lakeview. There were no paved or even graveled roads in those days; one had to follow the tracks out through the sagebrush. When you came to a forks you took a compass direction and decided which track showed the desired direction west. I had prepared for the trip with two jeep cans of gasoline, food and sleeping bag, but I only had to sleep out one night.

When I completed the *Mines Handbook* field work in 1940, I was moved to the Portland Office and promoted to senior geologist. Peggy and I rented a house on NE 45th Street just north of Burnside in Laurelhurst, and our daughter, Sally, was born while we were there. Later we bought (for $6,400) a lovely old house in Laurelhurst at 3925 Couch Street. Early in 1941 the department moved from cramped and dark offices in the Oregon Building to the 7th floor of the Woodlark Building on 9th and Alder.

In succeeding years, I helped make a survey of the limestone deposits in the Willamette Valley, compiled the bulletin on the manganese deposits of Oregon, mapped in the Butte Falls quadrangle north of Medford and in the Ochoco quadrangle east of Prineville, and edited and contributed to the *ORE-BIN*, the monthly publication of the department.

Early in 1943, the state legislature appropriated $20,000, which was matched by Coos County, for a survey of the economic possibilities of the coals in that area. I was in charge of the project, which was probably my most important one for the department, and was assisted by Ewart M. Baldwin as geologist and Ralph S. Mason as engineer. Between April, 1943, and June, 1944, we mapped the 650 square miles of the Coos Bay

79

quadrangle, and examined some 160 coal deposits. Most of our work was done in heavy coastal rains. In making a topographic survey of the very important coastal section of rocks, Ralph and I had to use old aluminum lithograph plates for plane table sheets.

We made detailed maps of four of the most promising prospects, and hand drilled some of the shallower seams to depths of as much as 55 feet in places.

The publication, late in 1944, of *Bulletin 27, Geology and Coal Resources of the Coos Bay Quadrangle*, also ended an era in the department. Earl Nixon had left, and the department mining engineer, Fay W. Libbey, was the new director. I took leave of absence and, with help of a small legacy from my father who had just died, was able to go back to Berkeley and in six months finished up my Ph.D. dissertation on the geology of the San Juan Bautista quadrangle.

When I returned to Oregon, I found that the department no longer had weekly staff meetings, in which we were briefed on what each one of us were doing and planned to do. Soon, none of us knew what was going on. My friends from eastern Oregon would come into the office and say, "John, I hear the department is doing, or planning to do such and such," and my answer had to be, "Oh, is it?"

I was given the grueling task of compiling a 10-year *Bibliography of Oregon Geology* (Bulletin 33). It took me six months, on and off. I had long had a plan that I would work in the field for at least ten years before I went into teaching, feeling that field experience was invaluable to a teaching career. I had sat under too many young professors who had gone directly from college into teaching!

Ray Treasher had left for work with the Army Engineers in California. Ewart Baldwin soon left to join the University of Oregon. Wallace Lowry took a job at Virginia Polytechnical Institute. Teaching jobs were very scarce in the west, but I was able to get a job at Pennsylvania State College now that I had obtained my "union card." I left early in September, 1947, for the East.

I left Margaret with her mother and Sally to sell the house in Laurelhurst and join me at Christmas. Imagine the courage it took for her to make this move without any help from me!

Concentrate 9a

Talks and Lectures

In keeping a record of the talks given, I have missed several years, but this is a good sampling. The number of times a particular talk was given that year is noted in parentheses. Some of the various groups to which I have given talks are listed at the end.

1940
Geology of the Ochoco Mountains
Chromite deposits of Oregon
Iron resources of Oregon

1941
First aid to fossils
Work of the Oregon Survey
Can Oregon minerals promote the defense program?

1943
Oregon mines for victory
Physiographic subdivisions of Oregon
Coal resources of Oregon

1945
The faults of California
Oregon's volcanic history (4)

1946
Oregon's volcanic history
Coal resources of Oregon (2)
Oregon's forgotten resources (2)
Frontiers of science (2)
Geology of Oregon (8)
Thar's more than gold in them thar hills (4)

1947

Minerals of Oregon (15)
Volcanoes I have known (2)
World outlook for gold, silver, copper, lead, zinc
Geology of the Wallowa Mountains (2)
Volcanoes of the Oregon Country (4)

1948

Volcanoes I have known (5)
Geology of the John Day Region
Oregon, an earth-science laboratory

1949

Volcanoes I have known (4)

1950

Volcanoes I have known
Some interesting Northwest minerals (2)
The making of mountains (2)
Why is a geologist? (2)

1951

Tectonics of the San Juan Bautista quadrangle
The seminar as a senior "polishing" course
Conservation and mineral resources

1952

Eruptive rings of the world
Geology of the Capitan quadrangle, New Mexico
The Carrizozo malpais

1953

Mineral resources and geology of a part of the Navajo Indian
    Reservation, New Mexico (7)
Animals of the past
Some interesting northwest minerals
The mineral economy of New Mexico
Bentonitic shales in the upper Mesa Verde formation (2)
Geology of the Fort Defiance and Tohatchi quadrangles

1954

Rocks and minerals of the Navajo Indian Reservation (2)

1955

New Mexico mineral production
The making of a mine
The art of geology
Geologic thinking in the discovery and extension of ore bodies
Geology of the Tohatchi quadrangle

1956

The ultimate resource (3)
Scenic geology of the Navajo Country
The effect of science on contemporary American thought

1957

Science and general studies
The case of the persistent sea (2)
Scenic trips (2)

1958

Scenic trips (2)
The case of the alternate hypothesis (2)
Geology of the Columbia River Gorge
Idea construction
Effect of science on contemporary American thought (2)
Geology of the Pacific Northwest
The International Geophysical Year and us (2)
Geology in industry (2)
Geology of northwestern Oregon

1959

Perspectives from earth
Indian mineral industries
The International Geophysical Year and us
Oregon coast geology (2)
Challenge of books
Northwest Oregon geology (3)
The tree of knowledge (2)
Field trip leader

Inside the earth
Columbia prehistory

1961
The origin of the ocean basins
Frontiers in earth sciences
A geologist looks at the future
A geologist in the Navajo Country
The IGY and you
The ultimate resource
Geological evidence for evolution
Science and American thought
Eruptive rings and volcanology

1964
Mohammed Khan speaks three languages
One year in Pakistan

1970
Seven keys to the past

1975
The Magnificent Gateway: catastrophe and change in the
    Columbia River Gorge

1982
Geology of the Columbia River Gorge (2)
Geologic features noted by Lewis and Clark

1985
Snake River geology
Portland geology (2)
The cataclysmic Bretz floods (5)
Geology of the Columbia River Gorge (2)

1986
Commencement Address - UC Berkeley Geology and Geophysics
    Departments

No dates available:
Perspectives from earth
Ultimate volcanoes, past and present
Chemical prospecting
Rogue River neighbors
Introduction to caving
New Zealand - from the northeast to the southwest Pacific
The science of scenery - landscape appreciation for laymen
The Columbia River Gorge revisited
Cracking Davy Jones' locker
Quaternary catastrophes in the Northwest
New techniques in prospecting for ore deposits
History of geological ideas
Wonder about the world
Careers in geology
The role of field trips in natural science education
Geology and the construction industry
The ecology of science

✳

Chapter 10

Pennsylvania State College 1947-1949

At Pennsylvania State College (PSC), I was Associate Professor and Director of the Geology Summer Camp ($4,250 for 11 months). At least I would never be an assistant professor! We moved into a little house (no more than a summer cabin) in Shingletown Gap, about nine miles east of the college, that Dr. Bonine, whom I replaced, rented to me. It was not a good choice. It was drafty, the heating was inadequate, and although it had a scenic location in the woods, when the snows came, several times I had to dig out 10 to 20 inches of snow to get the car out of the driveway.

Sally came down with a severe infection, and we almost lost her before we could get a doctor. Towards the end of the winter we were able to buy a house located directly across from the college stadium which was warm and cozy and had a nice backyard where Margaret's mother could do the gardening she so loved.

I soon found out that the PSC geology and mineralogy departments were as badly split as the California departments of geology and paleontology. I firmly believe that in both cases this was largely a result of physical separation in different buildings (Berkeley) or in different parts of the same building (PSC), although personal feuds also had a part.

The split was so bad at PSC that when I wanted to talk to P.D. Krynine, head of mineralogy *and* a Berkeley graduate (who was therefore very *sympatico*), I had to be very sure that the head of geology, Frank Swartz, didn't see me duck into Krynine's office!

PSC had about 11,000 students in 1946, a large proportion being veterans returning from World War II. They were competitive and hard-working and teaching them was a pleasure. The town of State College, however, had a population of only 5,000, and the "town and gown" split was very evident in the treatment we got from the locals. This was perhaps a minor irritant, but it was constant, and soon convinced us that we could never settle down as "Easterners."

It was another incident, however, occurring at the end of the first year, that made me decide to begin looking elsewhere for employment. Since my training had been largely in field geology, I wanted a field geology problem for my personal research project.

What I came across seemed very appropriate. Dr. Bonine, the man I replaced, had spent several years with his students in mapping a large part of the Bedford quadrangle, 50 miles south of State College, and his notes and maps were available. At his suggestion, I agreed to complete it for publication.

To get the ball rolling, I spoke to Ashley, the head of the state survey in Harrisburg to seek financing for a month of field work after summer camp was over. He agreed to pay me $8 *per diem*.

I presented this program to Swartz, and his reaction was "No, I want you to do differential thermal analyses on clays." I protested that I was a field not a laboratory man, and that I didn't know anything about DTA. He hemmed and hawed a bit, but didn't tell me outright that I could not proceed with my own project.

So, after a strenuous eight weeks running my first geology summer camp in Stone Valley with 80 students, I had planned to spend a month working in the Bedford quadrangle. On my second day in the field, I ran into two young men with Brunton compasses on their belts.

"Well, what are you two geologists doing here?"

"We are working under Dr. Swartz, mapping the Bedford quadrangle for our master's theses."

That was *it*! I decided then and there that I'd better go out West again, and when I got back to town I started the grapevine operating.

The summer camp in Stone Valley had an elaborate arrangement, consisting of a large dining and meeting hall in which we gave evening seminars, and about ten permanent screened cabins. We soon found out the reason for the screens: I had never in my life seen so many different kinds of insects as were on those screens each night!

The 80 students consisted of about 65 engineers and 15 geologists. We gave the engineers a six-week program consisting of learning to use the plane table and making a five-foot contour interval map of three or four square miles of the Manor Hill anticline. Then we took the geologists and immersed them into two weeks of mapping the geology of the anticline and making a two-mile long traverse across it for a cross-section.

The area abounded in fauna: deer, squirrels, turtles, and snakes! Garter, king, copperhead, and rattlesnakes were all frequently seen. A six-foot king snake lived near the cabins, and often was seen looping around in the trees over the path. The students caught a five-foot rattler

87

and brought it in alive, tied with shoestrings to a pole. After displaying and photographing it, they skinned and ate it that night for supper.

Wayne Felts joined the faculty that year, but only stayed for one term, finding it even more difficult to get along than I did. Bob Folk was among the graduate students, and even then was working on the limestone classification that so enhanced his distinguished career.

John Ferm was another graduate student who assisted me at summer camp. He was the first to take me out to scout out the site. I was driving up the Tuscarora quartzite ridge that separated Nittany from Stone Valley on a curvy but *paved* road when he exclaimed "Dr. Allen, this is a bad mountain road, you will have to drive very carefully!" I wished I could have taken him over some of the roads in Curry County!

I taught a full load the second year, as well as conducting and attending field trips. We would take six station wagons to the eastern part of Pennsylvania where we saw the iron mines at Cornwall, old chromite pits, and the fantastic zinc deposits at Franklin Furnace.

We also visited one of the large coal mines south of Pittsburg, where we rode in on cars for two miles, then crabbed along for several hundred yards beneath a 36-inch roof, and finally reached the face, where the giant automatic mining machines were operating. On these trips we were able to examine in outcrop nearly all of the geologic formations exhibited in Pennsylvania, from the Cambrian to the Permian.

It was not until the middle of the second year of summer camp that I received a phone call from Jack Workman, president of the New Mexico School of Mines in Socorro. One of my applications had been accepted. I had been appointed full professor and head of the geology department there, and I started in four weeks.

When I turned in my resignation to Dean Steidel, head of the School of Mineral Industries, his comment was, "Allen, you are a damn fool to leave here and go to such a small school!" In some ways, as it later turned out, it *was* jumping from the frying pan into the fire, but I never regretted it for a moment.

Concentrate 10a

Institutions I Have Known

Between sessions at the 100th Anniversary Convention of the

Geological Society of America, October 29 to November 3, 1988, I began to write down some of my thoughts on institutions, their fantastic variety and remarkable continuity. I have lived though 80 percent of the life of the GSA, and have been active in it for more than half of that time.

Institutions are the knots which keep the web of civilization from unraveling. All cultures appear to have three basic kinds of institutions: family, religion and law—however, the second two have frequently been merged.

These three are supplemented by thousands of other institutions, large and small, that form an intricate network which defines and stabilizes a modern culture. Institutions have a life of their own and the first three have life spans measured in hundreds and thousands rather than tens of years, and constitute the oldest components of almost every culture.

Most institutions today are called clubs, societies, institutes or associations, but other English terms for them abound. A glance through *Roget's Thesaurus* suggests the importance that our language gives to them:

A. *Educational*: academy, school, lyceum, seminary, college, university, institute, foundation, etc.
B. *Social*: club, society, association, party, faction, denomination, class, side, crew, team, band, caste, family, community, fraternity, brotherhood, order, etc.
C. *Political*: parliament, legislature, senate, house, jury, court, commission, committee, etc.
D. *Religious*: church, creed, denomination, communion, ministry, priesthood, monkhood, clergy, etc.
E. *Commercial*: shop, store, mart, emporium, fair, bazaar, exchange, burse, hall, bank, exchequer, treasury, factory, depot, etc.

One could also list many other categories, such as:

F. *Professional*   H. *Altruistic*
G. *Honorary*   I. *Athletic*

(Some institutions belong to more than one category.)

From the cradle to the grave every individual is shaped and directed by the institutions to which he belongs and the people whom he meets within these institutions. One is born into what might be

89

called "innate" groups (family, neighborhood), and soon initiated into others (day care, kindergarten). The early institutions are imposed; it is only during the teens that an individual begins to be able to make lifelong friends and join groups of his own choice.

An individual can do little to change or modify from within the early groups, and cannot change directed groups very much. In optional groups or institutions one begins to be able to make changes and one is in turn substantially changed by them. It is here that the direction of a career is finally set.

Institutions are normally initiated by groups of people with common interests (sometimes inspired by a charismatic leader!) who draw up rules, a charter, a constitution, or bylaws so as to pursue those interests in an orderly fashion.

As the institution grows larger, divergent interests are accommodated by division. After a hundred years, the Geological Society of America is divided into six geographical sections, ten special interest groups and eight associated societies. Less frequently, special interest societies may combine for the common good, as did the original 12 of the present 21 member societies within the American Geological Institute.

During the last 70 years, I have participated in more than 60 institutions and have helped create or been involved in the formative stages of several. It may be that this has been as long-lived a contribution to our culture as anything else I have done. Most of those in which I have been a member, like the Geological Society of America, originated within the last 100 years.

Following is a list of more than 60 institutions I have worked for, belonged to, or supported, listed in approximate chronological order within ten categories:

A.   *Educational*: Patterson Grade School, University High School, Boy Scouts of America (patrol leader, assistant camp director, camp director, and later, council training chairman, Philmont instructor), University of Oregon, University of California (Berkeley), Toastmasters Club, City Club, Geological Society of the Oregon Country (editor, president), Oregon Museum of Science and Industry (board), Red Cross (swimming and life saving instructor), Pennsylvania State College (associate professor, director of summer camp), New Mexico Institute of Mining and Technology (department chairman), University of California

(Santa Barbara), Portland State College (I founded the geology department, chairman of geology department), University of Hawaii, University of Peshawar, Pakistan (department chairman), Whitman College, Northwest Museum of Natural History (charter member, on board), Columbia Basin Education Project (charter member, on board).

B.   *Social*: Neighborhood dance club, Sigma Pi Tau fraternity, Condon Club, Theta Tau, Rotary Club, Scrooby Club, Camera Club, Coriba Club (originator), Ferdinand Society (charter member), Society of Miscellaneous Oregon Geologists (SMOG) (charter member), English-Speaking Union, Emeritus and Retired Faculty of Portland State (ERFOPS) (founder, editor, on board).

C.   *Political*: Milwaukee County Emergency Hospital (receiving room orderly), National Park Service (Ranger Naturalist), Oregon Department of Geology and Mineral Industries (field geologist, senior geologist), New Mexico Bureau of Mines and Mineral Industries (senior geologist), Nevada Bureau of Mines (research associate).

D.   *Church*: Unitarian, Presbyterian (deacon, clerk of session), Congregational (trustee).

E.   *Commercial*: Eugene Guard (newspaper route), Elliott's Grocery Store (delivery boy), Plant Nursery (budding), McAlister farm (milking cows), hop yard (stripping hops), Chase Gardens (flower delivery), Union Pacific Railroad (carpenter's helper on bridge building gang), Kuner-Empson Cannery (canning sauerkraut), Rustless Iron and Steel Company (prospecting for chromite).

F.   *Professional*: American Institute of Metallurgical and Mining Engineers, National Association of Geology Teachers (president), American Association of Petroleum Geologists, Geological Society of America, American Geological Institute, Oregon Academy of Science, New Mexico Geological Society, American Association of Professional Geologists.

G.   *Honorary*: Phi Beta Kappa, Sigma Xi.

H.   *Altruistic*: Red Cross, Rotary, Nature Conservancy (board), 1000 Friends of Oregon, Friends of the Columbia River Gorge.

I.   *Athletic*: Boy Scouts, University of Oregon swimming team, Red Cross (swim weeks), Eugene Obsidians (mountain climbing).

Concentrate 10b

The Galaxy of Recreation

*Two hundred ways to spend your time,
either by doing it or by watching it.*

Introduction

The remarkable number and variety of ways humans have devised to use their spare time has always fascinated me. With the exception of the Arts, these activities seem to be the only ones that repay only personal satisfactions for most participants and observers. Of course, professional sports certainly can give substantial financial rewards.

For tens of thousands of years before recorded history, humans survived by hunting and gathering; by fashioning weapons; by use of fire for warmth, cooking, and ceramics; by travelling in a nomadic life, to new hunting grounds, by boats; and later by raising goats, sheep and cattle, developing horsemanship (stirrups); and survival in warfare by knives and armor. After agriculture (growing crops and settling down) developed, government and law (politics), money and accounting (trade), architecture (building), and engineering (the wheel) developed.

Humans must have discovered very early that if they had time left after making a living they could use it for recreation, which probably began with the Arts: language, storytelling (history), drums, horns (music), dance, painting, sculpture. Many of these were integrated with religions and served other nonproductive needs. Later with the invention of alphabets and writing, language developed into literature, storytelling into drama, drama and song into opera.

Humans developed offensive weapons to wage war, using rocks, sticks, clubs, spears, atlatls, blowguns, poison darts, dogs, horses and elephants, canoes and ships, swords, pistols, guns, cannon, warships, tanks, airplanes, rockets, and atomic bombs. Then defensive devices

92

were invented to counteract offensive ones, using dogs, shields, armour, walls, moats, castles, trenches, Maginot Lines, radar.

When not engaged in war, humans developed competitive sports and contests, using balls and specialized tools such as boxing gloves, balls, bats, clubs, poles, cabers, mallets, rackets, cestas, javelins, saddles and stirrups, lassos, skis, sleds, and racing boats and cars.

Over millennia, human ingenuity has evolved a fascinating multitude of sports and games for every time and situation. There is not an hour of day that some sort of contest cannot be viewed or undertaken. Surely, man must have built into him from the ancient past a proclivity for sports. When and how and why did this originate? Did sport contests begin and continue as preparation for or as a substitute for war?

I have just read a marvelous collection that describes more than 250 children's games, tells where and how they are played, and gives all the rules. Jack Macguire published it in 1990 as *Hopscotch, Hangman, Hot Potato and HaHaHa* (Simon & Schuster).

I have never seen a complete thesaurus of sports but I wanted to see just how many different ones I could think up myself, and, as a scientist, to indulge myself by trying to classify and index them. If I had added in the children's games listed in *Hopscotch*, I would have doubled the 200 in my list.

Suggested Classification

A Ball Games & Sports		31
B Card Games		7+
C Table Games (Paper, Board & Men)		11
D Field & Track Sports		32+
E Gambling Games		11+
FIce & Snow Sports		12
G Motorized Sports		11+
H One-on-One Games & Sports		30
IProfessional Sports		12+
JSpectator Sports		12+
K Solitary Games & Sports		17+
L Water Sports		14+
M Non-Motor Wheeled Sports		2+
N Other Amusements		6+
Total:	208+	

Categorical List:

A. **Ball Games & Sports** (31)

badminton, billiards, bowling, baseball, basketball, bocce ball, cricket, croquet, curling, football (rugby, American, Australian, Canadian, college), golf, handball, hockey, hurling, jai alai, korfball, lacrosse, lawn bowling, marbles, pinball machines, polo, soccer, softball, table tennis, tennis, volleyball, water polo

B. **Card Games** (7+) *(See Hoyle for many others!)*

bridge, canasta, cribbage, pinochle, poker, solitaire, tarot

C. **Table Games** (11)

backgammon, Battleship, chess, dominos, hangman, mahjong, Monopoly, noh, Parchesi, Scrabble, tic-tac-toe

D. **Field & Track Sports** (32+)

archery, bull-riding, calf-roping, cross-country, dog-racing, fox-hunting, hiking, hop-skip-jump, horse (bare-back, racing, riding, roping), horseshoes, hurdles, javelin, jumping (high, long, rope), marathon, parallel bars, pole-vaulting, relay racing, rings, running (50m to Marathon), shot put, speed walking, throwing (javelin, discus, hammer, horseshoe, caber)

E. **Gambling Games** (11+)

baccarat, bingo, chemin de fer, keno, lottery, lotto, parimutuel, poker, roulette, slot machines, *and*, of course, betting on other events!

F. **Ice & Snow Sports** (12)

ice (boating, hockey), luge, skating (figure, speed, barrel jumping), skiing (slalom, downhill, Nordic, cross-country, jumping), tobogganing

G. **Motorized Sports** (11+)

automobiles (formula, mud, drag, swamp, crush, crash, off-road), boatings (many kinds), light planes, motorcycles, snow cats

H. **One on One Games & Sports** (30)

arm-wrestling, backgammon, badminton, Battleship, billiards, board games, boxing, bowling, checkers, chess, fencing (saber, foil, épée), flying (stunt, speed), hangman, handball, horseshoes, jai alai, karate, pool, Scrabble, snooker, sumo, table tennis, tennis, tic-tac-toe, tiddlywinks, tug-of-war, wrestling

I. **Professional Sports** (12)

billiards, bowling, boxing, cycling, football, golf, hockey, jai alai, rodeo events, soccer, tennis, wrestling

J. *Spectator Sports* (12+)

automobile racing (many kinds), bowling, baseball, basketball, cricket, football, golf, korfball, rodeo, soccer, tennis, track (many events)

K. *Solitary Games & Sports* (17)

body-building, cats cradle, crosswords, electronic games, fishing, hopscotch, hiking, hunting, jumping rope, orienteering, parachuting, puzzle solving, sail-planing, solitaire, cards, walking, yoyo

L. *Water Sports* (14+)

diving (numerous events), motor boating (speed, outboard to super), rowing (single, crew), sailboarding, sailing (ketch to 12m yachts), scuba-diving, surfboarding, water polo

M. *Non-Motor Wheeled Sports* (2+)

bicycling (several), roller-skating

N. *Other Amusements* (6+)

archery, dancing, fishing, hunting, skeet, target-shooting

The classification could have other categories such as "Child Sports" and "Team Sports."

Chapter 11

New Mexico School of Mines & Bureau of Mines and Mineral Industries: 1949-1956

When the Penn State summer camp ended, Peggy and I flew out to Socorro on a quick trip to size up the place and sign the contract. State College had a DC-3 plane that came in once a day and took us to Pittsburgh, where we transferred to a larger plane. We had to transfer again in Chicago to a Constellation.

The plane to Chicago was late, and we just barely made our connection. We had to sit in jump seats behind the pilot's cabin, facing backwards. Flying across Colorado we dodged thunderstorms for an hour and the up-and-down drafts were severe. Looking down the length of the Constellation, we could watch the floor undulate as the ship flexed.

The return trip was uneventful, but the next two weeks were not, since we had to pack and ship our belongings, and rent the house, which could not be sold on such short notice. After driving cross-country for six days, we arrived in Socorro on a Friday night in late August, 1948, and booked in at the Val Verde Inn. Margaret, during the unloading of the car, twisted her ankle on a step, and was incapacitated for several days.

Clay Smith, geology professor at the School of Mines, asked me to accompany him on a scouting trip the next morning, in preparation for writing a guide book for the forthcoming Geological Society of America convention in Albuquerque. The two of us left before dawn in a surplus army five-by-five truck with four-wheel drive for a locality 17 miles across the Rio Grande River and into the back country. After driving for several miles across a wide upland flat underlain by Mancos shale, we parked and hiked up a ridge to examine the geology.

Soon after noon, one of the daily summer thunderstorms thoroughly soaked us, and a sheet flood poured across the flat. When we returned to the car and tried to start out for home, we bogged down in the mud— all four wheels buried to the hubs. For seven hours, until nine that night, we tried to release the car by digging down and putting on the chains, which ended up digging us in only that much deeper.

We had had no lunch or dinner (Clay had assured me we would be back soon after noon), and at nine we started hiking the 17 miles back to town. By thirty minutes after midnight we had made ten of the 17 miles, when we saw lights which turned out to be a couple of our co-workers in Jack Workman's brand new Dodge power wagon on a rescue mission. Our wives had finally persuaded them to come out after us—fortunately we had told them where we were going. Once they reached us, Clay insisted that we go back the ten miles and pull out the truck, which we did with both winches in action. Clay and I went ahead in the truck, after eating a can of stew they had brought along—our first food in 20 hours.

On the way back, the desert tracks had been washed out at the edge of a wide arroyo, leaving a ten-foot vertical embankment. Clay and I turned upstream and found a crossing a few hundred feet above, came back down, and then joined the tracks across the wash. The car following us saw our tail lights ahead of them, and followed us over the brink! It took another two hours to get the Dodge back out of the gulch! Fortunately it was not damaged. We never did tell Workman about this caper.

We were fortunate in being able to buy for $5,000 a small brand-new house on Mines Road, halfway between the town and the school. It was the only new house that we have ever lived in. Payments on the house were difficult to make, since for two years we also had to make payments on the house in Pennsylvania, before it was finally sold.

Our lot was enclosed by adobe walls and built on sand and gravel. We put in a lawn in front, by hauling in silt, and even added a sprinkler system. About every three years we had to dig up the sod and take out a few inches beneath, since the spring dust storms added a few inches every year.

The great plague of the lot was "goats head," a mat of native vegetation with horrendous spiky fruits that grew out over the gravel and had to be peeled back regularly. Another inconvenience here was that about once a year, a summer flash flood would come through. The walls protected us to some extent and the house floors were about three feet above the ground. Neighbors who didn't have this protection were frequently flooded.

We joined the local Presbyterian Church and I sang in the choir. I became an elder and eventually clerk of the session. The year the church celebrated its 75th anniversary, I compiled a short history of the church from the records.

Socorro was a town of about 3,000 people, half of them Spanish-

American and half "Anglo" (the term for anyone not of Spanish or Indian origin). The School of Mines had about 200 students and 20 faculty members, nearly all with a strong scientific bias. The geology department had about 15 majors. It previously had been headed by George Vorbes, another Berkeley man, who had once been my head teaching assistant there.

The Director of the Bureau of Mines was Pat Callaghan, a 1928 graduate of the University of Oregon. The school president was Jack Workman, a physicist who had made a name in developing the proximity fuse during the war. Geologists in the Bureau consisted of Frank Kottlowski, later to become director, Max Willard, Brewster Baldwin, Bob Weber, and Frank X. Bushman, ground-water geologist.

In spite of its small size, the school was a frequent stopping place for eminent visitors, and had an excellent reputation due to a succession of outstanding geologists who had graduated or had taught there in the past. The New Mexico Geological Society was very active, with an annual field trip that drew as many as 250 participants forming a caravan of 100 cars! I was field trip chairman one year, and learned the logistics of running large field trips the hard way.

In 1950, we added a new professor, Stewart M. Jones, to the staff, and I began work mapping the Capitan quadrangle, located across the divide in the Sacramento Mountain between Carrizozo and Roswell. I thought everything was going along fine in the department, and was aghast when Workman called me in one day and told me that I was "not advancing the department" fast enough, and refused to renew my contract!

Pat Callaghan, probably jeopardizing his own job, immediately hired me at the Bureau of Mines as senior geologist, to head up a two-year study, under a $40,000 contract with the Navajo Nation, of the geology of the two 15-minute quadrangles on the reservation, and make an economic mineral survey of that part (3,500 square miles) that lies in New Mexico. We were very fortunate in obtaining Robert Balk to map the Fort Defiance Quadrangle while I mapped the Tohatchi quadrangle.

I was also fortunate in finding, as a field assistant, John Schilling, who had just received an M.S. for a study of a molybdenum deposit in northern New Mexico. (He later became head of the Nevada Bureau of Mines.) We measured 20,000 feet of sections across the Mesa Verde Formation in the southern end of the Chuska Mountains, establishing the inter-tongueing nature of the sandstone units on the southwest side of the San Juan Basin. The resulting *Bulletin 36, Mineral Resources of the*

Fort Defiance and Tohatchi Quadrangles, New Mexico and Arizona was a unique publication since there were no topographic maps of the reservation. Its large map was printed in color upon photomosaics, on a scale of 1:48,000.

Besides the areal geology, stratigraphy, and mineralogy, the text included lists of climatic data, vegetation, and Navajo names for geologic terms. Petrography was done by Balk and Max E. Willard, and ground water was covered by F. X. Bushman. Balk helped illustrate it with some his superb pen and ink sketches.

A tragic finale to the project was the death, late in 1953, of Robert Balk. In flying out of Albuquerque to take the final color separations of the map to the printer in Baltimore, his plane flew into a cliff north of town.

While living on the reservation for over a year, first at Nakaibito (Mexican Springs) and later at Tohatchi, Margaret and I had the opportunity to meet many fine Navajos and get slightly acquainted with their culture and personality. I had worked with Indians at Agness and that experience helped a lot. The first thing to learn is that time is not important! Probably the second is not to infringe on their privacy and let them speak first.

In doing my field work, I would frequently come upon a hogan, complete with dogs and children. I was careful not to get closer than a hundred yards to them but would stop my jeep, get out, sit down on the running board or a stump, and get out my pipe for a smoke. After a few minutes, one of the men would come up, and I would offer him my pack of Bull Durham. He would light up, and then, assuming that he could speak English (many of the old ones could not), I would tell him what I was doing in some detail.

At first he might only answer with grunts, but eventually he would begin to make comments and ask questions, and it was then that I was able to ask directions, where certain rock-types were, where coal seams were, what the best trail to get to a certain place was, and so forth.

One Navajo friend we met was a beautiful girl who had been queen of the tribal fair the year before. She visited with us several times, and told us that she was a medicine woman, which she had achieved by studying under her grandmother for a year, after paying her $600 for the tuition. She knew the location of all the different pigments used, all the medicinal herbs, and was a fountain of information.

I learned that the Navajos have a very sophisticated vocabulary when dealing with objects that had importance in their lives. Just as the Eskimos have dozens of words to apply to the different kinds of snow and ice, so do the Navajos have many words to apply to the different kinds of springs, creeks, and arroyos, and to the kinds of pigments, minerals, and rocks of value to them.

I also found out that Navajo was not a language that could be learned in a few months. It is highly inflected, like Chinese, and with many more compounded words than German. I met only one white man who could speak it fluently, Father Bernard Haile, who had lived at St. Michaels Mission in Fort Defiance most of his life. He compiled a cultural dictionary of the Navajo language, which was a great help to me, but it didn't help me learn the language!

At the end of the first summer season, I made a report before the entire Tribal Council in their great meeting hogan at Window Rock. I read the text a sentence at a time, it then being translated by the son of the chairman of the council, who had been working with me as a field assistant. It took 90 minutes to give the report, which I could have read off in ten minutes. Navajo is *not* a compact language!

During 1951, before moving to the Bureau, I taught the first of three summers at the University of California at Santa Barbara under Bob Webb. At that time the school was still up on the hill above town.

I arrived in very bad shape, since in loading the car in Socorro I had slipped a disk, and drove much of the way under heavy sedation. I had to lecture on crutches for the first three or four weeks.

Fortunately I found a doctor in Santa Barbara who did not believe in fusion of the disk, but treated me with heat therapy. But I have had to take special exercises once a day for half an hour ever since. It was in Santa Barbara that I first gave my favorite course "Minerals in World Affairs," which I later taught for 12 years at Portland State.

Among the many experiences in Socorro, one stands out. I was asked to assist a young Ph.D. from Columbia University who had spent the summer mapping a quadrangle in southern New Mexico. His new assignment was to make a detailed map of the perlite deposit south of Socorro. (Perlite is an expandable natural glass that, when furnaced, makes a very light aggregate.)

He needed someone to run the plane table and I volunteered. He would wander over the deposit while I took shots at his stadia rod and plotted the locations and elevations on the map. Every once in a while he would come in and place his geologic information, contacts, dips, and strikes of flow planes on the map. I noticed that his information did not match with what I could see, and after pondering this a bit, asked to see his Brunton compass.

The declination on his compass was set 12 degrees *west* of north, which is correct for New York, but not for New Mexico, where it is 12 degrees *east* of north! All his directions were thus 24 degrees off, both for the perlite deposit and for his completed geologic map. He left the Bureau soon after, and I heard he became a broker in New York.

During my four years with the Bureau, I began to accumulate my "Laws of Field Geology," a summary of all the frustrations that face a field man. Later I found it very useful in teaching field methods and field geology courses at Portland State.

One geologist, Dick Jahns, came to Socorro almost every spring on his way to study the pegmatites so abundant in New Mexico. One year he arrived when Max Willard, his longtime friend, was out of his office. Dick got a two-foot piece of chemical tubing, tied a knot in one end, blew it up at a water faucet to a foot-long sausage, and then placed it in Max's desk drawer, folding over the free end, and closing the drawer on it. When Max arrived, we were all hiding in our offices and listening. When Max opened the drawer, and the free end squirted him thoroughly, he burst out: *"Dick Jahns is in town!"*

Dick always was able to entertain us with a good story, and I'll never forget the various high jinks about Cal Tech he told us, such as the one when the students bricked up his office door while he was on vacation, or the one when they hitched a 20-foot aluminum pipe to a compressed air canister and lofted oranges into Pasadena, giving rise to all sorts of speculations by meteorologists about local aberrant cyclones.

My first contact with the Moslem world came when three visiting economic geologists from Afghanistan, who had just completed their degrees at Utah, arrived for a trip through New Mexico. I was delegated to spend a week with them, visiting outstanding mines such as Chino copper, Cuesta molybdenum, Carlsbad potash, and San Juan Basin uranium, and learning something about their culture.

Two of them were apparently of royal blood and the third a commoner. They certainly treated him as a patsy! He insisted on stopping at the appropriate times to make his prayers and was very careful of what he ate, but the other two said they had become "Jack Moslems" and didn't bother.

The beginning of the end came when Jack Workman asked me to go for a ride with him. He drove out of town and stopped and asked me whether I would take Pat Callaghan's job since he no longer could get along with him. I well remember what I said: "Dr. Workman, do you really think I would do that? After Pat had saved my job for me when you fired me?" Workman was a completely unpredictable man, with few scruples. One day he would be all gracious and friendly, the next day he would pass you in the hall without a word.

I had always wanted to eventually return to the Northwest and I had long ago alerted my friends in Portland that I would be amenable to offers of work in Oregon, especially in teaching. My luck was in, for at about this time I received a letter from Will V. Norris, Dean of Science at Portland State College, asking me whether I would be interested in coming there to start a new department of geology.

Of course I said yes, and since the request came to and not from me, I was able to ask for certain prerequisites as necessary before I came. I was to be given a large geology laboratory in the then-under-construction Cramer Hall, and several thousand dollars for start-up equipment. We packed up and left Socorro late in the summer of 1956.

Concentrate 11a

Allen's Laws of Field Geology

During my 20 years as a field geologist, I gradually came to understand and appreciate some of the immutable laws of nature which affect field geologists. As they occurred to me over the years, I wrote them down, and I now share this collection with you. Your appreciation of their deep philosophical significance will be in direct proportion to the amount of time you have spent in constructing geologic maps in the field.

1. **The basic law of science (Murphy's Law):**
   If anything can go wrong, it will.

2. **Laws of recognition:**
   a. The more you know, the more you see.
   b. You see only what you are looking for.
   c. You can't see something you are not looking for.
   d. When investigating the unknown, you do not know what you will find.
   e. Because of their different backgrounds, two geologists, looking at the same outcrop, will seldom agree upon the same interpretation.

102

3. **Laws of complexity:**

   a. The geology of any area is always more complex than you think it is going to be.

   b. The complexity of the geology is proportional to the area of outcrop in the area.

   c. In mapping complicated structures, the interpretation may be considered valid if not more than 50 percent of the mapped dips and strikes need to be discarded in order to obtain a correspondence with hypothesis.

4. **Law of accuracy:**

   a. The care and accuracy taken in mapping should be inversely proportional to the distance from the main roads and the edge of the map. Your superior will check your work along the main roads; your map must agree with work done by other geologists in adjacent quadrangles.

5. **Law of efficiency:**

   a. The curve of field efficiency is bi-modal, peaking at 9:00 a.m., with a smaller peak after lunch. It drops to near zero after 4:00 p.m.

6. **Laws of frustration:**

   a. The key outcrops and fossil localities are usually found at dusk, in the most inaccessible part of the area, on the last day of the field season.

   b. Whenever specimens must be collected and photographs taken, they usually are those in the most inaccessible part of the area, and the photographs don't turn out when they are developed.

7. **Laws of specimens:**

   a. The weight of a hand specimen is directly proportional to the square of the distance from the car.

   b. The number of specimens collected is inversely proportional to the abundance of the rock types represented in the area. The result of this is that the season may end without the collection of a specimen of the dominant rock-type. The psychology behind this ancient law has for many years been represented in the mining industry by the term, "Mexican sample."

8. **Laws of note-taking:**
   a. When writing your report at the end of the field season, the information you need the most is not to be found in your notebook.
   b. The most important notes and sketches are the most illegible or unintelligible.

9. **Other miscellaneous laws of value:**
   a. *Allen's Axiom:* When all else fails, read the instructions.
   b. *Woodward's Law:* A theory is better than its explanation.
   c. *Finagle's Law:* Once a job is fouled up, anything you do makes it worse.
   d. *Gumperson's Law:* The outcome of any desired probability will be inverse to the degree of its probability.

Concentrate 11b

The Tyranny of Things

An uncle of mine was, for many years, chief steam engineer for Electric Bond and Share Corporation in New York, designing steam power plants in such then exotic places as Hong Kong, Buenos Aires, and Singapore. When he was home, he and his wife lived in a large apartment in downtown Manhattan. In 1929 during my *wanderjahr* I stayed there for several weeks while trying to get a job on a boat back to the West Coast. I marveled at the elegant furniture, pictures, art objects, and oriental rugs in what seemed to me to be an over-furnished apartment.

My uncle's wife died several years later, and when in 1964 I came through New York and tried to visit him, I found that he was about to leave on a trip but he again offered me his apartment. It was tiny—and as barren as a hotel room! Only three or four hangers of clothes in the closet, only one drawer in the dresser occupied.

At least once a year after my uncle retired, he would visit us in Portland and always arrived carrying only a brief case. If it was cold and raining, he would buy a sweater and raincoat, wear them, and then give them away when he left. I finally got up nerve enough to

104

ask him about this style of life and he said he had learned to travel
with as little as possible during his active days. He told me "John,
beware of the tyranny of things—the less you have to care for, the
more freedom you will have!" I suspect that this was in part his
reaction to the over-acquisitiveness of his beloved wife. I never knew
what happened to all those gorgeous apartment furnishings!

My wife, Peggy, and I were married in 1933, and during my first
ten years as a field geologist we lived in 12 different houses in eight
different towns. When we moved, everything we owned would go
into our car or into a small box trailer towed behind it. During the
first 33 years of marriage we moved 30 times. However, for the last 26
years our home base has been a Portland apartment house, and stays
away from home have been shorter, from a week to six months, so
when we would leave for a while, we never moved our accumulated
things. Now they fill to overflowing our apartment.

We have found several ways for trying to cope with these accumu-
lations in a continual fight against the aggregation and tyranny of
things:

- One effective way to keep things under control is to make frequent
  moves—it worked for us in the early days. Each time you move,
  you have to decide whether something is *really* useful, necessary,
  and worth the cost of moving it.

- Although we have never had a garage sale of our own, we have
  visited many of them (and bought things there). Very few people
  want to go to this extreme unless they must vacate a house.

- At regular intervals we try to weed things out and give them to
  Goodwill or other charitable agencies. We find the tax deduction a
  pleasant side effect of such donations.

- Everyone needs a hobby and most people have them. Hobbyists,
  almost by definition, are collectors of things! I have collected
  stamps, coins, chess sets, rocks and minerals, hi-fi equipment, old
  (19th century) geology books, guns, swords and knives, and hats.
  But note the word "have." Nearly always I pursued my hobbies
  one or two at a time, made my collections one after another, *in
  sequitur*, and once I had learned all I wanted to know about the
  objects in a collection, I got rid of them and started on a different
  collection. This generally takes from five to ten years for each
  hobby, so I have learned a lot and had a great deal of enjoyment

from my hobbies. Right now I'm still on knives and hats.

- Books are for us a major problem, and our apartment shows it, with eight bookcases (30 shelves, about 100 linear feet) in three rooms. My tiny office at PSU has 140 linear feet of shelving, to the ceiling, on three walls. I turn in to a local bookstore or give away several cartons of books every few months in order to make room for the new.

  During my early years (1956-70) at Portland State, I would send a few cartons of technical books to the library each year. Cataloging is now so expensive that they no longer can afford to shelve outdated textbooks, so I give them away to students. We now have visits from our adult grandchildren who tag the books they would like to have, so that we can later mail them a carton.

- Magazines are also a major problem—how many times have you heard of someone who wants to sell a complete set of the National Geographic Magazine going back to 1914? I still have the ancient Geographic issues on horses and dogs!

  We like to try out new magazines and sometimes subscribe to more than we have time to read. Within the last ten years we have tried out and quit *New Yorker, Yankee, Asimov's Science Fiction, Analog, AIPG Bulletin, AIME Bulletin, GSA Bulletin, Science, Health, Insight, Newsweek, Saturday Review, US News and World Report, Scientific American, National Geographic,* and many others I no longer remember.

  Currently, we take *Time, Modern Maturity, Good Housekeeping, Reader's Digest, Consumer Reports, Smithsonian, Natural History, Discover, Wilson Quarterly, Journal of Geological Education, Geology, Geotimes, Oregon, California, Washington* and *New Mexico Geology* magazines, *American Scientist,* and *Oregon Scientist.*

- The proliferation of magazines has recently been overwhelmed by the proliferation of mail-order catalogues which fill our mail box two or three times a week. Our forests dwindle as the lumber industry supplies the paper for them. I throw away 10 to 20 pounds of magazines every month, and an equivalent poundage of catalogues every week. That is nearly half a ton of slick paper per year for one family of two!

  For several years I have formed the habit of sending back all "business reply mail" envelopes offering something I don't

106

want with a notice "Please take my name off your mailing list" next to my address. One can get rid of many unstamped pleas without spending a stamp by writing the national address clearing house.

- Incidentally, a year of the *Oregonian* newspaper (with all the ads) would make a pile more than ten feet high weighing more than half a ton. I was delighted when our apartment house recently put in facilities that allow us to separate newspapers, tin cans, and glass for recycling.

Concentrate 11c

Good Fortune, Not Misfortune

I bought a personal computer in 1983 and this now obsolete Kaypro changed my life—since writing suddenly became a pleasure rather than a chore. My first publication from it, in 1985, was the original version of *Bin Rock and Dump Rock*. I had been writing this in pencil for more than 15 years, but had hesitated to start the chore of typing and retyping it. That was when I began writing the concentrates about what I remembered of my life. As I wrote these, I gradually began to realize how fortunate I have been to have lived most of my life in the most affluent country (the USA), in the best part of that country (the Northwest), and in the best times (this century) that the world will ever see again. My misfortunes pale by comparison. Perhaps it will be worthwhile to summarize the times I remember as fortunate, arranged more or less chronologically.

I Was Fortunate Because:

- I was raised by highly educated, caring parents, who took a lot of time to see that I was happy, and only stood me in the corner or switched my legs when I really deserved it. They read to me, took me to the zoo, to Volunteer Park, on trips to Puget Sound, Estes Park and Triangle Lake, and even before I could read, kept me supplied with lots of books and later with knowledgeable tutors.

- They taught me responsibility by assigning certain chores around the house; I nearly always helped wipe dishes after meals, and for

107

ten years, I was in total charge of keeping four fireplaces and a furnace supplied with wood. My parents encouraged me to take a wide variety of outside and weekend jobs, to deliver the family bill payments, run a newspaper route, pump gas at a nearby station, strip hops and bud scions at nurseries, milk cows on a farm, deliver on grocery and flower trucks.

- I was able to work up through the Boy Scout ranks from Tenderfoot to Eagle Scout with 36 merit badges, which gave me excellent preparation to handle the diverse exigencies and emergencies I met during my 20 years as a field geologist. The Scout Oath and Scout Laws have served me well as lifelong guides. As a result of my scout training I was able to pay my own way through college by running Red Cross "Swim Weeks" and serving at three Boy Scout camps as assistant and camp director during four summers.

- I never had to borrow money, either in high school, college, or later after marriage. During my first married year at Berkeley, my mother sent me a Chinese box, enclosing fifty $1 bills, with directions to use them only for special events such as trips to San Francisco for meals and movies. Many years later my Uncle Louis began to periodically send us checks for $200. He was that same uncle who gave me a lesson on how not to let material possessions clutter up my life.

- I had exceptional teachers in Margaret Goodall (English) and Edith Pattee (French and Latin) in high school, and in college, George Turnbull (Journalism) and Warren D. Smith, Howell Williams and N.L. Taliaferro (Geology). In later years I had outstanding mentors in Warren Smith, Ian Campbell, Earl K. Nixon, and Pat Callaghan, all of whom contributed substantially by helping with career changes and other problems.

- I changed my major from journalism (the art of infringing on other peoples privacy) to geology (the fascinating study of how the earth and life evolved during eons of time). I was turned on by Warren D. Smith's charisma, and took my *wanderjahr* to meet many other incredibly enthusiastic geologists at six universities across the country.

- I married my loving wife, Margaret, who for 60 years has made homes for us in more than 30 different motels, apartments; and

108

houses in six states (and Pakistan); has raised an elegant and successful daughter under these mobile conditions; and has tenderly taken care of me under an incredible variety of conditions.

- Earl K. Nixon of Oregon, director of the new Department of Geology and Mineral Industries, sent me to my first professional job in Baker with the instruction: "John, I want you to examine and map all the mineral deposits in Baker County for a mines handbook, and I will come over and check up on you in six months. All your advancement and promotion will depend upon two things: first, the number of new ideas you come up with, and second, the amount of overtime you put in."

- I realized, after 20 years of experience in the field, that I was finding people more interesting than rocks, and was then able to move from field geology into a second career of teaching.

- I discovered I loved teaching, could build up classes to nearly 600 students, and achieve national recognition as a fine teacher. I was thus able to start and develop a well-recognized Department of Geology at Portland State. During a year at the University of Peshawar, in Pakistan, I really learned how the other nine-tenths of the world lives. We were able to route the trip west through Japan, Bangkok, Hong Kong, and India, with a four-month trip home the following summer through Iran, Turkey, Greece, the Cyclades, Italy, Austria, Germany, Switzerland, France, England, and Ireland.

- Since retirement and appointment as emeritus professor, with all the perks that implies, I was able to take up a third career of writing which has kept me busy and productive, and has satisfied my ego by publication of my two books (*Magnificent Gateway* and *Cataclysms on the Columbia*), a geology column for four years in the *Oregonian* ("Time Travel") and several other publications every year, adding to the more than 200 published items in my bibliography.

- I have a successful and loving daughter who wanted me to tell her the "whys" in my life, thus spurring me on to this endeavor. More importantly, she has presented us with two successful and active grandchildren who in turn have given us two lovely great-grandchildren.

109

- My wife and I have both been able to live to a ripe old age in comparatively good health with few financial problems.

Concentrate 11d

Frustrations I Have Known

"When to the sessions of sweet silent thought
I summon up remembrance of things past,
I sigh the lack of many a thing I sought,
And with old woes new wail my dear times' waste:
Then can I drown an eye, unused to flow,
For precious friends hid in death's dateless night
And weep afresh love's long since cancell'd woe,
And moan the expense of many a vanished sight:
Then can I grieve for grievances foregone,
And heavily from woe to woe tell o'er
The sad account of fore bemoaned moan,
Which I now pay as if not payed before
But if the while I think on thee, dear friend,
All losses are restor'd and sorrows end."
—*Shakespeare, Sonnet #30*

We have been taught that one learns and grows by overcoming disappointments and frustrations. I never thought much about this until last week, when my doctor told me that there was little hope that I would ever get rid of the asthma which has cut down so markedly on my activities. He said the inhalants I am using can keep me going, but I should not expect any improvements.

Yes, I am certainly frustrated at not being able to work at the office for more than a couple of hours at a time, drive for more than a hour or so, or walk more than a couple of blocks without taking a treatment. This is the first time that such a condition has so strongly affected Peggy, and it really has been hard on her which adds to my own frustration.

I am sure that frustration has an effect upon one's work and even health. Because of this, I have always tried to put any such discontent out of my mind, to swallow it, to forget it, and in most cases I think I have been successful in these efforts. Fortunately, during my career

110

the gratifications have so greatly outnumbered the frustrations that I seldom think about the latter.

In looking back, I can immediately remember nine major frustrations, three of which come under the heading of "unfinished business"—cases where months and even years of work came to naught:

1936 High Plateau chromite mine. While working for Rustless Steel, I located a high-grade chromite body (by far the largest I found in nearly two years work) and made a deal with the owner to buy it for $8,000. I cabled my boss for the money and instead he sent a mining engineer to complete the deal. The engineer tried to get it for less than that and as a result so irritated the owner that the deal was off. This property later produced nearly $2 million worth of chromite. I was so frustrated that when an opportunity came to join DOGAMI (at a lower salary), I snapped it up.

1939 Dissertation on geology of the West Coast chromite deposits. After spending two summers mapping the San Juan Bautista quadrangle, I had to leave Berkeley and go to work, first for the Park Service at Crater Lake and then for Rustless Iron and Steel Corporation prospecting for chromite from Twin Sisters Mountains on the north to San Luis Obispo on the south. I examined several hundred deposits and, after leaving Rustless in 1938 I spent several months writing up the literature on chromite and describing the West Coast deposits. I presented an outline of this dissertation to my Ph.D. committee chairman, Dr. Taliaferro, at Berkeley and he said to go ahead, so I finished a 200-page tome. When I sent it to Berkeley, it was rejected on the basis that it was not detailed enough on any one deposit to qualify as a dissertation. Fortunately, I was later able to take a leave of absence from DOGAMI and complete the San Juan Baustista quadrangle for my Ph.D. in 1945.

1948 Bedford Quadrangle, Pennsylvania. When I went to Penn State College, Dr. Schwartz, department head, told me that he wanted me to study clays. I said I was a field geologist and wanted to finish mapping the quadrangle that Dr. Bonine, whom I succeeded, had begun. After the first summer camp which I directed, I drove down to the area and right away ran into a couple of students with Brunton compasses on their belts—geologists. I asked them what they were doing there and they said that Dr. Schwartz had assigned the quadrangle to them.

1955 Capitan Quadrangle, New Mexico. I spent two long summers mapping the complicated geology of this 15-minute quadrangle, but was unable to complete the map by the time I moved from New Mexico back to Oregon. While working on this map, I wrote a paper on a structure at that time unrecognized in this country, called a "decollement." It was rejected by the American Association of Petroleum Geologists (AAPG) editor, and I found out later that it had been censored by a geologist who had also mapped in the area and did not believe in such structures. I did write a field trip guidebook on the area, which was published and republished, but the completed geologic map of the Capitan quadrangle was never published.

1959 AUGER Program. The Department of Geology at Portland State worked very hard for several months preparing a grant application to help establish an AUGER Institute at PSU (Applied Urban Geology, Education and Research). It failed. This was long before urban geology and environmental concerns had become popular. I have always regretted that we missed the boat on this, since we could not get funding for this leading-edge proposal.

1965 The Polluted Professor. When one of our faculty was co-opted as the president's assistant, the department searched for a replacement and found a highly recommended full professor from an Eastern school who was willing to fill in. His interview demonstrated that he was affable, knowledgeable, and capable of teaching in the needed fields, and we hired him. I even rented him my house when we moved into our Ione Plaza apartment. What the letters of recommendation and the interview did not tell us was that he was an alcoholic who went off on "lost weekends" and failed to show up for Monday classes. Were we frustrated! After repeatedly filling in for him, and warning him that he must attend therapy sessions (which he never did), he finally picked exam week for one of his bouts, and failed to show up for the final exam in our largest class. When he did finally appear, I had ready for his signature a letter of resignation. He groggily signed, saving me from having to go through a long termination procedure.

At first he was very angry at what he felt was my tricking him into signing the letter, but he later did join AA and reform, got another job

at a Southern university, became chairman, and wrote me long letters
in appreciation that I had shaken him up enough to make him reform.
We have had a pleasant correspondence ever since. He was a nice
guy when he was sober.

1974 Retirement. I became 65 in August, 1974. In the fall of that
year the university declared a financial exigency, because of a $1.2
million shortfall due to under-realized enrollment. In order to make
up this money, everyone over 65 was fired, tenured or not. Two
months later, the law forbidding such firings until age 70 went into
effect, but that didn't help me. I was furious at first, but later realized
I had a chance for a third career as a writer.

1975 Geologic Hazards. An educator with geologic background
approached me to help him write a book for secondary school use on
how to prepare for, and what to do during and after the occurrence of
as the title stated, *Hazards of Earth, Air, Fire, and Water.* I agreed, since
I had just written a summary of volcanic hazards for a proposed
American Institute of Professional Geologists (AIPG) publication.

I wrote a table of contents, preliminary outlines and bibliographies
for ten chapters, totaling 250K of disk space and proceeded to send
the "co-author" copies for his editing remarks. After a few encourag-
ing exchanges by mail, he disappeared and I was never able to get in
touch with him again. And the AIPG never published my summary.

The lesson I learned about frustration was to forget it, swallow it,
and for heaven's sake never let it rankle.

1987 Time Travels. During the summer of 1987, my editor at the
Oregonian began to turn down my columns or edit and criticize them
extensively. She began to write up the best geology stories herself,
rather than turning them over to me for a "Time Travel" column as
she had been accustomed to do. When I finally objected mildly about
the way I was being treated, she published, without my knowledge or
permission, the farewell column that she had in my backlog file,
which I had written after my auto accident several months before to
be used in case something happened to me.

I don't think I have ever in my whole life been more angry. It took
me nearly a week to cool down. She had abruptly and arbitrarily
terminated my four-year love affair with "Time Travel," and left me
with little to occupy my time. Being angry for a long time is not good

113

for your gut, apparently, because in December I was operated on for bleeding colitis, and put on a diet which excluded smoking, liquor, and citric acid (did you know that nearly all soft drinks contain citric acid?). Just when I had reached the time when I felt I could enjoy my pipe and scotch on the rocks more than ever before!

Two such events in a period of a few months really further upped my "stress score" and sapped my vitality. I came down with a peculiar type of long-lasting low grade flu that has affected my balance.

Concentrate 11e

Professional Ethics for Geologists

Science has been defined as "any branch of systematized knowledge, considered as a distinct field or object or study"; a profession is "a calling in which one professes to have acquired some special knowledge used by way either of instructing, guiding or advising others, or of serving them in some branch of learning or science."

The main thrust of this essay is to emphasize that idealism should and can be the essence of professionalism; that the true professions exist chiefly to protect and benefit society as a whole.

All professions (law, medicine, clergy, education, as well as science) have at least the five attributes listed as follows:

1. *A systematic body of knowledge* that is internally consistent.
2. *Professional authority* recognized by clients and based upon extensive education and competence in practice. Such authority must carry responsibility (which is where ethics come in).
3. *Community sanction* or the official granting of authority beyond that conceded by the client or employer. This can result in monopolistic powers and privileges recognized by citizens or governments.
4. *A professional culture* that consists of common standards of values, norms, symbols, and activities. A unique social structure commonly develops, resulting from association both formal and informal in work groups, research groups, professional associations and societies—a behavior pattern of its own which sometimes extends even to dress (uniforms, clerical garb, lab coats, Brunton

114

compass, and G-pick).

5. *An ethical code* requiring the members to deal fairly with their employers, clients, and fellow practitioners alike.

None of these are foreign to geology—the first and fourth are well developed and may be the dominant attributes. The others have not been nurtured by geologists to the same degree as in some other professions, although none are completely lacking.

The "ancient body of systemized knowledge" is by far the most important, and includes (this is where the ethics begin to come in) the obligation to see that the "body of knowledge" involved is: a) properly unfolded and employed in the service of employers, clients, and the public, b) available to qualified researchers and students, and c) that there is free opportunity and proper climate for continuing growth and development of the knowledge, by way of colleges, universities, research organizations, lectures, discussions, field trips, institutes, professional meetings, or on-the-job training.

"Professional authority" is actually quite generally confirmed by the faith of the client in the skill of the minister, doctor, or geologist. This is not so for the ordinary purveyor of services, where the customer himself can judge the quality of service. However, geologists need to develop this faith.

Every profession has incursions of unqualified "experts" into their field. In geology, the full utilization of our training and experience in every needed and proper field has not yet been attained, so that, without using geology, mining engineers still may estimate mineral reserves, petroleum engineers estimate oil reserves, highway engineers lay out road plans, developers build condominiums on beach sand or landslides, well drillers locate water wells.

"Community sanction" involves official granting of licenses to operate, such as required by the medical, engineering, legal, and perhaps unfortunately, less commonly the geological professions. It is an attempt to protect the public from self-styled "experts," "quacks," or "doodlebuggers" who prey upon them.

The "professional culture" of geology has been established and maintained by several large and a multitude of small specialty organizations, some important ones being:

American Geological Institute
Geological Society of America
American Institute of Petroleum Geologists
American Association of Professional Geologists
National Association of Geology Teachers
and nearly 20 others, most of them in specialties.

Most of these organizations have regular meetings, field trips, publications, and regional divisions, and several of them have their own ethical codes. Most of them require qualifications for membership which can be quite rigorous.

Ethics has been called the "science of the ideal human character." An ethical code for geologists must deal with the responsibility assumed with respect to their own work, the work of other geologists, their employers or clients, their employees, the public in general, and to his or her own self.

With respect to his own work, the geologist should:
- not take on a task that is *not* within his own province of competency
- make each report as complete as time will allow
- carefully separate facts from inference
- never pick his facts to suit his hypotheses

With respect to the work of other geologists, he should:
- use quotes, rather than plagiarize
- give credit where credit is due
- be meticulous with acknowledgments
- never slander or libel (thou shalt not gossip, belittle, or underbid!)
- never work with unethical people

With respect to one's employer or client, the geologist should:
- keep his information confidential
- be loyal, especially after the report is turned in, except when the employer or client turns out to be dishonest himself
- always be ready to clarify or summarize results

- never use one's work for land-grabbing or job-hopping
- watch out for personal conflicts of interest

With respect to one's employees, the geologist should:
- always be sure to give them credit for their work

With respect to the public, the geologist should:
- always get permission to meet with the media
- never exaggerate or sensationalize his work
- advertise his work only in professional magazines or with a calling card.
- be willing to refer his client to another geologist if he cannot handle the case

With respect to his own self, the geologist should be careful to apply the Golden Rule and maintain his own integrity.

"Above all, to thine own self be true,
and it must follow as the night the day,
thou canst not then be false to any man"

—Polonius in *Hamlet*

Problems in geological ethics
(I used to use these as points to ponder in my economic geology classes.)

1. To what extent should I continue to oppose an action or program authorized by my superior or my company when I do not agree with the program: a) on ethical grounds; b) on moral grounds?

2. I am offered a more attractive position with a competitor company in exploration work which will encompass the same area which I have examined for my present employer and about which I have confidential information gained in the employ of my present employer. What should be my decision and course of action?

3. I am severing connections with a company after some time of service. What reports, maps and notebooks am I entitled to take with me?

117

4.   I have an active interest in a mining property prior to taking a job with a company engaged in exploration. What are my responsibilities to the company, if any, regarding this property in which I have an interest?

5.   I am called in as a consultant on a new mining property and am offered a percentage interest in the property if I will write a geological report on the property and promote it to some buyer. Are there any questionable ethics involved?

6.   While in the employ of a company or after leaving its employ, I wish to publish an article either of a popular nature or on scientific findings based on experiences during my period of employment by the company. What are my responsibilities to the company?

7.   I have advance information of a confidential nature of my company's dealing with another small company listed on the stock exchange. Can I ethically purchase stock in this company to take advantage of the almost certain rise in the value of the stock?

8.   I am sent to examine a mining property as a guest of the owner, and I notice that his claims do not cover the whole deposit. Should I stake out the open ground for my company or notify the owner?

Chapter 12

Portland State College, Early Years: 1956-1962

After the flood of 1948 which wiped out the Vanport Campus of two-year-old Portland State College, it was moved, for five years, into local shipyard facilities. In 1953, it finally moved into "Old Main," the former Lincoln High School building on SW Broadway between Market and Mill Streets. It is now known as Lincoln Hall.

By 1956, the school had grown to 2,800 students, all housed in the one building, with a cafeteria and gym in the basement, auditorium, library, and administration on the ground floor, and classes in the two upper floors. Already it was splitting at its seams, and the first quarter of a new building, later to be called Cramer Hall, was under construction on the block to the immediate south.

The only science degree offered was in General Science. Since 1948, one course in geology had been taught, first by John Dart, then by Ruth Keen and Ralph Mason. My office in "Old Main" was shared with Irwin Lange and was located on the top floor in the back of the chemistry laboratory. I taught the beginning geology sequence to about 60 students in a small classroom on the second floor, which also had to serve as a laboratory. I had to use my own extensive collection of rocks and minerals as specimens for the laboratory.

My family moved into 1162 SE 58th Avenue on the west slope of Mount Tabor, a house which Margaret had picked out before I got to Portland. It was a lovely old house, with a full basement where I had a shop. We had a large and elegant living room, dining room, kitchen and TV room on the first floor, and three bedrooms and bath with large closets in the upper floor.

Daughter Sally finished her last two years of high school at Washington High, and in 1958, went to Mills College in Oakland, California. Although her applications had been accepted at both Holyoke and Radcliffe, she chose the West Coast. During several of the years we lived on Mt. Tabor, Margaret taught as a substitute in the city high schools, which meant that she had to be ready on call at seven each morning, so

I could take her to her assigned school if she got a call.

Being back in Oregon, Margaret rejoined her PEO Chapter W (a sorority alumnae club). I rejoined the Geological Society of the Oregon Country and the City Club, and I again became active in the early efforts to establish the Oregon Museum of Science and Industry.

When the northwest quarter of what is now Cramer Hall was completed during the summer of 1957, I moved into the laboratory that had been promised to me: Room 1—a large room, 50 x 26 feet, where I built, at one end, an office retreat out of steel bookshelves. The second course added to the curriculum was entitled "Elements of crystallography, mineralogy, petrology, and structural geology," nine hours for the year. I had already found out that it was easier to split off a course than to add a new one and was ready to begin splitting!

During the next five years, the fall term enrollment in geology rose as follows: 160, 171, 189, 232, and 345! Bob Van Atta joined the staff part-time in 1957 and full-time in 1958; Gus Armstrong came in 1960 and Miriam McKee started part-time in 1961. We added 15 hours of new courses in 1959 and 24 hours in 1961, the faculty of three and a quarter people by then was teaching 72 hours of courses. With no graduate assistants to teach the labs, our contact hour load was between 18 and 25 hours per term (now it is six to nine hours!).

We found time, however, to take the beginning class on a full-day field trip up the Columbia River Gorge in the fall, one to the coast in the winter, and a three-day camping trip to the John Day Country in the spring. In addition, we took the beginning labs on three trips in the Portland area during the year, and most other classes went on weekend trips as well.

For the first few years, the field trips were taken with personal and student cars, but as the caravans grew in size it became more and more difficult to find parking spaces at appropriate stops. Irwin Lange used to go along on many of these trips, and he assumed the duty of herding the cars into the smallest possible space so the crowd wouldn't have to walk too far and take too much time at each stop.

When the number of cars grew to more than a hundred, we finally began to use buses. We found that students filling a bus could take all the necessary overnight gear along by dividing the crowd into cooking parties of five, and allowing each party two cartons for food, one tent, and a knapsack and bedroll apiece. We eventually had 11 buses on some of the trips!

I think that I am most proud of the senior seminar course, initiated in 1957, which was specifically designed to give the students skills in the oral and visual presentation of geologic material. It was patterned after the Toastmasters program, as I had been a Toastmaster for several years.

Each student filled out a "critic sheet" after every talk, and 40 percent of the grade was on presentation! This seminar has contributed greatly to the ease of presentation of our graduates. The other course that I am proud of was the course in field methods where the student learned how to use a Brunton compass and plane table and alidade in topographic and geologic mapping.

It was during this period that the general studies program was started at Portland State. I was on the committee which set up the guidelines and learned a great deal from the skillful way in which the chairman, Philip Hoffman, conducted the meetings. For several years I taught a full-year course on the subject, entitled "Origin and Development of Scientific Thought," to anywhere from 50 to 150 students. In preparing for this course, I felt that I had really finally earned my Doctor of Philosophy!

One fall during this period, I acted as guide (and roustabout) on a bus tour to Alaska. It was a 27-day trip, through Banff and Jasper and up the Alaska Highway to Anchorage, then Mt. McKinley and Fairbanks; returning to Whitehorse, where we took the train side-trip to Skagway and back, then down the Rocky Mountain Trench, winding up at Harrison Hot Springs and Seattle.

By 1963, I was ready for a sabbatical and began to investigate how best to take advantage of one. Sally had married Scott McNall in 1960, and after two years in Portland, she finished college at PSU. With our new grandson Miles, they moved to Eugene, where Sally worked on her M.S. while Scott worked on his doctorate at the University of Oregon. We were at last free to go anywhere.

Concentrate 12a

Guidelines for a Committee Chair

The unwieldy and inefficient committee system seems to be, in spite of its inadequacies, the best known way of running a democratic institution. It has, however, been my experience that there are committees and then there are committees, and that there are certain principles which tend to speed up the process of decision-making. Here are my observations on what I personally think makes a good committee.

Committee size: Any number above three tends to slow down the work to be done, but for adequate representation, perhaps five or seven are the best numbers. Any more than this becomes burdensome in ways too numerous to mention. With larger numbers it is best to do most of the work in subcommittees.

Responsibilities of the chair: The chair must do most of the work to be done and make most of the decisions, *without letting the committee members realize that he is doing it!* His chief skill should consist of an ability to bring out opinions by questioning, and then devise a consensus statement that, ideally, satisfies all the members *without* taking a vote. Votes should be taken only as a last resort, and the odd number of members frequently permits the chair to make the final decision.

The chair must draw up an agenda and send it to the members before each meeting. He must work with the secretary to draft the working preliminary and final decision statements, which should be presented in print in the agenda for the next meeting so that they can be discussed, amended, polished, and approved. Work will be facilitated if the chair will see that as many preliminary decision statements as possible (some of which he may want to write himself even before discussion) are included in each agenda as working drafts.

Responsibilities of the secretary: The secretary must arrange a meeting time amenable to all, and set this time up for definite, regular weekly (or sometimes monthly) meetings at the same time and place. For the first few meetings each member should be reminded ahead of time, until attendance becomes automatic. Roll should be kept and those not in attendance should be noted in the minutes for each meeting.

The minutes of each meeting should include a complete record of all decisions taken but *not* of the discussions and varied views expressed during the meeting. These minutes should be duplicated and distributed not only to the committee members but also to all other persons and groups who might possibly be interested in the decisions being made. The secretary will also be responsible for

122

preparing copies of the agenda to be sent to the committee members well before each meeting.

Policies and procedures: Too many committees become immediately immersed in details, and never get around to finding out what they are really supposed to be doing!

1. A committee will have *only* such powers as it *assumes*, never more, and only infrequently less. At the first meeting, have the charge to the committee printed in the agenda, and begin to establish tentatively, and as soon as possible firmly, the field of influence within which the committee should operate, its limitations, and its relationship with other committees, groups, and individuals.

    Set up an operational chart showing these relationships, and be sure that constant communication is maintained with related groups and individuals. Perhaps they might give you an idea in return!

2. Next, establish firmly *in writing* as many of the basic policies as possible, to which the committee can refer in later decision-making. If done early, this can eliminate much time by making many, if not most, decisions routine.

3. Then decide on the order of importance and urgency of businesses to be accomplished, and set up a tentative schedule for the year's operation. Then and then only is the committee ready to begin to get the work done.

4. During the year, each committee member should consider it part of his assignment to consult with as many faculty members as possible on the problems of the committee. He should constantly "feel out" the sense of faculty opinion. If this is not done, and if the minutes are not widely disseminated, the decisions are likely to be voted down when they come before the senate or faculty. The more people that can be reached and persuaded beforehand, the more chance of acceptance by these bodies.

Concentrate 12b

The Anatomy of Success

I have usually been successful in my endeavors and I am happy with the way most of them have turned out. I feel that, in general, I

have had a very fortunate life with few setbacks and disappointments, most of which I have been able to overcome. They have been
minimal compared with the successes.

I need to acknowledge that a large proportion of my accomplishments have been indirectly a result of the great care and constant
consideration given me by Margaret, my wife of 65 years. Without
her constant love and faithful attendance I would never have done
half as many things or visited half as many places. I owe more than I
can ever say to her accepting, noncomplaining, helpful, thrifty,
cherishing assistance.

During our first ten years of married life, we lived in 16 different
towns, and she never ever made a single complaint. When I took my
first full-time teaching job at Penn State in 1946, I had to leave her in
Portland in September, with her 75-year-old mother and out eight-
year-old daughter to, sell the house and move our furnishings and
join me in December. She did it!

I was fortunate to be endowed with enthusiasm (eventually to
become the most important weapon in my teacher's arsenal) and a
generally sanguine outlook on life. Whenever a possibility for change
was presented, I could usually look forward to new places and
challenges with keen anticipation. Examples: my *wanderjahr*, our
move across country to Pennsylvania State College and into teaching,
a year with SEATO in Pakistan, the teaching and research jobs at
Santa Barbara, Hawaii, Walla Walla, Socorro, and Reno.

I had, undoubtedly learned from my father, a sense that I should
not express my emotions in front of others. He was a very repressed
Irishman whose most extreme curse when furiously angry was
"Confound it!" I'm afraid that my daughter, during her early years,
regarded me in much the same way that I regarded my father, with
respect but with only a modicum of affection. I still find it difficult to
give way to my feelings upon the loss of loved ones.

I don't know from whence it came, but in spite of varied health
problems, and possibly because of them (asthma, allergic migraine,
ruptured disc), I was able to develop endurance, stick-to-it-iveness,
and persistence which has repeatedly made the difference in whether
I completed or abandoned a project. As a student, it allowed me to
work for nine years on my Ph.D. thesis and still come back with a
second dissertation after the first had been turned down. As a field
geologist, it allowed long traverses and the development and maintenance of physical fitness from regular exercise, especially the last 20

124

years. As a teacher, it enabled me to put up with 15- to 25-hour-per-week teaching loads without the help of graduate students for laboratories or grading. As a writer, it helped me in editing and retyping manuscripts from five to eight times.

Although I had distinguished educators and ministers among my forebears on both sides of the family, I never inherited any high monetary ambitions, nor looked forward to being an outstanding journalist, geologist, teacher, or administrator. Perhaps this helped in reinforcing my ability usually to accept things as they came, rebound after an upsetting change or apparent disaster, and continue without letting it get me down.

Examples of low points: turndown for Rhodes Scholarship, Brown chromite fiasco, PSC Schwartz fiasco, turndown of department head and dean offers at Texas A&M and dean offer at PSU, firing from NMIMT, turndown of Capitan paper, bad back injury, unfinished Capitan map, Lounsbury fiasco, car accident.

Of course, I have had enough high points in my life to keep my spirits up and on which I still can look back with elation. Perhaps listing them will give an impression of my priorities. Eagle Scout (1924); first swimming letter, Spaulding Cup, Order of the "O" and Phi Beta Kappa, my marriage, chromite bulletin, the birth of my one and only daughter, Wallowa Mountains bulletin, dissertation passed, president GSOC, *Who's Who in America 1960*, round-the-world-trip, president NAGT, Neil Miner Award, citation by OAS, *Gateway* book, "Time Travel" column in *The Oregonian*, *Cataclysms* book.

During my formative years at home I enjoyed nurturing surroundings with relatively strict rules but moderate discipline. My mother used to repeatedly admonish me to operate on the Greek principle of *juste milieu* or moderation in all things. Later, I came to understand that it applied to beliefs as well as actions, and for most of my life I have tried consciously to maintain a middle position between opposite extremes with the result that I was consistently under attack from both sides. She and my father also were always telling me not to "go off half cocked" and to "think before I jumped." All my life I have had to fight the tendency to go into things without adequately sizing up all the possibilities.

Both my parents tried to instill the work ethic in me at an early age, which was evident as I was expected to help wash dishes, and later to fill the cellar every fall with wood and keep the three fireplaces and wood furnace supplied at all times. I paid for my second bicycle with a five-mile, 70-house paper route that I had for two years. I spent my Saturdays for the same period delivering groceries from a grocery truck.

Disciplinary habits were reinforced when I joined the Boy Scouts in 1922 at the age of 14, and since the scoutmaster had been a captain in the war, he continued to give us drill and discipline. I rose through the ranks to Eagle in less than two years. As a result of Merit Badge training (Eagle scout, 36 Merit badges, later Wood Badge, Silver Beaver), I developed a tendency to try new things and an ability to handle them when I did. Another early habit was reading science fiction, which I believe helped keep my mind flexible and enabled me to consider outrageous hypotheses at times when they were usually regarded as anathema. Even more of my indoctrination in self-discipline I owe to college athletics. I made three college swimming letters (backstroke) from placing with seconds and thirds. I found that if I practiced for two to three hours a day, six days a week, I didn't have to come in last. Today, if I let up for even one day on my morning exercises, which I have taken regularly for more than 20 years, I can feel the aches start to take over.

I found out very early that I had the ability to plan, organize and carry out complicated programs. Undoubtedly this was due to my early training in leadership, first in scout troops, then in directing scout summer camps (Siuslaw, Blue River, and Catherine Creek). I also ran several Red Cross Swim Weeks.

My later executive jobs consisted of geologic field work director for a survey of West Coast chromite for Rustless Iron & Steel, Coos Bay coal survey, field camp director for 60 students from Penn State, geologic mapping of the Tohatchi and Fort Defiance quadrangles on the Navajo Reservation, and planning and executing one- to three-day field trips from PSU. I was general chairman for the sixty-ninth meeting of the Cordilleran Section of the Geological Society of America, with 600 people taking seven field trips and presenting 250 papers at 27 sessions. Of course, building the PSU department from one to eight faculty (1956-1974) while teaching classes of up to 800 students per term took some organizational and executive ability.

During many of my 20 years as a field geologist, it was my habit to get out in the field as the sun came up. During my 18 years as head of the Geology Department at PSU, I nearly always got there in the morning before anybody else did. This was part of the "overtime" ethic given to me by Earl Nixon, which inevitably led to many new discoveries. Examples of new ideas I am proud of: "first aid to fossils," field-mapping on photo-mosaics for the Navajos, Capitan decollment, scenic trips to the geologic past, high Cascades graben, laws of field geology, eight then-undiscovered calderas in Oregon, and those over 200 "Time Travel" essays.

Another principle to which I have always tried to adhere is "moderation in all things" (I wish I could find the Greek phrase!). Over the years I have seen its value demonstrated in doing exercises (I tried jogging, but it was too violent), in eating (I keep my figure by shoving away from the table three times a day), in drinking (I've only been drunk once in my life, and never take more than one or two drinks at a party or one at home), and in taking medicine (I have always taken just as little as the doctor would let me).

I am sure that any success I have had as a teacher is a direct result of another important characteristic with which I have been blessed—enthusiasm for my subject and ability to project that enthusiasm to others. And I can't discount luck as part of my success, which I believe is simply being in the right place at the right time. I met Peggy early on, and we stuck it out. I always found new jobs when I needed them. I don't remember ever having been out of work.

Of course, my lifetime has been during just the right span of years to take advantage of all the momentous and exiting happenings that have occurred since the turn of the century. I saw the first automobiles and airplanes come to Eugene. I built one of the first radios in Eugene. I saw the first autogyro in Oregon. In 1929, I crossed the country in a Model T Ford I bought for $50 and later flew in DC-3s and Constellations. I saw early TV, radar, jet planes, etc. Starting with Sputnik, I saw the space age unfold. I have said many times that if I could have picked a time in all history to live in, I would still pick my own lifetime.

I also lived in the best country in the world through the best time that the world has ever known or will ever know again. I think our civilization reached its peak several decades ago. We are losing the moral fiber that brought us to this peak, we are losing ground in the availability of natural resources, and we have let the population explosion and the entrenched bureaucracy get completely out of control. The former wonderful environment of the Northwest is now mostly logged off and polluted. Read what happened towards the end of the Roman Empire.

I have lived at the right time for a geologist, too. I began when field geology was basic, and I was essentially a field and economic geologist for my first 20 professional years. Field work is now being gradually replaced by black boxes and maps by computer imagery.

Although I was trained in the 1920s and early '30s as a rigid geological uniformitarian, I have lived through the revolutions of neo-catastrophism and plate tectonics and the development of the fantastic tool of radioactive dating.

As far as success with human relationships goes, I have found that for the most part, the geologists I have come across have been compatible as friends because of their outdoor profession. My lifelong policy of accepting everyone as honest and reliable *until they prove themselves otherwise* has been especially valuable. This way you don't spend your time and energy doubting or worrying about people. A corollary to this is when you lend money, consider that you are *giving it* and forget it. Then it's a pleasant surprise if you get it back.

Fortunate as I have been to last as long as I have, I still can't help but believe that no matter how relatively mediocre a life you lead, if you just live long enough, you come to be appreciated. I never considered myself a hotshot geologist and I don't think many other people did either, but now I am being referred to as the "grand old man of Oregon Geology"!

Concentrate 12c

A Tribute to Pierrot

If and when I get to heaven, I will not be wholly happy unless our miniature poodle Peri is there to greet me. We have lived in an apartment for 30 years, and when people ask us how we like living there, we still answer, "We like it well enough, with two serious exceptions—we can have neither a pet nor a fireplace."

I had an amiable Airedale for a while when I was seven years old—I called him "Dale" and that is about all I remember about him. I also have a very vague recollection of a collie in the family for a while. We have had many cats who are pets that allow you to serve them, but who only show signs of affection when they are trying to get something from you. Our daughter Sally once had a white angora rabbit named "Fluffy."

Our cats ranged from part angora "Gabriel," a house pet for many years, to a striped tiger-cat we had in Pennsylvania. We had carefully trained it to a leash for our drive to New Mexico, but it escaped en route, never to be found although we drove back many miles. An eerie red-striped cat regularly visited us at Agness, but she went wild every time she smelled a certain bearskin rug of ours that had once had an adventure with a visiting polecat. But our poodle Peri is quite another story.

While I was teaching summer session at Santa Barbara in 1951, we decided to get Sally a dog since she was 11 years old and could help take care of it. Because we were moving around so much, we chose a miniature poodle. The first puppy we found turned out to be a hypochondriac, too sensitive for a pet, so after a week of putting up with her megrims we sent her back. We then chose a black and white unregistered miniature who wasn't quite ready to leave his mother, so we arranged to have him shipped by air to Albuquerque a few weeks after we returned to Socorro.

The day he was to arrive, we drove 75 miles to the airport, claimed the puppy, and opened the travel cage in which he had been crated up for many hours. And this tiny wooly mite of a poodle, no bigger than a shoe box, was so delighted to see us that he couldn't lick our faces enough, and won our hearts at once. We named him Pierrot, after the pantomime character and because of his black and white coat, but when he learned to chase his fluffy stub of a tail, spinning around in a circle when especially happy, we naturally shortened it to Peri.

For 12 years this valiant mite, weighing only 15 pounds, never failed to guard our homes in both Socorro and Portland, challenging intruding dogs ten times his size and several times getting bitten by a neighbor Great Dane for his daring. He quickly learned to tell the sound of our car and would announce its coming while it was still a block away.

He was Sally's pet until she left for school in California, but once when she came home and a visiting swain gave her a hug, Peri became furiously jealous (or protective?), nipped him on the ankle, and got kicked across the room by the surprised suitor.

Peri had a vocabulary of at least a dozen words, and if we carelessly used such words as "go," "dinner," "walk," and "outdoors," he would go into an ecstasy of jumping up and barking. On the other hand, if we mentioned the dread word "bath," he would instantly disappear, and we would have to hunt under all the furniture in the house to find him. But after his bath, he loved to be combed and brushed, and he would prance proudly around displaying his delightfully woolly pelt.

Peri could speak, sit, lie down, and roll over. He could tell when we were getting ready to leave him alone, and he would retire to a landing halfway up the stairs to lie there shivering. After we had left the house, he would go upstairs and if we had carelessly left a bedroom door ajar, he would pull back the bedspreads and wipe his muzzle back and forth across the pillows (doggy comfort behavior?).

"Kennel" was another forbidden word resulting in instant disappearance since Peri never forgot the trauma of getting his shots. We later left him at another pet hospital when we had to leave town, and after the first time, all was well. He would actually get out of the car and trot up to the door by himself; they must have treated him well there.

Both Peri and I were most comfortable when he was lying to the right of my big chair where I could drop my hand onto his head and rub or scratch his ears. That I still miss the most.

By 1963 he was near my present age of 88 (in doggy-years), and, like me now, was getting a little creaky in the joints and slept a lot. That summer, I was appointed by SEATO to a teaching position at Peshawar, West Pakistan, so we had to find some friends to care for him during our absence. We never saw him again, but he will have a secure place in our memories as long as we live.

Chapter 13

Pakistan Interlude The Orient, 1963

My sabbatical application was granted, and early in the spring of 1963, I applied for a Fulbright grant to teach in Holland. By then Bob Van Atta was fully competent to carry the department chairmanship for a year, with the help of Augustus K. Armstrong, who had arrived the year before.

The Holland job didn't work out, but at the last moment the secretary in charge, in Washington, called me to say that there was a position available as chairman and professor at the University of Peshawar, Pakistan, under the South East Asia Treaty Organization (SEATO) exchange program. I would get half my salary and all my travel expenses for myself and my wife.

Fortunately, Paul Hammond was to be added to the PSC staff. He needed a place to live, so we were able to rent our house to him. We really had to scurry around to get our passports and visas, and pack six steamer trunks of belongings to be airfreighted, but we made it in time to spend ten days in Japan before flying to Hong Kong and then to Bangkok for briefing at the SEATO headquarters.

As VIPs we flew first class (for the only time in my life!) to Hawaii and on to Tokyo. We had reached the point of no return on the flight when the captain came on the line: "Sorry, folks, but there is a malfunction in one of the engines, and we'll have to fly south (for 1,200 miles!) and land on Wake Island for a checkup! Please no smoking for the next two hours, as we will be dumping gas in order to land there!"

The somewhat anxious waiting ended with a perfect landing on the short runway, which we used up completely. While the ship was being checked out, I ran over to the adjacent reef and picked up ten different species of coral which I added to the collection in Peshawar.

While in Japan we had time to take a tour of Tokyo and a trip, in a private sedan, to Myanoshita where we stayed at the magnificent old hotel set in lovely gardens. We also toured Sakurijima, where the great Buddhist statue dominates the temples, and Hakone State Park, where we were able to take a trip on the lake and visit the hot springs on the edge of the caldera. We then took the fantastic bullet train to Kyoto, where we stayed in a ryokan and visited the ancient temples of this old capitol.

The only time we saw Fujiyama was when we passed by it on the plane to Hong Kong. We also caught a glimpse of an erupting volcano on a small island south of Japan. It was only a few hours to Hong Kong, where we stayed in a hotel across the street from the famous Peninsula Hotel and took trips across the bay to Hong Kong island and a loop trip north to the Chinese border. There was a water shortage at the time, and baths were available for only two hours in the afternoon. On our trips we could see that the reservoirs were nearly exhausted.

At Bangkok, the headquarters for SEATO, we were really treated as VIPs. Margaret's guide to the sights and shops was Supisha, a royal princess working for SEATO. We were entertained by the Pakistani ambassador and took trips on the klongs (canals), to the cobra pits, and visited dozens of the spectacular *wats* (Buddhist temples) which decorate the city. I used up two rolls of film on the gorgeous idols, buildings, and decorations, all gold-leaf covered or covered with broken bits of porcelain.

We left Bangkok on the inaugural flight of Lufthansa, accompanied by a horde of Japanese dignitaries and others. One delightful young woman, who turned out to be the wife of a Scandinavian diplomat, was able to converse in French with us. They handed out all sorts of goodies to the first class passengers en route.

We landed in Calcutta in a terrific rainstorm, and the plane bounced about 50 feet into the air on first contact. We didn't get off here but disembarked a few hours later in Karachi. We stayed over for a day to meet the diplomats and get our permits and visas before taking another flight for the 1,000 miles north to Peshawar.

Chapter 14

Pakistan Interlude:1963-1964

We were met at the airport by a large delegation from the University of Peshawar, including most of the geology faculty and some represen tatives from the American AID and Fulbright programs. They hung leis (made of tinsel rather than flowers) around our necks and escorted us to Dean's Hotel for a night. We then moved into the campus Guest House, where we stayed for a week while our own house was being prepared and furnished.

Peshawar, a city of some 1,250,000, is located about 15 miles from Jamrud Fort at the mouth of the Khyber Pass, and the University is on the Grand Trunk Road about halfway between. In order to go shopping, we had to take a tonga (a one-horse, two-wheeled cart) and drive the seven miles into town to one of the bazaars. The American Air Force station was located another five miles south of Peshawar. We were taken there many times by our friends to visit the AFEX store to supplement our diet with some American food and even once or twice to have a meal at the Officer's Club.

We rented several pieces of furniture (beds, divan, tables, chairs) from the furniture factory where we later bought our two magnificent camel chests for $125. We bought drapes, sheets (we didn't need blankets as the temperature was still in the nineties during the day and rarely went below 75 at night), kitchen utensils, and dishes. We had shipped four footlockers by air freight, but they didn't arrive for several weeks, so we lived out of our suitcases.

Our cook-bearer at the guest house, Nabi Baksh, a Ghurka whose father had been a cook for bigwigs, apparently took a liking to us. He insisted on following us and resigned from university service when we moved into the faculty quarters. He was a treasure, and we were envied by our British friends, who told us we were paying him far too much at 100 rupees a month—about $20!

We also had a sweeper who came every day to wash the concrete floors, a *dhobi* who came to do the wash in the compound, a *mali* who cut the grass (with a sickle) and took care of the flowers, and a *chowkador*— a retired army man who brought his own *charpoy* (a bed-frame with canvas cross-webbing) every night and slept on our front porch with a shotgun to keep off the *dacoits* (raiders from the adjacent "Northwest Territories"). Each of these was paid about two rupees a day (40 cents).

The geology department was in the Science Wing, a massive building which extended for 1,500 feet along the east side of the University. It was nearly a mile from our quarters. I bought a bicycle for $25 and rode to work each day. Nabi also used it to go to town for shopping, and when we left I gave it to him.

Geology was on the ground floor and anthropology was on the upper floor. My staff consisted of three lecturers, Mohammed Attaullah Khan, Arif Ali Khan Ghauri, and Masud-un-Nabi Naqvi; a clerk, Shaukat Ali; a special technician, Qamar Abbas; a driver for the Land Rover, Umrao Khan; and three laboratory attendants.

There were 29 undergraduates and four final-year students—Qasim Jan, A. Malik, M.A. Riaz, and Akhtar Zaman—who were completing their M.S. degrees. Ghauri and Qasim Jan later came to the U.S. and got M.S. degrees here. Jan has since returned to Peshawar and has published a number of papers.

A word here about language. Most of our students were Pathans from the Tribal Territories, whose native language is Pushtu. This meant they had to spend much of their time in grade school learning the national language, Urdu, so they could go to high school. Then, when they went to the government high school, if they wanted to continue to college, they had to spend much of their time learning English, since the University taught in English. The result was that by the time we got them they didn't know much about science, and their English wasn't all that great either.

When we were examining students who wanted to major in geology, I would ask them about physics: "What is the smallest unit of matter?" They would answer "The atom" but had never heard of protons or electrons, much less the multitude of other subatomic particles. I would ask them about biology: "What is the smallest unit of life?" They would answer "The cell" but had never heard even about the nucleus, let alone mitochondria or chromosomes. Their texts must have been nearly 50 years out of date!

I taught two classes to the final-year students: Economic Geology (based upon a text by Bateman) and Crystallography and Mineralogy (Dana). Both books I had brought with me since I had been told that there was no library to speak of. I also brought my old portable typewriter, which I sold when I left, as I did my Brunton compass. We went out in the field as often as possible, but in the Tribal Territories we were restricted to the roads since those who got off the main highways were vulnerable to harassment or capture by the Pathans.

We took trips to the coal mines near Kalabagh, the salt mines south of Bannu, and examined impressive stratigraphic sections exposed in the Salt Range. The students wanted to bring their bearers along to carry their gear, but as I pointed out to them, I was carrying all my gear, so if the professor did, they wouldn't lose face by doing so too.

The bureaucracy was incredible. If I needed another box of pencils, the clerk had to write out a requisition in five copies, all signed separately, and then he would disappear for the rest of the day. I found out that he had to stand in line for hours at about four different offices in the university, getting further signatures on up to the vice-chancellor! Later in the year I took the requisitions myself, since I was the professor and I didn't have to stand in line.

Whenever we wanted to take a trip, we had to go the police station and get a permit and then check in when we had returned. If we wanted to cash a check at the bank, it took an hour or so waiting for all the formalities to be observed.

As a result of this, whenever we were in town we would stop off at the American Consulate, which was next to the great Peshawar Fortress. There we could cash my paycheck, get our mail, and send our films back to Portland. We had been given an APO number before we left the States, which we were allowed to keep, and this was a boon since the local mails were highly unreliable. An airmail stamp was worth a day's pay so why wouldn't a clerk rip them off?

Whenever there was a holiday (I couldn't get the students to go on trips on holidays!), we took off on a trip with our British and American friends. There were innumerable holidays, lasting from one day or one week to one month (Eid or Marhoram), so we did get to see a lot of the country even though we didn't have our own car until after Christmas. Besides numerous trips through the Khyber Pass (every time a visitor arrived, this was the first thing they wanted to do), we took trips to Swat, Baragali, Lahore, Abbottabad, Rawalpindi, Bannu, Parichinar, and Lyalpur. I made one flight to visit the Pakistan Geological Survey headquarters at Quetta and was horrified to find that the fine buildings and laboratories built with AID and Colombo (Canadian) funds were scarcely occupied. The labs were empty, and the officials were sitting behind clean desks doing nothing.

One memorable trip was to Swat, an isolated valley about the size of the Willamette Valley about 75 miles north of Peshawar. The main crops seemed to be mustard (gorgeous in the spring) and poppies (for opium). It was still a separate principality, ruled by the Wali of Swat, and we stayed in the hotel in the capital, Saidu Sherif and visited the emerald mines, which was another source of income. We went to the government emerald dealer and he poured sacks of emeralds into our laps! I bought one tiny perfect hexagonal prism for $10.

We took a trip up the Swat River to Mingora and beyond, but the mountains, which rose for two miles above us, became so steep and there were so many slides on the narrow road that we didn't get very far.

Another trip was with the anthropology head, Dr. Ahmed Hassan Dani, to Sangao, where there was a microlithic dig in a cave used by the Soan culture (250,000 to 50,000 years ago), with 14 layers of hearth. The material for the artifacts came from a large quartz dike in the schist across the valley. The town of Sangao covered about half a square mile, and the street was so narrow that we had to leave the car and walk through town. We were given tea by the elders (with a ring of wide-eyed children watching from the outskirts) and several of the populace were delegated to carry our gear during the two-mile walk up to the dig.

We also visited a dig near Charsadda where the mound of the old city of Pushkalavati (700 B.C. to 460 A.D.) was being excavated. Artifacts of the Kushan culture consisted of small statues of Buddha, small replicas of stupas, lapis rings, and tons of shards from pottery of all kinds. We had already seen another Kushan city in Swat that reputedly had been destroyed by Alexander's army, in spite of a great stone fort a thousand feet up the hill above the town site. I climbed up the hill to the fort, and found, in a room near the entrance, a pile of rounded granite pebbles undoubtedly used for slingshot ammunition. The famous Kushan city of Taxila, near Rawalpindi, was an even larger excavation.

On a trip to Lahore, I was thrilled to stand in front of the Museum at the Gun of Zam Zamma, where Kipling's book *Kim* begins. Inside the museum is a marvelous collection of Kushan sculptures, most of them done in the soft schist of the region. The great fort and palace built by the Mogul kings in Lahore was equaled only by the fantastic mosque whose courtyard can hold 10,000 worshippers.

One of the best trips was our Christmas trip to Lyalpur to stay with PSC friends, the Ralph Boyds, who were working there for AID. By this time, I had been able to get hold of a Volkswagen which had been driven cross-continent from Germany by an American who was visiting his son at the air force base. He didn't have time to go through all the red tape of having it shipped back, so he appointed me as his shipping agent, with the provision that I could use it until I came back myself. Actually, I paid him for it with a US check (strictly illegal) and he sent me the owner's certificate when the car got to the states.

At any rate, we celebrated an early holiday at home, where Nabi cooked a gorgeously decorated Christmas cake with a lighted house on top and Santa Claus standing in the door, and then we took off one morning with our entire staff seeing us off. The Boyds had a fine house, with completely American furnishings (we hadn't seen an electric stove washing machine, dishwasher, etc., since leaving home!), and they entertained us royally. At one party we had a team of dancing girls (actually eunuchs dressed as girls) perform for us. We rode on a camel and drove around town to see the sights.

During the spring, the 50th anniversary of Islamia College (high school) was the outstanding celebration of the year. There must have been a thousand people gathered beneath the colorful *shamianas* (canopies) which covered much of the great field in front of the old college building. At night it looked like a great Christmas tree with strings of electric lights. Ayub Khan, the president of Pakistan, gave the main address, and the Khattock dancers gave their famous sword dance.

Another event, which I didn't get to see but Margaret did, was the wedding of the vice chancellor's daughter to Ayub Khan's son. The stories Peggy tells of the magnificence of this event are really something! We were also invited to the Pakistani Air Corps annual review in Abbottabad. We sat in the second row, right behind the generals!

Towards the end of April, my students stopped coming to classes. I asked them why, and they said they always spent all of May studying for their exams. I talked with the vice chancellor (president of the University) who told me that yes, this was so, and that I was to prepare syllabi of my courses, which would be sent to other universities so they could then send professors to administer the examinations.

Apparently there was so much chance of bribery and nepotism that this system was necessary! The vice chancellor then told me that when I turned in the syllabi, my job was over, and I could leave whenever I wanted to. He asked me urgently to stay another year, but since repeated bouts of dysentery had caused me to lose nearly 40 pounds (I was back to my college weight of 130 pounds!) I decided that discretion was the better part of valor and took preparations to leave.

First, I had to drive the Volkswagen to Karachi, a trip of 1,000 miles.

137

I took Masud with me as an interpreter, and we spent four days on the road since I wanted to make a side trip to see Mohenjodaro. This adventure took a whole day travelling over muddy narrow roads and along the top of dikes. Even though we nearly got completely mired several times, it was worth it. This ancient city has been partially excavated (around a much later Buddhist stupa which capped the mound) and shows the narrow streets and sewage systems beneath the tiles, in addition to the wells and the tiny rooms of the 10,000 inhabitants.

After making the complicated arrangements to ship the car to Portland, I returned to Peshawar to find the "Chinese Packers" building a six-by-six-by-ten-foot crate into which all our worldly goods were to go. We were entertained at a number of going away parties where we were again decorated with leis. We said a sad farewell to our servants and gave them departure gifts. Then we enplaned to Karachi where we had to spend several days checking out with the consulate and getting appropriate visas for our stay in Tehran.

Concentrate 14a

From Pakistan to Afghanistan
The Khyber Pass

The Khyber Pass, a 30-mile route through the rugged 3,000-foot-high Hindu Kush Range between Afghanistan and Pakistan, has an ancient and romantic history bound up intimately with the 150-year presence of the British in India.

The Hindu Kush Range is in Pathan Tribal Territory, and although the Pakistani government pays the tribes each year to keep peace and order, it stations armed guards along the highway and at the border. Those who travel through the pass must obtain written permission from the authorities in Peshawar, must not stray more than 50 feet from the main highway, and must take no photographs.

Peshawar is located about fifteen miles east of tribal territory and the entrance to the Khyber Pass at Jamrud Fort; the University is located about halfway between on the Grand Trunk Road, which goes all the way to Calcutta. Because of sporadic raids from Pathan *dacoits* in 1963, all university residents hired a guard or *chowkador* to stay on their porch at night. He carried a shotgun and a bandolier from his

138

former service in the Pakistani army. Our guard knew almost three words of English—when I would drive up late in the evening, he would open the garage door, come to attention, and salute with "Good evening, *Sahib!*"

I had occasion to make the trip to the border several times during the nine months that I was teaching at the University of Peshawar, as all visiting tourists just had to see this beautiful gorge for themselves, and I had a Volkswagen to accommodate them.

The pass lies in a narrow and rugged canyon bounded by steep slopes and cliffs. High on these slopes and on the still higher ridges are at least five forts; the largest of them, Fort Shagai, was then occupied by Pakistani troops.

The three routes through the pass consist of the ancient unpaved camel-caravan trail in the bottom of the canyon, the railroad a few hundred feet above it, and the "modern" paved highway still higher on the north wall. Besides the forts on the ridges and crests, there are several small adobe-walled Pathan villages at wide places in the bottom of the valley. Landikotal, the only Pakistani village in the pass, lies a couple of miles east of the summit and owes its existence to the smuggled goods that are sold from many small shops near the highway.

A bridge at the border is bounded on the west by the Afghan headquarters, whose loud speaker beams propaganda to the tourists in the parking lot on the east side and to the Pakistani troops in their headquarters. By slumping down in my seat, I was able to take a furtive picture of a squad of neatly uniformed troops undergoing inspection.

For several hundred feet west of the parking lot, the rocks of the north wall of the highway are painted with colorful emblems and medallions representing dozens of the companies and battalions of British troops who had fought their way to this border and helped maintain it during the British Raj. I was really excited to recognize familiar names I had read in Rudyard Kipling's *Soldier's Three*, the first of his books about India.

Chapter 15
Pakistan Interlude: Iran and Europe 1964

After the short flight from Karachi, we were met at the Tehran airport by our longtime friends, Howard and Lois Anderson. "Andy" had been there for several years, working as petroleum geologist for the oil consortium, and they took us to their lovely home with a true Persian garden of incredibly large and beautiful rose bushes.

They had planned several trips for us, and we did take a trip up into the Caucasus Mountains and saw the complicated geological folding and the interesting Iranian villages before I came down with a bug I must have caught in the Karachi hotel dining room.

We visited the fabulous collection of crown jewels in the subbasement of the national bank, where there were long ropes of pearls, bowls of rubies as big as hens eggs, a two-foot terrestrial globe whose continents were studded with rubies and the oceans with blue sapphires. Most of the week, however, was spent close to the bathroom!

When we flew to Turkey, we landed in Ankara, but did not leave the airport, and reboarded for Istanbul. We stayed in the delightful old Park Hotel on the hill east of the Golden Horn. Here we crossed the bridge to visit the great covered marketplace in downtown Istanbul, but the high point in our stay there was the Hagia Sophia Mosque.

Another college friend of ours, Bob Van Nice, had spent many years studying this ancient Christian church and making a detailed study of its architecture. Unfortunately he was not there at that time, but his name was an *open sesame* for us and we spent half a day wandering around the great central nave, corridors and balconies.

We went down into the great underground reservoirs which underlie much of the hilltop and spent half a day in the Topkapi Palace, now a museum with incredible collection of porcelain, jewels, and the jeweled dagger made famous by the movie *Topkapi*.

A boat trip up the Bosphorus to the mouth of the Black Sea showed us the Frankish castles built during the Crusades and the numerous elaborate villas built along the shore.

140

We had wanted to visit Palestine and Egypt, but we found that we did not have the inoculations for typhoid fever required, so our next stop at Athens, Greece, may well have been the high point of the entire trip. Athens, with its lovely Acropolis and ancient museum and agora, took a lot of time to tour. The trips to see Delphi, Corinth, Epidaurus, and especially the legendary capital of the Minoan civilization were experiences of a lifetime.

We climbed up through the great stone gate with its guardian lions, saw the possible tomb of Menelaus and the beehive tombs (all fashioned from hard quartz conglomerate), and wandered up over the Acropolis. Later, in the museum, we saw the famous golden mask of Menelaus, and many other millennia-old artifacts.

A three-day trip on a small steamer to Hydra, Mykonos, and Delos was all of the Aegean Sea that we had time to visit. Delos was the most impressive with sights such as the remnants of the great statue of Zeus and the lion statues, the little lake with a single palm tree where Aphrodite is supposed to have been born, the great amphitheater, and the mosaic pavements and underground cisterns capturing part of that very sophisticated civilization.

Mykonos, with its glaring white buildings, tiny church, unique windmills, tiny port with a resident pelican, shops, and friendly people will long be remembered. We left Greece with great regret.

Arriving in Rome, we checked in at the Hotel Ingleterra, just a block from the famous Spanish Steps. Our first visit, of course, was to St. Peter's Basilica, where we actually got a glimpse of Pope Paul VI in his car. We spent hours in the fabulous museums in the Vatican, saw the glorious Sistine Chapel and the Pantheon. The old agora, the Byzantine church of St. Mary of the Angels, and the Colosseum took another day. We walked the length of the Via Veneto, stopping for lunch en route.

The next day we took off on a bus tour to Naples, Pompei, and Capri. The Amalfi drive along the rugged coast was fantastic. We stopped overnight in Sorrento, and the next morning we took the boat trip to Capri, which took us into the famous Blue Grottos, and on a tour of some of the great villas, stopping for lunch at the villa of Axel Munthe, now a museum.

We took the train from Rome to Florence the next noon and arrived at a small hotel, the Nuovo Atlantico, before dinner. Beautiful Florence was the high point of our stay in Italy, for sure, and we spent three and a half days there. I was fascinated by the variety of semiprecious stones used in the construction of the Duomo, and by its great bronze doors.

141

Half a day in the Ufizzi Galleries was scarcely enough. We crossed the Ponte Vecchio and climbed up to the Michelangelo Park which has a famous view of the golden city. The Church of San Croce, the National Galleries, Santa Maria del Annunziato, and many more will long be remembered.

We had to take the bus to Pisa to get to the airport for a short flight to Venice and saw the Leaning Tower from the bus. Coming down to the airport, Venice was an incredible sight in the reddish late evening haze. We took the *vaporetto* to the island, and when we arrived, the Pension Flora arranged a special dinner for us, although it was nearly ten o'clock. We spent most of a day in the St. Marco Square, went up in the campanile, visited the cathedral, the Bridge of Sighs, took a *vaporetto* tour around the canals and one to Murano to visit the glass factories. We even had a hamburger at Harry's Bar!

An early morning flight took us to Vienna where we stayed at the Pension Elite on the west side of the Ringstrasse—very convenient to the center of the city, and just a few blocks from the University. Our reservations were only for two days, but by changing rooms we were able to stay there for six days, all the while visiting palaces (Schonbrun, Belvedere), museums, and the opera (Carmen).

Salzburg was the next stop—we stayed at the Hotel Mozart, attended a violin concert in the Marmorsaal of the Mirabel Schloss, saw an Aicher marionette show and a Fledermaus opera. We rented a car and drove through the Alps to Hallstadt where we went through the salt mines, and upon return had dinner at Winklers atop the Monksberg. The next day we spent in the old castle and fortress on the hill south of town.

In Munich, we stayed at the Link Motel Pension across from the railroad station and took in a concert with an old friend, Claire Roselius. We spent the following day at the Deutches Museum where we saw the original Madgeburg spheres and Leewenhouk's early microscope, and we also prowled through a simulated coal mine. The next day we spent at the Nymphenburg Schloss and the Ludwig Hunting Lodge built for Amalie.

In Zurich we stayed near St. Peter's Church, whose bells ringing the changes awoke us at seven. The antique shops were incredible! We rented a car and drove into the mountains, having lunch at Meiringen in the quaint Pension Flora.

Geneva was another high point. We stayed at the Montana Hotel and shopped for my Heuer watch (which I still have). I went to the University to find Marc Vuagnat, another old friend. We spent a day taking a boat

Mother with six week old John, Seattle, Washington, 1908.

John at three years old, Seattle, Washington, 1911.

House at 1855 Alder Street, Eugene, Oregon, 1918-23. "Now occupied by Delta Upsilon, parent fraternity of my colony of Sigma Pi Tau."

John at nine years old, Eugene, Oregon, 1917.

John, Betty, Bob, Grandfather, Aunt Carolyn, Granny and the Maxwell at Central Point, Oregon, 1920.

1916 Trip to Triangle Lake, Oregon, in Chalmers Touring Car—John is standing on the running board.

John, at 20, 1928.

"My sister Betty's wedding to Charles Gilbert in Eugene, Oregon, 1937." From left: Margaret (wife), John, Anna Davy (groom's sister), Eric Sr. (father), Eric Jr. (brother), Betty (bride, sister), Charles Gilbert (groom), Hugh Davy (Anna's husband), Sally (mother), Bob (brother), Velma (Bob's wife).

1933 visit of 3 aunts from Milwaukee to Eugene, Oregon. Back: John, Aunt Amy, Sally (mother), Aunt Carolyn, Eric Sr. (father), Margaret (wife), Aunt Marjorie. Front: Betty (sister), and brothers Bob and Bill (Eric Jr.).

In Milwaukee, Wisconsin, for high school graduation trip. From left: Uncles Chester, Hugh and Reeder, Josephine (grandma), Eric Sr. (father), and Aunt Amy.

The Condon Club, a geology honorary at U of O, Eugene, Oregon, 1921. From Left: Chuck Marlatte, John Allen, Earl Turner, Farrel Barnes, Harold Fisk, Tom Thayer, John Butler, Ed Schenk.

Part of the crew as we scouted the cliffs from the Columbia River, 1931. From Left, Meredith Sheets, Ed Thurston, Dr. E.T. Hodge, Dick Bogue.

Left: Red Cross Swim Week, Summer 1928, La Grande, Oregon. John on left with Bill Clark.

Right: John, in the field with plane table. Deschutes River, Oregon, 1928.

John's "Mess Kit Lid" as spoken of in Concentrate 3a, enhanced with soot.

"Camp Adventist," beginning of Gorge/ Mt. Hood summer trip, Troutdale, Oregon, 1931.

A regular sight—a breakdown of the Model T, somewhere in Illinois. Wanderjahr, 1928.

"The offending part being held by my two companions," Wanderjahr, 1928.

Above: John, well equipped for Gorge work, Oregon 1931.

Right: Start of big trip up Mt. Hood, Oregon, 1931. "I traversed up toward the X then dropped down onto Reed Galcier on the other side."

"Margaret, the Dodge, and plenty of snow greeting us on arrival at Crater Lake, Oregon," June, 1935.

San Juan Bautista, Castro Flats Camp, California, 1934. "With Bob Coats on right, and our matching 1925 Dodge Coupes. We may look good, but boy was it cold!"

Above: "Margaret's and my 'home' at Crater Lake, Oregon," Summer, 1935.

Left: A typical "round the lake" tourist boat tour with Wizard Island in the background, Crater Lake, Oregon, Summer, 1935.

Walter Fry and canine companion on left, with John, at Agness, Oregon, 1936.

A typical pack train south of Agness, Oregon, on the Illinois River, 1935-36.

Bob Owens, left, and companion, "building one of our Agness field shacks—all in one day!" Oregon, 1936.

US Mail boat at Crooked Riffles on the Rogue River near "Singing Springs Ranch" in Oregon in the 1930s.

A typical view of the weekly supply run loading up for Agness, Oregon, 1936.

Trip to Sourdough—"We're seen here waiting out the crest of the Applegate River in spate," west of Grants Pass, Oregon, 1937.

John, while employed at Rustless Iron & Steel Company, Grants Pass, Oregon, 1937.

A couple of student geologists and John on a University of Oregon summer trip led by Dr. Warren D. Smith to the Wallowa Mountains, Oregon, 1939.

A frequent sighting at Penn State Summer Camp. Sally is amongst some geology students and a rattle snake. Stone Valley, PA 1949.

Above: John, approx. 1945.

Right: "Some of the guys in New Mexico with the visiting 'jack-Moslem' Iranians amongst us." Pictured: John Schilling, Bob Coats, Said, Arnold Buzzolini, Shah, Kahn, and John, 2nd from right.

John with students during a field trip to coast while teaching
summer session at University of California-Santa Barbara, 1951.

"Our sweet and beloved Peri, 1953-1963, here, sporting a new haricut."

"Our Socorro, New Mexico, home, 1949-55. One of the few we purchased."
Photo taken in 1955.

Examining Four Corners. "I'm in Utah,
photo taken from New Mexico." 1954.

John and Jaguar, Albuquerque
Airport, New Mexico, 1955.

John, with his endeared red Dodge pickup, is getting a closer look at the ruts left by travellers on the Oregon Trail during field work for DOGAMI east of Burns, Oregon, 1958.

John at Bay Ocean, Oregon, on Portland State University field trip, early 1960s.

John, as instructor, at National Boy Scout
Camp Philmont, NE New Mexico, 1954.

John and Margaret at friends' patio party in Peshawar, Pakistan, 1963.

"Our friends, Dr. & Mrs. Ralph Boyd at Christmastime," in Peshawar, Pakistan, 1963.

Left to right: George Mahlin, John, Neal Fakrion, and Clair Stahl in the Wallowa Mountains, Oregon, June, 1972.

John at right and others in New Zealand for International Geological Congress, 1976. Dr. & Mrs. Gordon Oakshot are in the back at left.

John, as General Chairman, posing for a Geological Society of America photo during 1975 meeting held at Portland State University, 1975.

John and Margaret, Christmas 1991, Portland, Oregon.

John and Margaret, Summer 1995, Portland, Oregon.

tour around Lac Leman looking at all the marvelous *chateaux* along its shores. Marc took us to his home in Dordigny, where his wife, Anne Marie, served a marvelous dinner. The next day we took the train to Zermat and the Gornergrat, with its view of the majestic Matterhorn, Castor and Pollux and Monte Rosa. Marc had arranged a trip for me into the Jura Mountains with a graduate student. His English was nil, but we got along fine with my fractured French and a little German. The sixth day, July 4th, Anne Marie took us to Chamonix, where we rode the *teleferique* to Mont Blanc and Le Plain des Aiguilles. In the afternoon we visited the church at Assy, planned and executed by famous artists. The next day we went to the American Church and shopped in old town again.

At Lausanne we spent most of the day at the Exposition, visited the Cathedral, and saw the famous Lion of Lucerne.

Paris was our next stop. We stayed at the Hotel Baltimore, only a few blocks from the Arc de Triomphe and Champs d'Elysées. Our four days in Paris were spent walking, and riding buses and the metro. Starting with a city tour, we visited Napoleon's tomb, the Latin Quarter, Notre Dame, the Eiffel Tower, the Sorbonne, the Cluny Museum and church, the Pont Neuf, Galleries Layfayette, Montmartre, Cathedral Sacre Couer, Place Pigalle, Place Concorde, Musée Jean de Paume, Montparnasse market, the Bourse, the Tuileries Palace and, finally, the Louvre Museum.

Flying to London, we arrived at the Regent Palace Hotel, next to Picadilly Circus, soon after noon. Visited Burberry's, Harrods, Simpson's, Dunns, Fortnum and Masons. The next day it was St. Paul's, the Old Curiosity Shop, St. James Park, 10 Downing Street, Scotland Yard, and the Queens Guards show at Buckingham Palace. We took a two-hour launch trip down the Thames as far as Greenwich. The next day we toured Westminster Abbey and lunched in St. Stephen's Tavern. We saw *Who's Afraid of Virginia Woolf* that night, and later visited Mme. Tussaud's Wax Museum, Baker Street and Regent Park.

We rented a car and drove to Cambridge where we stayed in a 400-year-old house in Barrington with Raymond and Bridget Allchin, archeologists we had met in Pakistan. After visiting the Cambridge Colleges and meeting the geologists there, we then drove to Oxford where we checked in at Mitre Hotel (no longer in existence) and had high tea. We spent most of the day visiting the various Colleges there and then returned to London.

It took us much of the next day, spent mostly waiting at the airport,

143

to fly via Air Lingus to the Shannon, Ireland, airport. We stayed overnight at the International Motel in Limerick, and rented a car to drive to Killaloe where we stayed at the Lakeside Hotel, just across the Shannon River from the old church where many of my ancestors are buried. The Dean of St. Flannan's Cathedral showed us the church records with their names inscribed, and we saw some Allen tombstones in the cemetery. We then drove to Newport and had tea with a relative, Mrs. Annette Coffey, who directed us to Killeen Farm where my cousin Matthias Allen and his family live. We stayed until tea, then drove back to Killaloe for the night before taking off for Dublin.

The drive took only four hours, traveling through the green country-side with high hedgerows much of the way. We checked in at the Ormund Hotel, right on the river, and spent the afternoon shopping. The next day we visited Trinity College Museum and Library where we saw the famous collection of eighth to tenth century illuminated manu-scripts, including the *Book of Kells*, before driving back to Tipperary by way of Cashel, with its historic castle and church on "The Rock." After dinner in Tipperary, we drove back to Limerick. On our way to Shannon the next morning to catch our international flight home, we stopped at Bunratty Castle, which was then not as much of a tourist trap as it later became.

Thus ended the most significant year of our lives!

Concentrate 15a

Mohammed Khan Reads Three Languages (While Johnny Can't Read One)

(Abstracted from a 1964 talk to the City Club of Portland.)

Introduction

The cultural program of SEATO (the Southeast Asia Treaty Orga-nization) made important contributions to the educational progress of the less well-developed of the eight member nations, with very small expenditure.

Three exchange professors and several tens of graduate students and lecturers from Australia, France, New Zealand, the United

144

Kingdom, and the United States went each year to Pakistan, Thailand, and the Philippines where selected senior professors were given positions of authority, frequently acting as heads of university departments. At Peshawar, a succession of geology heads from Cambridge, Harvard, and Portland State built in five years time a respectable curriculum and reputation.

After spending only nine months in an Asian country, one cannot understand very much of its culture, society, and educational processes, although one is expected upon return to tell about the impressions and ideas gained during this short period of time. In the different world of Pakistan, history, religions and cultural development are so unlike ours, that the first month was mostly involved in getting over cultural shock.

Orientation

Separated from Afghanistan on the west by the Hindu Kush Range and from India on the east by the Great Indian Desert, West Pakistan extends for 1,500 miles from the Arabian Sea at Karachi to the provinces of Kashmir, Dir, Chitral, Swat, and the Russian and Chinese borders in the Himalayas. Peshawar, with a population of more than 150,000, is located in the northwest near the mouth of the famous Khyber Pass into Afghanistan.

After partition from India in 1947, Moslems formed a new nation consisting of two parts, separated by 1,500 miles. East Pakistan (later to become Bangladesh) has an area less than that of the state of Washington, with a population of 55 million, or more than 1,000 souls per square mile. West Pakistan, with an area larger than Texas, has a population of 45 million, or about 145 person per square mile. Away from the Indus valley and its tributaries, the land is largely comprised of mountains and desert. In comparison, Texas has a population density per square mile of 37, Washington 44, and Oregon 28.

History

The prehistory of Pakistan is represented by successive layers containing microlithis white quartz scrapers and blades found in a cave 100 miles north of Peshawar. Man did occupy northern Pakistan during the Stone Age perhaps more than 50,000 years ago. The history of Pakistan began 5,000 years ago, when a great city of more than 100,000 souls existed on the banks of the Indus River 200 miles north of its mouth on the Arabian Sea. Moohendojaro is the world's oldest known metropolitan area. It was excavated in the 1920s by John Marshall and Mortimer Wheeler. The rectangular street system, large buildings, and drainage and sewage accommodations indicate a degree of sophistication unknown elsewhere at this early date. Numerous clay seals with impressions of animals and symbols suggest that there was a written language as yet to be deciphered.

The "Sub-Continent" (a term commonly used to denote pre-partition India) was repeatedly invaded and conquered through the passes in the Hindu Kush from Afghanistan, Russia, and China. Alexander destroyed the city of Udegram, 100 miles north of Peshawar, in 326 B.C. This city, now in the autonomous kingdom of Swat, was protected by a castle on a ridge 2,000 feet above. Just inside the walls above a "Grand Stairway" I found a cache of rounded quartz pebbles of ideal size for use in slingshots.

Evidence of the Buddhist expansion during the late centuries B.C. and early centuries A.D. appear everywhere in the ruins of dozens of monasteries and stupas in sheltered canyons throughout Pakistan. These originally had inner chambers for relic depositories containing a casket with a piece of bone from Buddha. The outside of each stupa was originally covered with hundreds of statuettes of Buddha.

During this period, King Asoka carved his philosophical ideas and legal edicts on rocks which can still be read by scholars in the Kharoshti language. At the same time, the art form known as Ghandara, which had strong Greek affinities, produced hundreds of carvings representing in detail the life story of Buddha.

The Buddhist period was ended by the invasion of the Huns in 450 A.D. followed by the gradual rise of the Moghul kings during the first centuries of the second biennium. The Moghuls built highways and forts, and their remains still lie in splendor in the tombs they constructed.

The Pathans

The Hindu Kush Range has been dominated throughout history by the Arab Afghan ,or Pathan tribes, who have never been completely subdued, either by the Greeks, the Moghuls, the British (during their 150 years of occupation), or by the Pakistani government. As did the British, the present government pays each Pathan chieftain an annual subsidy so long as they keep peace among themselves and do not raid the lowlands. This system seems to work, and a few at a time, the tribes are beginning to join the government. The tribes gain in return

146

new schools, roads, dams, irrigation, and electrification.

The Great Partition

Until Pakistan separated from India in 1947, the population of Hindus, Sikhs, and Moslems had lived pretty well together under British rule. Partition caused one of the greatest migrations in history, as Hindus moved out of Pakistan and all but a few Moslems moved out of India. Religious differences and mob actions during transport killed some million Hindus and Moslems, which has affected the thinking and actions of both states since that time. Kashmir, for instance, still under India, is 85 percent Moslem, and is a constant thorn in Pakistan's side. When the United States gave military aid to India to help them defend themselves from Chinese aggression, Pakistan objected that this gave aid to their own enemy. The present Kashmir boundary is armed throughout its length.

Pakistani Culture

Pakistan is occupied by an amazing assortment of racial types, held together only by their religion, Islam. Color ranges from very dark to very light, height from short to very tall. Grecian profiles still suggest Alexander's conquest. A few Mongolian features appear, especially in the Hazara tribe. Dark skins from the south and east mingle with lean aquiline features from the west. Although Islam rejects the caste system which is the curse of India, it still does exist in Pakistan. A "sweeper" still has no chance of bettering himself. Nomads daily pass through Peshawar, making a living from goods smuggled across the border from Afghanistan. Camel trains still come through regularly. Traveling herds of goats and sheep (fat-tailed) are met on most of the roads.

Villages in the tribal territories are feudal towns under a chieftain and, until recently, made much of their living by raiding other towns or the fertile valleys. Valley villages are agricultural, relying on several crops a year of grains, sugar cane, cotton and jute fiber, and opium poppy. Although one does see elaborately painted buses and taxis and can travel in two-wheeled one-horse tongas, mechanization is minimal. One sees only one tractor per hundred farms, plowing is done with wooden plows, as it has been done for more than 2,000 years. Corn is threshed by hand with flails. Brahma cattle pull two-wheeled wooden carts. Although humans are the chief beast of burden, donkeys carry tremendous loads. Little girls collect and dry manure for fuel.

A village, which occupies one square mile of tightly-spaced mud-construction huts, will contain as many as 5,000 people; anything less than 50,000 is still called a village. A city such as Peshawar (sixth largest in Pakistan) may contain 125,000 souls. It is a walled city, and the fort built originally by the Moghuls is still occupied by the army, with the American Consulate in a building across the street.

In the bazaars, most businesses are small one-family operations, with frontages perhaps ten feet wide, selling one product only. Peshawar bazaars are famous for number and quality; especially for copper and brass goods, furniture, and cloths in astounding variety. In the shoe bazaars you can have any kind of footgear made to order in a couple of days, from sandals and curly-toed native shoes to European dress shoes.

Food

The basic diet is coarse wheat grain ground between six-foot-diameter discs of garnet schist. It is made into flat cakes similar to tortillas, or a heavy coarse bread an inch thick and a foot across known as a "nan." Rice is also a staple, but the only meat that the ordinary person ever obtains is an occasional scrawny chicken or a piece of goat or water buffalo that has died of old age. Mutton and beef is almost unobtainable. Fruit (oranges, limes, apples) and vegetables such as peas, string beans, cauliflower, tomatoes, beets, radishes, onions, and potatoes are available in season only.

Education

Since partition in 1947, with the help of SEATO, UNESCO, and United States AID, the Pakistani government has made a tremendous effort to haul itself rapidly into the 20th century. The already extensive irrigation system is being modernized, new power dams are being built, and electrification is becoming widespread although still erratic. Small industries are receiving all sorts of help, and the network of paved roads is being extended.

The government has recognized that the success of all these developments depends upon raising educational standards, a difficult thing to do for nearly ten million people, only ten percent of whom were literate in 1951 and sixteen percent by 1961. Literacy, by the way, is defined as the "ability to read with understanding a short statement on everyday life in any language." With the exception of

148

new factories, the largest building projects in the country are new schools, colleges, and universities. In 1947, there were only two universities, in Lahore and Dacca, and only a scattering of primary and secondary schools. Since then building projects have included four new universities, numerous technical colleges, hundreds of secondary schools in all parts of the country, and literally thousands of primary schools, including one in almost every village.

In Peshawar city alone there are now thirty primary, eight lower middle, three middle and eight high schools, five colleges (two for women) and the University of Peshawar. Schoolboys can be recognized by their gray *shalwar* and *kamise* (shirt and baggy cotton pants) and school beret. Faculty in the primary and secondary schools seldom have master's degrees. The oldest college in north Pakistan is Islamia College, now surrounded by university buildings. It celebrated its 50th anniversary in 1963. We met a number of college and university students who delighted in asking us questions about American ways and kinds of education. Some of them were regular visitors to our home and became good friends, inviting us to visit their family homes in their village.

The University of Peshawar

The University of Peshawar is located in the country, halfway between the city and the mouth of the Khyber Pass at Jamrud Fort. Like Portland State, it was founded in 1955 with about 2,000 students and now has more than 7,500 students with majors in 18 departments and seven professional schools. There is very little graduate work. The Administration Building is a large concrete structure two blocks long with an auditorium holding about 1,000 students. Commencement ceremonies are impressive, with the faculty in full academic regalia and addresses given by high government officials. At the one we attended, Ayub Khan, President of Pakistan, spoke beneath a *shamayana* (awning) which covered three acres.

The Science Block was actually three blocks long, and the geology department occupied a new wing which was completed in 1963. There were 45 students taking an honors or three-year geology curriculum, 24 were first-year, 14 were second-year and seven were third-year students. Faculty consisted of a professor (myself), and three lecturers (instructors). The British educational system has one professor as department head, with much more power than a professor in the States. Readers are the equivalent to associate professors,

149

senior lecturers to assistant professors, junior lecturers to our instructors, and demonstrators to teaching assistants.

Students take nearly all their non-geology courses while in junior college and only geology courses at the University. I found that my students' preparation in mathematics, physics, chemistry, and biology was highly inadequate, but the better students had nearly as good a geology background as our own four-year students. Their deficiencies in liberal arts, however, were even more apparent.

I taught two courses to third-year students, but I considered that my chief contribution, other than planning and organization, was seeing to it that all students spent a full day in the field each week during the year. We made three short trips each week, and spent Christmas vacation on a ten-day trip. I also tried to persuade students that monthly examinations were a valuable part of the learning process, not just something to pass at the end of the year.

Unfortunately, I got the impression that all this educational endeavor led to less efficient results than one might suppose. When I visited the new offices of the Geological Survey of Pakistan in Quetta, I found that the general attitude was that a degree gave one carte blanche to sit behind an empty desk in a secure civil service position for the rest of one's life. The Americans who set up this survey found it almost impossible to get these so-called geologists out in the field— they spent their time battling all the red tape one needed to go through to get anything done.

Problems

Severe problems face Pakistan, and beneath the friendliness and gaiety, their love of color and poetry, I could frequently sense a quiet desperation with which I could wholly sympathize. I can list some problems, but lack answers.

1. **The climate.** It is impossible by our standards, with temperatures above 100°F for at least five months of the year.

2. **Population growth.** It cancels much of the progress made since partition. The average income is $73 per year; in Peshawar the average wage was 42 cents per day.

3. **The influence of the Mullahs.**They realize that every advance by the population means a loss in their influence and power.

4. **The lack of resources.** The absence of minerals and timber and an

150

unfavorable import-export ratio—jute is the only important export—are problems.

5. **Language diversity and low literacy.** Although Pakistanis do not speak as many local dialects as Indians, they speak Bengali in east Pakistan, Pushto in the Tribal Territories of Northwest Pakistan, and Punjabi in southwest Pakistan. The national language, however, is Urdu, and, fortunately, the universal language of the educated is English.

A chieftain's schoolboy son from the Hindu Kush, speaking Pushto at home, spends most of his time in grade school learning to speak and read Urdu, so that he may go to high school. There, he spends much of his time learning to speak and read English, so that he may go to the University.

This Mohammed Khan (John Smith) who graduates from the University reading three languages is probably less than one out of several thousand of his 45 million countrymen.

Chapter 16

Portland State University: 1964-1974

We arrived home on July 27, 1964, in time to prepare for the next school year. My Volkswagen, which I had bought in Pakistan, had arrived in good shape, along with our large crate with all the possessions we had taken over and those purchased there.

The following year, while I taught summer session at Santa Barbara, we decided to move into an apartment in the Ione Plaza and soon sold the house at 1162 SE 58th.

My class in general geology had grown so large that we decided to try teaching it by closed-circuit television, and I spent much of the summer taping two of the three weekly lectures for the fall term. The third hour was given live in the Old Main auditorium and was used for exams, explication of the mechanics of the course, and lectures which were derived from the question cards that students got credit for handing in. I usually got 30 or 40 cards a week and could cook up a lecture by organizing the questions. In this way we could teach the course without adding more sections and overloading our meager staff of only four faculty.

During the next four years, this class grew from 200 (the largest classroom available) to nearly 700. Besides taping the new lectures for the following terms, I usually was able to revise at least two of the old lectures each term, but at the end of the third year, it grew too cumbersome and I gave up the chore.

By this time the older lectures were out of date (the rocks don't change, but our ideas concerning them are in a state of constant flux), and after four years I decided that it wasn't much fun to lecture to a little red eye on the camera. So, when Tom Benson was added to the faculty in 1968, I gave up the television course and handed the class over to him. By this time we had seven faculty, so it could be done.

An innovation in 1965 was the establishment of annual student-chosen awards: John P. McKee Award (usually a Brunton compass) to the best field geologist, and a Service Award to the "most valuable to the department." These seemed to help keep up department morale.

During the summer of 1966, I taught general geology at the University

152

of Hawaii. Gordon McDonald rented us his house in Kailua, since he lived on the big island during the summer and let me use his Volkswagen to drive across the island each day to work. I had a class of about 35, about half of whom were high school students. They were really sharp and kept the college students, who were just taking their science requirement course, on their toes. At the end of the session we made a tour of the Islands, visiting Maui and Hawaii, where Gordon took me on a fabulous trip into Kilauea Iki crater and across Kiluea caldera.

In the fall of 1966, we made another very important innovation by hiring Gene Pierson as staff geologist. His duties encompassed almost everything except teaching, and he took a great load off the faculty. A fourth innovation the same year was the initiation of a class in geologic illustration, designed for art majors who needed science credits. Over the years, this resulted in the magnificent paintings and sculpture which now decorate our lobby.

It was also during this period that the regular field trip program began to be supplemented by trips for nearly every course taught. Between 1965 and 1971 we ran 161 trips involving 6,509 students, who spent 395 days in the field and drove 55,410 miles. During this same period the faculty spent 934 days in the field with the students. That's an average of 66 days a year or over seven days a month! The total student-miles traveled amounted to 1,815,053.

I attended the GSA Convention in Mexico City, November 9-17, 1968, where I was able to take a field trip to Popocateptl and Ixtlaciotl, the two highest volcanoes in Mexico. I managed the climb to 14,000 on Popo, but was the last to arrive at the final stop, still several thousand feet from the summit. We also visited archaeological digs, with artifacts dated at 40,000 years old. The outstanding sight in Mexico City was the Archeological Museum; no one should miss it.

Two events in 1969 brought maturity to the department. The first was the move of the department during the Christmas holidays into new space (from 7,000 to 20,000 square feet) in Cramer Hall, and the second was the initiation of a graduate program which permitted us to offer a master's degree in Earth Science and Geology. We granted the first degree in 1970, and by the end of 1974, when I was retired, we had granted 11 degrees.

On August 22, 1970, Peggy and I left for London and Ireland for three weeks. We took in the Wallace Collection, the British Museum, the Geological Museum, the Victoria and Albert Museum—all of which we had missed on the last trip. The last day we drove to Brighton and

153

Rottingdean before taking the Royal Scot to Perth.

We took a trip to Dundee and St. Andrews and a bus trip to Oban on the west coast. We also spent a day in Edinburgh, then on to Durham with its marvelous cathedral and castle. We took a taxi to nearby Hexham and Corbridge, with Hadrian's Wall encampment nearby.

On the sixth of September we flew to Shannon for a quick visit with our cousins at Killeen Farm, then back to London, where we spent another day in the British Museum, visited Buckingham Palace, and went up to Bletchly to visit Ian Gass, a geologist at the Open University, and then flew back to Portland on the 12th.

In November, we flew to Milwaukee for the GSA Convention, where we also visited our Allen relatives.

In the fall of 1970, to celebrate the occupation of the new quarters, and to prepare for the forthcoming convention of the Cordilleran Section of the Geological Society of America, my department at Portland State held an open house and banquet which drew nearly 200 visitors. The convention, in March of 1973, registered 729 geologists and students from all the western states, with 257 papers presented.

At the end of 1974, the University suffered a $1,225,000 deficit due to under-realized enrollment, and all faculty over 65 were arbitrarily retired. Fortunately, I was appointed Emeritus Professor, and have since retained an office and all faculty perquisites.

Concentrate 16a

What I Have Learned

Presidential Address to the National Association of
Geology Teachers, 1968

During the past year, the *Saturday Review* magazine has carried a series of articles by eminent individuals entitled "What I Have Learned." I have been fascinated by these distillations of lifetime experience, and although I have great doubts whether my own experience as a field geologist, teacher, and head of a department can add much to the record, I cannot pass by this once-in-a-lifetime opportunity without a few comments.

Perhaps this is because one learns so late! George Bernard Shaw is reported to have said, "What a pity that youth is wasted on the young. If I had known some of these things earlier, I might have accomplished more. So, in my role of teacher, I will try to pass a few ideas along, well knowing that one actually has to learn the hard way, by experience, and that elderly words seldom have much impact on the young. Surely they have been said before, probably better; but the ideas have been meaningful and helpful to me.

Success

When I joined the Oregon Department of Geology and Mineral Industries as a field geologist on my first regular job, my new boss said to me: "John, you will be paid for your day's work of eight hours. Any promotion or recognition you receive will depend upon two things: First, the number of new ideas you are able to generate, and second, the amount of unpaid overtime you put in." I still think that this is the most concise and accurate formula for success I have ever heard! Again and again I have seen students like myself, without really exceptional qualifications, advance because of their ability to undertake hard work and long hours.

Motivation

Of course it is easy and fun to work long hours if you are more interested in your work than in anything else. I recently heard a definition of work given by a six-year-old child: "Work is what I have to do, play is what I like to do!" I am thankful that I have been able to play most of my life.

If you can persuade your students that geology is fun, you have helped them to find the motivation that is an important component of success. I have referred before to the excitement of learning, which can usually only be inspired by the contagious enthusiasm of the instructor.

Communication

It is a constant marvel to me how teachers, people whose very livelihood depends upon their supposedly superior ability to transmit ideas, so frequently have such great difficulty in communicating with each other. I suppose this is because we are usually dealing with subtle ideas and minute distinctions. Perhaps other professions have even more difficult problems, but after a long faculty or committee meeting I sometimes doubt it.

We are, whether we realize it or not, regulated primarily by

155

decisions made on every level by groups of people who get together to agree on our laws, our economy, our education, and even our entertainment.

These decision-making groups, when more or less permanent, may be boards, directorates, courts, councils, cabinets, assemblies, houses, senates, and congresses or parliaments. When they are more ephemeral, they are called powwows, meetings, hearings, conferences, committees, forums, tribunals, sessions, caucuses, commissions, and conventions. The very abundance of such terms in our language suggests the importance of communication and compromise in our kind of culture.

The very first paper I published in the *Journal of Geological Education* in 1951, was concerned with the needs for developing speaking and writing skills among geology students. Throughout their careers they will be spending increasing amounts of time, as they rise up the ladder, in such groups as those listed above. The rate of rise will, in large part, depend upon their ability to communicate and convince others.

Teaching

We would not be here today, however, it we were not primarily teachers. We have the problems of exploding college enrollments, and, until very recently, of declining numbers of undergraduate geology majors. When more and more of the beginning geology courses are being presented to classes numbering in the hundreds, we have a obligation to search for all possible techniques of restoring as much as possible of that person-to-person relationship which we all feel is the most important factor of excellence in teaching.

We cannot abandon the opportunity of rousing a lifelong interest in these potential geology majors to the impersonality of a TV course or an auditorium of 500 students taught by an instructor. I do not have the answer, but surely there must be one somewhere.

The Ecology of Good Teaching

In essence, good teaching depends upon (a) the individual teacher, and (b) his administrative environment. Perhaps it can be summarized as follows:

A.   Faculty
     1. Personality

156

a. Enthusiasm for one's subject
b. Ability to transmit this to the students
c. Rapport with students and concern for individuals
2. Training
   a. Mastery of one's subject
   b. Broad philosophical and cultural resources
   c. Research orientation and continuing practice
3. Teaching Approach
   a. Emphasis on concepts and processes
   b. Constant use of field problems with research participation by students as early as possible
   c. Problem-solving orientation in each the classroom, laboratory, and field
   d. Integration of all the sciences into all geology courses at all appropriate levels
   e. Requirements of writing at all levels and public speaking at upperclass levels
   f. Flexibility and adaptability in the use of new concepts, methods, and approaches to teaching
B. Administration
   1. The best teachers should give the beginning courses
   2. All faculty members should teach at least one undergraduate course
   3. Field trips should be required in as many of the geology classes as is possible and appropriate
   4. All the faculty should serve as student advisors, and there should be an organized program for placement of students in graduate schools and jobs
   5. If at all possible, faculty offices and subdisciplines in geology should never be physically separated by location in different buildings or separate floors
   6. There should be regular weekly faculty meetings limited to 50 minutes and operating under published policies and procedures

One other function of a geology faculty is seldom mentioned, but can be very important to the department and to the school. This is community involvement. Faculty should be encouraged (and re-warded) for:
1. Visits to high schools and even grade school classes

2. Talks to community clubs and other organizations
3. Assistance in the activity of a student geology club
4. Cooperation with local state surveys, museums, etc.
5. Cooperation with the university school of education in presenting geology classes and organizing curricula for potential secondary school science teachers

Probably, what I have been trying to say is that in order to be of greatest service, every teacher must be as well-rounded as possible. The geologist of tomorrow must have not one, but many tools, not all of them strictly academic, with which to meet new challenges. All of the aspects of academic life that I have suggested can be important in preparing students for changing times. As Bill Rubey has said, "the jobs for which we are training students today do not exist yet. Most of the great advances in science today are being made by people working in more than one field, as is emphasized by the proliferation of such inter-disciplines as astrogeology, oceanography, urban and environmental geology, and many others.

Surely we should be concerned with all of these things, if we are to implement the expressed purpose of our organization: "to foster improvement in the teaching of the earth sciences at all levels of formal and informal instruction, to emphasize the cultural significance of the earth sciences, and to disseminate knowledge in the field to the general public."

Concentrate 16b

Time, Life, and Humankind

A sermon given twice on August 4, 1974,
at the First Congregational Church, Portland, Oregon

Introduction

I have been fortunate because my study of the history of earth and life on earth has bolstered my confidence in the gradual development of higher intelligence, higher aspirations, higher accomplishments, and greater perfectibility. One who has spent a lifetime studying the slow rise of life, in spite of uncounted failures and regressions, cannot doubt that we too can rise to a still higher state of consciousness. One who can look back into those depths from which we have risen cannot doubt that we are destined, in spite of pessimistic prophets of doom, to move on to better days.

I taught a course called "The History of Life," from its primeval beginnings to the present, and it reinforced my confidence in the ultimate meaning of life. In order to explain the fantastic ability of life to attain greater degrees of complexity and competence, I will first discuss the meaning and origins of *geologic time*, then review the *rise of life*, and finally try to summarize how the principles that produced this progress affect *mankind himself*.

Time

Possibly the greatest contribution geology has made to our culture is the concept of *geologic time*. Geology, a young science, began about the year 1800, when a British engineer with the distinguished name of Smith showed conclusively that rocks containing groups of *similar* fossil organisms could be matched up over wide areas, sometimes worldwide.

This meant that we could begin to construct a standard column of rocks, with the oldest at the bottom and the youngest at the top, which would enable us to tell the *relative* age of the fossils in the rocks. This in turn would give us their position in the hypothetical column (which, in total, measures about 72 miles thick). The fossils showed a gradual increase in complexity from bottom to top—invertebrates first, then fish, then amphibians and insects, then reptiles and birds, and finally mammals and at last, man. The very names given the primary segments of eras of the column denote this relationship: Paleozoic (Age of Ancient Life), Mesozoic (Age of Mediæval Life), and Cenozoic (Age of Recent Life).

For nearly a hundred years, geologists were largely concerned with the elaboration and refinement of this column, and were increasingly concerned with the multitude of events which had occurred, such as repeated advances and retreats of the sea over most of the continents and repeated folding up and wearing down of great mountain ranges. By no stretch of the imagination could all these events be fitted into the chronology of Bishop Ussher, a cleric, who in the mid-1600s had declared that the earth was formed in October, 4004 B.C. The Hindu scripture, on the contrary, states that one cycle of the universe (one day in Brahma's life) is 4.3 billion years, and that we are 2 billion years into the present cycle.

Numerous attempts to gauge the real age by rate of deposition of the column (100 million years), rate of accumulation of salt in the sea (100 million years), rate of cooling of the earth (40 million years) still left geologists feeling very cramped by even these vast time spans. Events on earth and development of life *must* have taken more time.

It wasn't until the turn of the century, with the discovery of radioactivity, that determinations of real time became possible. The natural breakdown by radioactivity of certain elements into other elements occurs at a known unchangeable rate. The measurement of the proportions of the mother and daughter elements finally gave real ages to rocks containing them.

The oldest rocks on earth are about 3.8 billion years old; unicellular organisms probably appeared 3 billion years ago, and abundant and varied life appears 600 million years ago. Dinosaurs dominated the earth 150 million years ago, mammals replaced the dinosaurs 60 million years ago, and fire- and tool-using man appeared only three million years ago. The Hindu estimate of time was very close to what we now believe.

Frankly, I cannot grasp these immense spans of time any more than I can grasp the immensities of space measured by the astronomers. Perhaps reducing the scale to one year will help! If the earth originated on January 1, unicellular life appeared on April 5, abundant invertebrate life on October 13, dinosaurs by December 19, abundant mammals by Christmas, and man on December 31, at eight p.m. Recorded history (6,000 years) began after 11:59 p.m, less than one minute to go. Christ came thirteeen and a half seconds ago.

Life

There are 92 natural building blocks—kinds of atoms which make up the universe. All matter is made up of these 92, or combinations of them. But all *life* is made up predominately of only four: hydrogen, oxygen, carbon, and nitrogen, although small amounts of sulfur and phosphorus and minute amounts of a few other elements are necessary for many forms of life.

Why these four? Of the five most abundant elements in the entire solar system, four are the chief components of life. Water (which makes up 60-95 percent of all life forms) is hydrogen and oxygen. The atmosphere is 20 percent oxygen and nearly 80 percent nitrogen. Carbon is present in smaller amounts in the atmosphere, in the oceans, and in the rocks. (The fifth element is helium.)

After the aggregation of the solar system from dust clouds 4.6 billion years ago, the earth cooled and two of the five gases condensed to form a primeval ocean. The atmosphere, which then had little or no oxygen, is thought to have been composed of hydrogen, the light gas helium (which later escaped into space), and combinations of hydrogen with nitrogen and carbon. Thus all the elements necessary for life were present.

In 1953, a scientist took a mixture of these elements and water and subjected them for a week to an electric spark discharge. On analysis, the resulting liquid was found to contain a complex mixture of amino acids, the basic building-blocks of life. Later experiments have shown that lightning strikes in shallow lakes or tide pools could have synthesized almost every major constituent of living systems. Since that experiment a myriad of hypotheses have been proposed to attempt to explain how these nonliving building-blocks could develop into self-duplicating organisms. This step is still the basic miracle of life; we may never find direct evidence of it. It took billions of years to occur!

We know that plants appeared first, since they produce oxygen, and most animal life depends on oxygen. As oxygen became a component of the atmosphere, animals could have then begun to evolve. This probably took 2 billion years! The earliest abundant record of invertebrate life appeared little more than half a billion years ago.

Suddenly then, we find thousands of different kinds of animals representing nearly *all* of the invertebrate groups fossilized in the rocks. Suddenly, they had developed the ability to secrete a hard protective shell, which could be preserved. From then on, evidence of increasingly complex life appears abundantly.

Today, over a million different kinds of animals have been classified (over two-thirds of them insects). *How* has this fantastic variety of life, which occupies every environment on land, underground, in the sea, and in the air developed? How has this thin and tenuous mantle of life, which we call the biosphere, that covers and permeates the surface of the earth come into being? No single act of creation could possibly be as miraculous as the complex and interwoven processes which we believe to have resulted in this awesome diversity in which every life form is beautifully fitted to survive in its own particular environmental niche.

Our knowledge of these complex biological processes is derived from an amazing number of lines of evidence. In addition to the fossil evidence, we have embryological, physiological, and biochemical data from present life for which resemblances can be traced throughout the great tree of life. Man himself has created, within historical or near-historical time, a great diversity of domesticated life: from Saint Bernard to Chihuahua, Percheron to pony, Jersey to Black Angus. Putting all this together, we find three repetitive themes occurring again and again throughout geologic time: from simple to complex, from small to large (especially increase in brain size), and from generalized to specialized.

These changes occur as a result of two processes. First, *organic variation* in a population (tall-short, brown eyes-blue eyes, etc.) and second, *natural selection* of those variations which are best able to survive competition in their particular environment. Fortunately there is always a variety of different kinds of individuals—some who are *able* to service and perpetuate the race. Thus, life is always changing. But what is most important is that it is changing in favor of the more complex, more specialized, better adapted forms. Those less able to compete with new higher forms eventually become extinct. Out of a total number of forms that have existed on earth, more than 98 percent are now extinct! Only a few of the branches of the tree of life now reach the top of the tree.

Humankind

Now, what is *man's* place in nature? What is *his* future? In 1936, I heard a French Jesuit priest, Pierre Teilhard de Chardin, speak on "Ancient Man" at the University of California. He was just back from China, where as a paleontologist and anthropologist, he had helped unearth the 350,000-year-old skull of Peking Man. Upon his death in 1955, it was discovered that de Chardin had written several books on the phenomenon of man, which had been unacceptable to the Catholic hierarchy. Fortunately, copies of the manuscripts had been left with friends who immediately saw to their publication.

De Chardin's ideas approximate my own ideas on man and his future. Even in translation they are not easy reading, but I will try to summarize them:

For de Chardin, all being is unitary, the universe is "convergent," steadily progressing toward an "Omega Point," which is Christ, the center and meaning point of the universe itself. Life is not a chance combination of material elements, an accidental product of world history, but the form assumed by matter when it reaches a certain level of complexity. The organization of the biosphere introduced a new order, characterized by special properties. Matter, when it became "vitalized," showed new qualities, such as the ability to reproduce, to increase in complexity or *degree* of vitalization.

Another trend is the "cerebralization," or increase in intensity of psychic activity that, for example, distinguishes the insects from the vertebrates. The great breakthrough in this latter characteristic occurred only a few million years ago at the apex of one small twig on the relatively unspecialized and primitive branch of mammals, the primates, and represents a specially favored axis of development. Only in this group did the cerebralization fully move over the threshold into reflection or consciousness. This change established on earth a *thinking* sphere, the Noosphere, superimposed on the Biosphere.

Man is unique among all life in having: 1) An extraordinary power of expansion over the entire earth by waves. 2) An extreme rapidity of diversification into a multitude of cultures. 3) A still greater multitude of diverse individuals with individual capabilities within each culture. 4) A remarkable persistence of germinative power, or reproduction ability. 5) A unique capacity for interconnection (by communication) between its separate groups that has resulted in a gradual coalescence of all groups.

It is this coalescence which generates an *ethnic compression*. As the population increases, it results in an increase in available energy, just as in the compression of a gas. The more mankind has compressed itself (by population growth), the more it is forced to find new ways of arranging its elements, ways that are the most economical of energy and space. This in turn should automatically be accompanied by better social arrangements since it inevitably increases each human radius of action and power of penetration in relation to others. Perhaps this is what the younger generation has been trying to tell us! The only coherent explanation of what is happening is the idea of an increasingly convergent world.

Perhaps our modern social distress is a result of this change from divergence to convergence which has now reached worldwide proportions. The Noosphere, like the brain in its evolution, is now folding in upon itself, and generating even greater psychic powers, as evidenced by the fantastic discoveries made by *group* (as compared to individual) scientific research.

Mankind may now have completed his physical development, but he is on the threshold of a new leap forward, a new kind of development of his psychic powers, a new understanding not only of the world, but of himself. The vast eon-long efforts toward cerebralization that started billions of years ago on the infant earth is being fulfilled in the direction of *collective organization* and social consciousness.

Just as we have seen in the history of life, the increase in complexity from atom to molecule, from molecule to protein, from protein to cell, from simple cell to specialized cell, from specialized cell to simple organism, and from simple organism to complex organism, so also can we see in recorded history this trend—as the Noosphere becomes more dense. From family to tribe, from tribe to city-state, from city-state to nation, from nation to empire. The League of Nations and the United Nations are, so far, abortive in attempts to continue the trend toward the future unification of man in the completion of the Noosphere, which will only be accomplished by universal acceptance of the principles enunciated by Christ.

Mankind, that youngest of all species, is still advancing with full vigor toward this goal; there are now more people of good will than ever before. We are still converging toward eventual maturation, toward full hominization. Hopefully science will enable us to understand and faith will keep our goals clear until we reach a common understanding and a common passion—until we have reached Omega.

Concentrate 16c

The Hierarchy and Language of Academe

Introduction

I have had friends who, when I told them that I taught three classes, asked me "What do you do during the other 37 hours of your week?"

I had to explain to them that each class in geology usually included three 50-minute lectures and two or three hours helping students in the laboratory. They were unfamiliar with academic jargon, and I had to translate much of this for them. I told them that in addition to these

15 to 18 hours of classwork, we must outline the next week's lectures, prepare and grade exams, read and grade student reports, keep office hours for advising students and consulting with visitors, attend several committee meetings each week, conduct several field trips each year, and, of course, work on research problems and write reports for publication. To climb the academic hierarchical ladder ("publish or perish"), a faculty member should do most of these.

During 40 years at PSU I have seen detailed descriptions of only a few of these rungs. I have also noted that the number of administrative members on the ladder has grown proportionally much faster than the student body or the academic (teaching) faculty.

I recently realized that a concise description of the ranks in the hierarchy might be a valuable essay to hand those friends who are unfamiliar with the language of academe and this stratigraphic organization which ranges from chancellor to student. I take the Oregon State System of Higher Education and Portland State University as models and exclude nonacademic administrators.

The first paragraph of each of the following sections consist of definitions, appropriately copied from *Webster's Collegiate Dictionary*.

Chancellor: "A head of some universities."
In Oregon, the chancellor is the head of the State System of Higher Education, and the university presidents report to him and the Board of Higher Education. In Pakistan the chancellor was the president of the University of Peshawar.

President: "A chief officer of a corporation, company, society, etc."
A president is in charge of all operations of each university and state college in Oregon. A provost, who is usually the second in command can act in the absence of the president. He is also dean of the deans, in charge of academic affairs. I note in the PSU phone book a provost, four vice provosts, two assistants to the president as well as presidential advisors. PSU also has a vice president for finance and administration.

Dean: "Any of certain college supervisors of junior students. 3. The chief administrative officer, under the president, of a college or university faculty or department."
A dean supervises the academic affairs of each school and college within the university, and all department heads or chairs

165

report to him. There are usually associate or assistant deans for various duties as well as a dean of students.

PSU has a dean for the College of Liberal Arts and Sciences (23 departments), and one for each the six schools: Business Administration, Education, Engineering and Applied Sciences, Fine and Performing Arts, Social Work, Urban and Public Affairs, as well as for Extended Studies and Summer Session.

Chair or Department Head: "... an office of authority, dignity, etc., as that of professor, or the like; as the *chair* of mathematics in a college. A chairman."

A chair is elected by the faculty of his department for a period of three years, a department head is appointed by the dean for an indefinite period. They supervise all the academic and financial activities of the department. I was head of geology at PSU for 15 years and chair for three years.

Professor: "One who professes, or publicly teaches, any branch of learning; especially a lecturing or teaching officer at a university, college or other seminary, on whom the title has been officially conferred by the academic authorities; as, a *professor* of mathematics."

Three professorial ranks begin with assistant, followed by associate and then full professor. A Ph.D. (Doctor of Philosophy) degree is nearly always a requirement for professorship. It usually takes four or five years to move up each step on the hierarchy.

Tenure is granted after five to seven years (probation) of satisfactory performance, which only assures that a professor cannot be fired unless he exhibits rank incompetence, moral deficiencies, or the university suffers from a financial exigency (that is how I was retired in 1974). In Europe, the only full professors are the department heads.

Adjunct professors are given faculty status and perquisites in return for limited services in teaching or research. Upon retirement, a professor may be voted emeritus status by his department, which then may supply him with an office and many faculty perquisites.

Instructor: "Specifically, in American colleges and universities, a

teacher of a rank inferior to that of a professor."
Instructors are usually faculty who have earned an M.S. or M.A. (Master of Science or Master of Arts) degree, but have not yet obtained their academic "union card"—the Ph.D. degree. They teach laboratories and lower division courses.

Student: "A person engaged in study; a learner; scholar."
University and most college students fall into five ranks, freshman, sophomore, junior, senior and graduate, depending upon the number of years of attendance and/or the number of courses (and credit hours) they have passed.

When seniors complete all department and school requirements, they are granted the B.A. (Bachelor of Arts) or B.S. (Bachelor of Science) or other degrees in some schools.

Undergraduate freshmen or sophomores usually take lower division courses numbered 100 to 299, while juniors or seniors take upper division courses numbered 300 to 499. Graduate students working towards advanced degrees usually take courses numbered 400 to 600.

A few graduate students in each department can help support themselves as "TAs" (Teaching Assistants) or "RAs" (Research Assistants). They are paid for part-time assistance to a faculty member for teaching in his laboratories or helping in his research.

Undergraduate courses are graded from excellent to fail (A, B, C, D, F), or by Pass/No Pass. Courses given grades of "fail" or "no pass" must be taken over and passed if credit is required. Many specified courses are required by the student's department and by his college or school. Maintenance of a certain "GPA" (grade point average) is also required for graduation. GPAs are calculated by equating four points for each hour of A, three for B, etc., adding them together, and then dividing by the number of course hours taken. Most courses earn three credit hours toward the 186 hours required for graduation with a bachelor degree. This means that an average student needs to take a little more than five courses (15 credit hours) per term for 12 terms or four years. I once had an older student who took my beginning geology class for an A; he received his B.A. degree from PSU in two years after taking up to 35 hours of classes each term for six terms!

Universities and colleges that divide the school year into two semesters rather than three terms figure credit hours differently. I taught in the semester system at Penn State and at Berkeley. There are advantages and disadvantages to both the two-semester and the three-term systems.

Chapter 17

Retirement I: 1974-84

Retirement came as a shock, and at first I felt some resentment at being so suddenly dumped, especially since the new law prohibiting involuntary retirement before 65 was passed two months later. However, I soon discovered, that, thanks to my appointment as emeritus professor, retirement had many attractions.

I had completed 20 years as a field geologist, 20 years as a teacher, and now I could start a third career as a full-time writer. I had an office only a hundred yards from our apartment, full use of mailing privileges, a xerox machine, and warm associations with faculty and students. My income, which was $21,000 at retirement, began to increase more rapidly than that of my still-working associates. It had, in ten years, more than doubled, and thanks to a good broker, my investment portfolio had more than tripled in value. But before beginning full-time writing, I took on three other jobs.

My first job after retirement began in January, 1975, when I went to Whitman College in Walla Walla, Washington, to take the place of Richard Clem, the geologist there who had died suddenly. I spent the second semester of the year teaching his courses and helping find a replacement, Bob Carson. Walla Walla is a lovely town; we made many friends and enjoyed the stay there very much.

The second job began in 1976, when I began a six-month stint at the Nevada Bureau of Mines as Senior Geologist. It was a fascinating job because John Schilling, the director (an old student of mine at both Penn State and Socorro), gave me eight different projects to work on, which meant that whenever I tired of one chore, I could shift to another. I was also able to go on all the weekend department field trips and thus got to see a lot of the state.

The projects included editing manuscripts on leaching copper ores and the urban geology of Reno, compiling indexes for Nevada stratigraphy and *Isochron/West*, a publication listing all dates of western U.S. rocks, etc., but the most important and interesting duty was the compilation of all the data on seven of the largest iron mines in Nevada.

This involved filling in the blanks on 13 pages for each mine, after translating the data into the metric system and then into code numbers from a manual used by the U.S. Bureau of Mines, so it could be entered into their computer file. I really learned the metric system at this time! Part of this entailed compiling the ore reserves from available maps and records. I was suspicious of some of this data, so we visited the mines on a series of trips and found that at most of them the owners had illegally scooped out and high-graded most of the reserves below the levels indicated before closing the mines.

My third job was six months back at Socorro, New Mexico, as a research geologist there for the New Mexico Bureau of Mines. The chief project was to write a third edition, completely revised, of *Scenic Trips to the Geologic Past, No. 3*, which I had first published in 1958. We really enjoyed visiting with all our old friends there and seeing the country again. We were able to get a small, new house near the campus, which was very convenient. Our friends supplied us with enough furniture to make it cozy. We drove back to Portland early in February, 1976.

On August 3, 1976, I left for New Zealand and Australia to attend my first and only International Geological Congress. I took a ten-day trip on the North Island before the meetings in Sydney, and an eight-day trip on the South Island after the meetings, and fell in love with the country and the people. I also took an engineering geology trip to Canberra to examine the environmental parameters which were taken into consideration when they laid out the development for this new city.

Upon my return, I continued work on my new book, *Magnificent Gateway*, and by 1978 was able to bring it to fruition. In addition, within the ten years after retirement, I was able to complete 44 other articles. After publication of *Gateway* in 1979, I began work on my next book, *Cataclysms on the Columbia*, which turned out to be an even more arduous chore. By the end of 1982, I had retyped the 200-page manuscript eight times!

The department had just bought a computer for our secretary, and within a few weeks she was handing back corrected copies of manuscripts within ten or fifteen minutes! We all saw the light, and within six months most of our eight faculty had purchased their own personal computers. I was among the first and haven't used a typewriter since.

After shopping around for a month or so, and doing a lot of reading up on the subject, on March 7, 1983 (a date which changed my life) I bought, for $2,351, a Kaypro II, with Perfect Writer software (later updated to PluPerfect) and an Epson MX 80 printer.

It was the best investment I have ever made, and I have never regretted this choice for a minute, although some of the other machines now in the department can do things mine can't, such as color and graphics. The Kaypro is a 1972 Chevy pickup of a machine, a "best buy" and strictly utilitarian (I have heard it called Darth Vader's lunchbox), but I have written 1500 pages (nearly half a million words) on it and it has never failed me.

It took me about a month, working up to five hours a day, before I learned enough to write easily on it (the first few chapters of this manuscript provided my learning exercise). Even after more than ten years, I am still learning new tricks in CP/M and PluPerfect. I haven't even opened the manuals on Perfect Calc and Perfect Filer yet, although I know that if I wanted to use them also, I could eventually learn to do so.

I felt like a sculptor who had worked in hard granite all his life, returning to clay. Writing was a joy, instead of a chore. Away with the onerous task of first writing by hand, revising, typing, revising, retyping *ad nauseam*. My correspondence multiplied manyfold, since I could set up my letterheads and closing ahead of time, PIP them onto a new letter, and only need to fill in the date, address, and message. I could write a perfect letter in ten minutes instead of half an hour.

Shortly thereafter I began writing my weekly "Time Travel" articles on geology for *The Oregonian*. With an estimated two percent readership of the 300,000 circulation, I had a class of at least 6,000 readers! I got from two to five letters every week and answered almost every one.

Concentrate 17a

How Do You Do?

Until very recently, this well-meant question baffled me! An octogenarian seldom does very well and must constantly guard against frustration by the multitude of onerous daily activities necessary just to keep on one's feet and present a cheerful face to the world. One is not about to tell anyone the repulsive details.

For several years, if things were going well, I would cheerfully lie: "Great!" Or, if I didn't feel too bad, I would say, "Pretty Good!" or, "OK." When I reached 80, I discovered another that satisfied me:

"Better than I ever, ever expected to be at my age!" Both my parents died in their 60s, and when I reached 70, I considered that I had it made; any further years were a bonus!

Recently I saw that lovely movie, *Driving Miss Daisy*, and the last scene gave me the reply that I have been using ever since. For those of you unlucky enough not to have seen it yet, in the final scene, the faithful old chauffeur is visiting his employer of 50 years who lies afflicted with Alzheimer's in the rest home, and she asks him "How do you do?" His reply is "Well, Miss Daisy, we do what we can!"

Concentrate 17b

Media Pessimism

To the editor of the *Oregonian*:

A grim and despairing picture of mankind can be derived from the stories seen and heard hourly and daily through all media, more than 99 percent of which describe a world of dissension, lawsuits, deprivation, starvation, intrigue, corruption, violence, crime, and war. How can anyone, brainwashed into believing the truth of such a state of affairs, live an untroubled life?

It is not surprising that youth, without a perspective gained through experience or knowledge of the real world, accepts this picture of society as normal and takes refuge in cults, drugs, gangs, and even suicide.

In the real world this grim picture is just not so, as an elementary statistical hypothesis could demonstrate. At the risk of my being called a bloody optimist, my experience leads me to believe that for the nearly five billion souls now alive, more than 99 percent of the time more than 99 percent of the people of the world live quiet, useful, hard-working, cooperative, friendly, courteous, even sacrificial lives. All very dull and certainly not news.

This percentage leaves 50 million people in the world who are in trouble for one percent of the time, or for an average four days each year. It follows then that half of them are above the average, being in trouble for longer periods of time. In Oregon, with a population of nearly three million, this would mean 15,000 people are unhappy for more than four days a year. Is this the bad news depicted by the

172

media?

Media bad news is so pervasive that the periodical *Reader's Digest* stands out as such a unique lighthouse in the night that it invites ridicule from sophisticates. A personal antidote to media unbalance might be for each of us to stop a moment and calculate what percent of my last waking day or week or month or year was occupied by events which disturbed me seriously enough to make me unhappy? One of our TV stations should conduct a telephone poll on this. I would bet on an average of less than one percent.

I can remember the times before electronic media and rapid transportation when our personal lives were more peaceful, even during the rigors of The Depression and World War I. A flood of bad news did not overwhelm us then as it can do today if we do not recognize the distortion that the media makes of human life.

Chapter 18

Retirement II 1985-1994

During 1985, I was very busy writing the weekly "Time Travel" column in the *Oregonian* newspaper, finishing a new book on the Bretz floods, giving lectures at least once a month, and leading field trips to the Columbia River Gorge and to Mt. St. Helens. Grandson Miles graduated from the University of Kansas in June. Amy attended art school in Chicago.

The second edition of *Magnificent Gateway* came out in December, 1984, and sold well. I wrote a "Volcanic Hazards" section for an *Issues and Answers* booklet to be put out by AIPG. An interesting experience of note was being called as a consultant on a court case regarding whether a sunstone deposit in Eastern Oregon was a placer or a lode mine!

Peggy was occupied with PEO and Alpha Xi Delta activities and her silver study and book groups. In May we flew to Kansas for the graduation and wedding of Miles. Three generations marched in the academic procession! It was a lovely outdoor wedding on the Coulter ranch in western Kansas.

Late in 1985, Peggy and I had driven to Coos Bay for the Nature Conservancy Annual Meeting and decided to make a return trip via Medford to see Eric, my youngest brother, who had been in very poor health since his stomach and lung cancer operations. We found him in poor spirits. He had recently lost his wife, retired from his job as editor, sold his house and moved into a "manor," and had still another operation. According to accumulated trauma points, he should have been long dead.

Eric told me that the *Mail-Tribune* wanted him to continue to write for them, but that he didn't have the energy to write on his portable typewriter. So I persuaded him to buy a word processor. He took my advice, and for most of 1986, we were able for the first time to have a weekly and even biweekly exchange of letters and developed a closeness which we had never had before.

Eric wrote 40 editorials during 1986 and was well into his autobiography when he had to return to the hospital, where he died unexpectedly on Christmas day. Peggy and I had planned to drive down to visit him

174

during the holidays, but I came down with a recurrence of the flu just before we were to leave.

Four days in May of 1986 realized first the zenith and then the nadir of my experiences since retirement:

Late in 1985, I was asked by the University of California Department of Geology at Berkeley to give the 1986 graduation address to the combined geology and geophysics students. I doubt whether I ever before spent more time in preparing a 20-minute talk. During the next months I wrote and revised "The Importance of Communication (You Can Take It—Can You Dish It Out?)" which went through five drafts before I felt it was up to snuff. I really felt that it was a great honor to speak at Berkeley, and I flew home the next morning feeling pretty high. The Greeks have a word for that: *hubris*.

The next Monday I drove my Volvo station wagon north on Highway 30 towards the testing station near Linnton to get the exhaust checked so I could apply for a license renewal. My vanity license plates which read "CORIBA," were given to me by some of my students when I retired in 1974, and I have kept them ever since. (CORIBA stands for Columbia River Basalt.)

I started to make a left turn into the station and woke up in the hospital! The car was totaled by a young female driver who apparently hit me broadside, and I had a hole in my head that had to be patched by putting together seven pieces of bone. I had a fairly short convalescence, but the hearing in my left ear was permanently damaged, and I have never regained my former energy.

The 30th anniversary of my founding of the Department of Geology at Portland State University was in February 1986. At the evening banquet, nearly a hundred alumni and friends gave a standing ovation to the founder. Soon after that, I received from the publisher my advance copy of *Gateway*, the book that I have been working on spasmodically for more than fifteen years.

The most memorable event during the rest of the year was the trip we took to Alaska in August on the cruise ship *Universe*. Traveling along the Inland Passage, we stopped at eight different towns, and aboard ship, we would have regular lectures by area authorities on the local history, biology, anthropology, etc. Unfortunately, Peggy and I caught the flu from another passenger and were unable to visit the Vancouver Expo.

In 1987, we took only one trip by car, a drive around the Olympic Peninsula, mainly to see the Makah Anthropology Museum at Neah Bay which is a time-capsule reconstruction of a village covered by a mudslide

175

400 years ago. The only other trip we made was by AMTRAK to Aptos, California, to celebrate the 50th anniversary of Bob and Betty Coats, at whose wedding I had been best man. While there, we visited the fabulous aquarium on Cannery Row in Monterey, the San Juan Bautista Mission, and drove through the quadrangle which I mapped in 1935-38 for my Ph.D. dissertation.

With the publication on November 5th of "Time Travel" number 200, I brought to an end my four-year stint as weekly columnist for *The Oregonian*. Sale of a xeroxed scrapbook of the first 100 columns raised about $2,000 for the Department's student funds. The book of the second 100 columns was out by Christmas.

My other book, *Cataclysms on the Columbia—A Layman's Guide to the Efects of the Catastrophic Bretz Floods in the Pacific Northwest* was finally, after nearly 15 years of gestation, published in hardback in June, 1986, and has been selling well, despite what we considered to be an exorbitant price of $20.00.

Peggy's latest venture is teaching spoken English to Asian and European refugees in a class sponsored by the English Speaking Union, of which we are members.

I made a final decision in 1986 to end the lectures I had been giving two or three times a month for so many years. My impaired hearing made it more and more difficult, and I couldn't help but remember the pitiful lecture I heard Dr. Hodge give several years after his retirement, when I said to myself, I must remember to quit while I am still ahead. So I did and have given no talks since then.

My only trip in 1988 was to the 100th Anniversary GSA Convention (7,400 geologists in Denver) where I was happy to renew bonds with numerous friends I had not seen for many years. Peggy and I had both our 55th anniversary and our 80th birthdays, made more memorable by visits of Sally and Scott from Kansas and their daughter Amy, and son Miles with his wife, Laura, from Minneapolis.

Although I gave up my weekly column in December 1987, I still write numerous essays. I serve on several boards and committees, mostly involved with the preservation and enhancement of the Columbia River Gorge, or with the ERFOPS (Emeritus and Retired Faculty of Portland State), a group which I founded several years ago and now totals over a hundred members.

In 1989, I found a new writing interest to keep me occupied. I started compiling, for the various agencies in the Columbia River Gorge, a series of capsule descriptions of geologic features. I found this to be a challenging exercise—getting down the important features at first in 2,500 words, then 1,200 words, 600, 200, 50 and finally 25!

Actually, this started when Graphic Arts Press asked me to do a geology of the Gorge for their coffee table picture book. Essentially, I condensed *Gateway* down to 4,500 words for them. Then they came back and said they could only use 2,500 words, which I provided. That gave me the idea that "capsulization" itself was a writing art of some importance, and I started experimenting.

About the same time, I sent a copy of the table of contents of my long-projected book "The Hundred Outstanding Geological Localities in Oregon" to Ellen Morris Bishop, the woman who took over the "Time Travel" column; she thought it was a great idea and agreed to do those in eastern Oregon if I would do those in western Oregon. I have written capsules varying from 400 to 1,000 words for 21 western Oregon localities. Unfortunately, Bishop had problems of her own, so her side of the bargain is still in limbo. I hope it doesn't turn out like the "Hazards" book.

In May of that year, we flew to Spokane for the meeting of the Cordilleran Section of the GSA—and were disappointed that so few familiar faces appeared; but Peggy had good visits with two of her oldest friends, one of them dating from her childhood in Spokane, the other from our years in Baker.

The following week, we flew to granddaughter Amy's graduation from the Minneapolis College of Art & Design, then flew back to Lawrence, Kansas, for her wedding to Francis Pearson. A lovely wedding in the University Chapel was followed by a sumptuous party in the yard of our daughter Sally's home. Her husband, Scott, had planted, groomed and decorated the garden to perfection, enlisting the help of groom, son, and best man, we were told.

Scott left Kansas in December for a new job as Dean of Arts & Sciences at the University of Toledo, Ohio. Sally was an assistant professor with tenure in the Honors Program, taught creative writing for the English Department, and assisted with the birth of a Woman's Studies Program.

The following July, Sally, Scott, and later Amy, Francis, Miles, and Laura came to Oregon, stayed with us a few days, and then proceeded to the coast. We visited them at the beach, and in October, again drove down the coast to Newport for a Nature Conservancy annual meeting, shun-piking back with nostalgic visits to Neah-Kah-Nie and Neskowin.

At home, we were kept almost too active. During November of 1990, for example, one or both of us attended one or more meetings of the following 12 organizations: Congregational Church, PEO, English-Speaking Union, PSU Book Club, Alpha Xi Delta, GSOC (Geological Society of the Oregon Country) and its PPP (Past President's Panel), Writer's Group (retired newspaper writers), SMOG (Society of Miscellaneous Oregon Geologists), Ferdinand Society (faculty who meet to smell the Four Roses and shoot the bull), Sigma Xi (science honorary), Geology Department Colloquium (visiting speakers nearly every week), and ERFOPS (Emeritus and Retired Faculty of Portland State). Now you can see why we have stayed for 26 years at the Ione Plaza on the PSU campus within walking distance of downtown Portland!

Over the years, I have been especially involved in GSOC, PPP, SMOG, Sigma Xi, Ferdinand, and ERFOPS because I was either a founder, charter member or past president of all of them. Also keeping me busy has been the publishing of 27 articles in 1989-90. Among them, 14 were printed in the *GSOC Newsletter*, five in the *Journal of Geological Education*, and two in *Oregon Geology*.

And, in 1991, I was rewarded for work done at least five years beforehand: I had convinced the Oregon Historical Society that they should republish Ira William's classic book on the Columbia River Gorge. It finally came out in June, using my geological introduction, and with my name imprinted on the cover of a most attractive volume!

In February, 1992, we bused with members of the English Speaking Union to Victoria, B.C., for a joint meeting with the Canadian chapter held at the Empress Hotel. I was able to spend a day in the wonderful Provincial Museum, just across the street.

Another outstanding event of 1992, which came late in March, was a week's visit with our daughter Sally and her husband Scott at the University of Toledo in Ohio. They have a lovely three-story turn-of-the-century home near the campus in an old, but not yet decayed residential district. They returned the visit with a ten-day stay here in early August.

But the real event of the year, for me, came in October. The luxurious 75-passenger shallow-draft diesel *Sea Lion* made an eight-day, 1,200-mile trip first from Portland to Astoria, then tracing the Columbia and Snake rivers to as far as Clarkston, Idaho. At that point, we boarded jet boats and continued 50 miles up the Snake, deep into Hells Canyon, to the mouth of the Imnaha River. The *Sea Lion* was one of a pair of Lindblad ships that were built in 1988 especially for plying western coastal and river waters.

During this trip, sponsored by the Nature Conservancy and billed as "In the Wake of Lewis and Clark," we passed through the locks of eight dams and made 18 stops for short side-trips by bus, train, or four Zodiac rubber boats carried on board. En route, a historian told us Indian legends and the history and stories of Lewis and Clark, Marcus Whitman, and Chief Joseph; a biologist pointed out and named the abundant wildlife and plants; and I described the geology.

If my publication rate since retirement in 1974 is an index of my productivity, I have been doing well:

1974	6	1975	3	1976	5
1977	3	1978	0	1979	4
1980	6	1981	6	1982	1
1983	4	1984	11	1985	5
1986	4	1987	3	1988	8
1989	13	1990	14	1991	9
1992	9	1993	7	1994	6

My total bibliography to date now consists of 222 articles, 53 of which were published in the *Geological Society of the Oregon Country Newsletter*, 32 in the bulletins of the Oregon Department of Geology and Mineral Industries and in *Ore Bin and Oregon Geology* magazine, and 18 articles in the *Journal of Geological Education*.

If the 200 "Time Travel" columns published between 1983 and 1987 were counted separately I would have over 400 citations.

Concentrate 18a

The Importance of Communication (You Can Take it–Can You Dish it Out?)

(An expanded version of this essay was given as a talk to the geology and geophysics students graduating from the University of California, Berkeley, on May 16, 1986)

Nothing has been more important to my intellectual development, and nothing has more consistently stimulated me than the subject of this essay—communication. Early on I read and reread Lancelot Hogben's "Loom of Language," Hayakawa's "Language in Action" and Korzybski's "Science and Sanity," and they affected my whole life.

The thing that most clearly distinguishes *Homo sapiens* from all other animals is not bifocal vision, bipedal locomotion, erect posture, and opposable thumbs; it is the use of language for communication.

Cultures are determined by their language, and language is in turn affected by environment. The Hopi language has more verbs than nouns; everything is process, moving and dynamic, and its effect is that Hopis have a quite different sense of time. Because they live in an arid region, they and the Navajos have dozens of words for different kinds of water; living in the arctic, Eskimos have even more words for the different kinds of ice and snow.

An old French saying suggests this effect of language on culture:

> *Si je connaissais plusiers langues,*
> *Je parlerais le latin à Dieu,*
> *Le français à toi,*
> *L'anglais aux oiseaux*
> *L'espagnol aux femmes*
> *Et l'allemand à mon chien.*

("If I knew several languages, I would speak Latin to God, French to thee, English to birds, Spanish to women and German to my dog.")

For at least a hundred thousand years the essentials of human culture were handed down by word of mouth; shamans and sages committed legends, customs, and religious rituals to memory so that they could be perpetuated.

During the last five millennia, three "unconformities" or revolutions in the history of communication have taken place—each as important to culture as Stephen Jay Gould's "punctuations" are to evolution. The first was the almost simultaneous inventions of writing by the Babylonians, Egyptians, Chinese and Central Americans. The second was the invention of moveable type by Gutenberg more than 500 years ago; and third, in the last 60 years, the introduction of electronic media.

We are now in the throes of a fourth revolution, engendered by computers, which is the most momentous and trenchant unconformity of all. Anyone with a computer and modem can communicate worldwide at a rate of 144 thousand signals per minute (2400 BAUD), and that rate is expected to be doubled shortly.

180

In words of this computer language, children and young adults download new software files and reprogram their RAM on hard or floppy discs. They add new chips, cards, a Winchester hard disk, a 9600 BAUD modem to their work station, and are now ready for SYSOP, e-mail and the Internet.

Although humans have a prodigious capacity for learning languages, it takes nearly five years to absorb basic English, and 10 to 15 years to achieve competence in the vocabulary of our culture.

Parents will vouch for the fact that many, if not most children suffer through their teens with a more or less complete inability to communicate with them. It is fortunate that this is nearly always a passing phase!

During the eight years of high school and college, many students learn basic French, German, Spanish or other foreign languages, but geology students must also achieve proficiency in the dialect of scientific language. If one has never thought of it as a new language, look at the *Glossary of Geology*, which contains 30,000 words, more than Shakespeare's entire vocabulary.

For four years, geology students absorb and organize geologic information, and upon graduation from college, they must start to emit it as well. They must use this new language among their peers, but the great danger they now face is that if their "geologese" is not layperson-compatible, the general public will not understand it.

Oregon has a tradition, initiated in the 1870s by Thomas Condon, the pioneer minister-geologist, of communicating geologic ideas through public lectures and articles in non-technical publications. The favorable "geologic climate" thus engendered in Oregon was one of the reasons why I was so determined to return there.

Nearly two-thirds of my publications have been directed towards the lay public. I have given more than 250 public non-technical talks over the years on over 100 subjects, and in the last four years, thanks to my word processor, I have had the privilege of writing 200 weekly geologic essays, each of 500 to 1,000 words, for our local newspaper.

I cannot urge graduating students strongly enough to give talks to the public as often as possible—it is the public which usually pays teachers' salaries. The public *needs* to know what geology is all about in today's technical world, and the public will supply the next generation of geologists. Civic, hobby and many other clubs are always delighted to find a speaker for their meetings.

A senior seminar course initiated at Portland State in 1957, patterned after the excellent Toastmasters Club manual, was specifically designed to give students skills in oral and visual presentation of geologic material.

Forty percent of the grade was on presentation and all members of the class filled out a critique sheet during each talk. Warned at eight minutes, speakers were cut off abruptly at ten minutes. The speaker's grade consisted of the average of the grades given by the students, averaged with the average of those given by the faculty.

Although each student only gave two or three talks each quarter, we were consistently gratified and sometimes amazed at how rapidly they improved. Later, their oral and poster presentations at GSA meetings nearly always rated far above average.

Every graduate will soon be required to give both oral and written reports to his boss or board of directors in which he must be able to translate his results into English.

I'll never forget my committee chairman's remark when he came out of the room after my final defense for my Ph.D. at Berkeley in 1945: "Allen, you'll never have to take another exam!" Boy, was he ever wrong! In the real world, you take a written exam every time you write a report and an oral exam every time you stand before your peers.

When I returned to Oregon with my degree, I found that the new director of the Oregon Department of Geology and Mineral Industries no longer held weekly staff meetings, in which we brainstormed new ideas and briefed each other on what we were doing and planned to do. Soon, none of us knew what was going on in the department.

My friends from Eastern Oregon would come into my office and say, "John, I hear the department is doing, or planning to do such and such," and my answer had to be, "Oh, is it?" Within six months, all four existing geologists had left the department.

As I originally planned, I had worked as a field geologist for more than ten years, and was ready to return to teaching. I had sat under too many young professors who had gone directly from college into teaching. Field experience is invaluable for a teaching career.

The opportunity came soon, at Pennsylvania State College. However, there I found that the geology and mineralogy departments were as badly split as geology and paleontology had been at California. In both cases, I am convinced this was a direct result of physical separation in different buildings as at Berkeley or in different parts of the same building as at Penn State. Physical separation inhibits

182

communication and breeds dissension.

The atmosphere was so bad at Penn State that when I wanted to talk to the head of mineralogy, P.D. Krynine, a Berkeley graduate and therefore very *sympatico*, I had to be very sure that the head of geology, Frank Swartz, didn't see me duck into Krynine's office at the other end of the hall.

In later designing the new geology quarters at Portland State, all ten faculty offices were located around the lobby, only a few steps apart. And in my 20 years as department head, I always insisted on regular weekly staff meetings.

Enthusiasm is a rare and valuable quality because it is contagious! It was almost entirely because of a charismatic teacher at Oregon that I became enamored of geology and changed my major from journalism at the end of my sophomore year. Your ability to communicate will depend in large part upon your enthusiasm.

Before I made this change, I bought a Model T and took a trip across the country, visiting departments of geology en route. The faculty in every department took in this youngster, not even a geology major, and made him feel welcome, spending hours telling about their work.

The people I met became lifelong friends, and I started building up a grapevine of friends who helped me get every job I have ever had. Attend every convention you can, not so much for hearing papers as for making new friends.

Fortunately, geologists are nearly always enthusiastic about their work. This marvelous by-product is that it is fun to work long hours when you are more excited about your work than in most anything else. I keenly remember that in New Mexico, when I used to get out in the field before sunrise, with dew on the cactus flowers and birds singing, I would say to myself, "I am being *paid* to do this!"

I recently heard of a perceptive definition of work given by a six-year-old child: "Work is what I have to do, play is what I like to do!" I have been able to play most of my life.

In summary, my charge to soon-to-be ex-students is to learn to translate geology into English and take every opportunity to speak to the public. Make lots of friends, and you will never have to spend months hunting for a new job—just turn on your grapevine.

If you plan a field career, whenever possible get a partner to work with you in the field. When dealing with other cultures, remember that they may have a different work ethic and sense of time. In economic geology, bin rock *or* dump rock is the bottom line.

If you plan to teach, get several years of field experience to learn the real world and build up you repertoire of stories. In your lectures, express your enthusiasm with geology. Constantly try out new ideas in teaching. Take your students on as many problem-oriented trips as possible so they too can learn in the field. Learn how to run a committee, since most academic decisions are made there.

And when you get into administration, as many of you will, have regular staff meetings and don't physically separate faculty offices. Assign your most enthusiastic teacher to the general geology course.

Concentrate 18b

The Case of the Counter-Clockwise River

This was originally published in Oregon Geology, *v.52, n. 3, p. 67-69, 1990.*

Introduction

A tiny creek appears just east of Cochran, a former Southern Pacific Railroad station located at the summit elevation of 1,808 feet in a little known pass through the northern Coast Range of Oregon. For six miles, the creek flows east to the town of Timber where the valley widens, and the creek, gathering water from several tributaries, meanders north for almost ten miles across narrow flood plains, and then turns northeast for four miles to Vernonia.

Within slightly incised meanders though a narrower valley, the river continues from Vernonia north-northeast for five miles, then north-northwest for five miles, and northwest four miles to the town of Mist. There it takes a six-mile arc to the west and southwest to arrive at Birkenfeld where it begins a generally southwest-trending and deeply incised meandering course for 25 miles to the mouth of the Salmonberry River, a stream which completes the oval, since only 14 miles upstream to the east, the headwaters of one of its tributaries begins just south of Cochran, within a mile of where our river began!

This is the peculiar 65-mile-long counterclockwise loop made by the Nehalem River around the heart of the northern Coast Range before it turns west-southwest for the last 15 miles through deeply incised meanders to Nehalem Bay and the Pacific Ocean. The width of the Coast Range between Forest Grove and Tillamook Bay is less than 40 miles; the Nehalem River valley is more than 90 miles long.

Policies and Procedures

The purpose of this essay is to develop multiple hypotheses, one of which might account for this apparently anomalous course of the Nehalem River, a minor geomorphic puzzle that has intrigued me for more than 40 years, ever since the publication of the first geologic map of the area (Warren, et al., 1945). Old-fashioned armchair geomorphic analysis, reading the contours of topographic maps, which I have sometimes indulged in since my retirement (Allen, 1975, 1989a, 1989b), can occasionally furnish valuable insights into the geologic history of an area.

I have heard that the course of the Nehalem River caught the attention of interpreters scanning satellite images, looking for "astroblemes," structures produced by the impact of large meteorites or comets. Although such a hypothesis (#1) can be quickly discarded, another hypothesis (#2) is suggested by similar drainage patterns that can form within giant calderas produced by great volcanic explosions.

Structural uplift or doming, as in the Black Hills of South Dakota, is a third more likely explanation (#3); its implications will be explored later. Still another hypothesis (#4) suggests that the Miocene Nehalem river, flowing east into the Columbia, was diverted north and then west by flows of Yakima basalt filling the ancestral Columbia River valley.

Geographic factors that can be investigated are statistics on relative rainfall, length, and gradients of stream channels, and changes of drainage divides. Geomorphic features to be studied include presence or absence of meanders (especially when incised), different valley-wall slopes and benches or terraces, upland surfaces of low relief (which used to be called peneplains), and barbed tributaries.

Along the Oregon coast, geologic and geomorphic features have been studied by Lund (1971,2,3,4,5), but within the northern Oregon Coast Range, possibly due to heavy vegetation, the geologic maps of Warren, et al. (1945) and Wells and Peck (1961) are the only ones that have been published, and no geomorphic studies have been made.

Areal geology and bedrock structure ("ground truth") must always be considered whenever geologic maps are available, since bedrock characteristics can affect drainage patterns and result in drainage changes due to differential erosion. Dipping strata can cause lateral migration of valleys. Vertical beds or a fault zone may result in a straight valley course. Tight folding may result in an Appalachian-type trellis pattern; domal uplift may produce a both radial and concentric patterns.

Geography

Careful map measurements on seven 15-minute quadrangles (Birkenfeld, Cathlamet, Enright, Nehalem, Saddle Mountain, Timber and Vernonia) give the length of the Nehalem River valley as 88 miles for a valley gradient of 20 feet per mile (1,808/88=20.5); repeated, more precise measurements which followed each meander gave a channel length of 121 miles. The average river gradient (1,808/121=14.9) itself is thus 15 feet per mile.

One tributary of the Salmonberry River rises near Cochran and joins that river which then flows 14 miles westerly to its mouth on the Nehalem at an elevation of 231 feet. The Salmonberry River thus completes the southwest 55 degrees of the 305 degree Nehalem loop, with a channel gradient of 113 feet per mile (1,808-231 = 1,577/14 = 113), 7.53 times that of the Nehalem. The area within this loop is nearly 300 square miles, the area within the Nehalem River drainage (excluding the North Fork) is a little more than twice that.

Average annual rainfall in the northern Coast Range is higher than anywhere else in Oregon: 110 inches at Nehalem near the mouth of the river; 130 inches at Glenora on the Wilson River ten miles southwest of Cochran. West of the main drainage divide of the Coast Range, adiabatic/orographic rainfall is greater than that to the east; and stream gradients are steeper since they travel a much shorter distance to the sea. Erosion on the west side of the northern Coast Range could well have been more rapid than anywhere else in the state.

Geomorphology

Barbed tributaries in the Coast Range can indicate stream capture of the headwaters of streams flowing east into the Willamette River. Barbed tributaries on both the South and North Forks of the Salmonberry River, suggests that at least eight miles of the Nehalem has been captured, and that the North Fork, before its capture at a point one and a half miles west of Cochran, once formed the headwaters of the

Nehalem River.

The result of such stream captures is that the Coast Range drainage divide here lies farther to the east than anywhere else north of Eugene. At its easternmost limit, the divide now lies within 12 miles of the Columbia River; south of the Nehalem drainage basin, the Coast Range divide lies 15 miles farther to the west. At its northern limit, the Nehalem drainage divide lies only two miles south of the Columbia River.

Usually, a stream will constantly adjust its course so as to run on the most easily erodible bedrock. The location of a stream, then, is nearly always a result of such differential erosion of the various kinds (stratigraphy) and the folding and fracturing (structure) of the bedrocks. Thus the stream may follow a bed of soft shale lying between more resistant sandstone layers; it may follow a zone of broken rock caused by a fault or sets of closely spaced joints.

Within the Nehalem drainage basin, upland areas of gently rolling surfaces can be observed on several of the quadrangles. These could be interpreted as remnants of a once continuous late mature or early old age erosion surface. Elevations on this surface usually lie between 800 and 1,200 feet, with few ridges and prominences rising above them to above 2,000 feet.

The Nehalem drainage divide is marked by several basaltic prominences reaching nearly 3,000 feet or more; among these are Saddle Mountain, Humbug Mountain, Onion Peak, Pinochle Peak, Rogers Peak, Larch Mountain, and Round Top.

Stratigraphy and Structure

The cast of our detective story must include the geologic formations making up the northern Coast Range, whose names and ages are as follows (Baldwin, 1981):

Miocene (5.3 to 23.7 million years):
    Yakima Basalt of the Columbia River Group
    Astoria Formation
    Scappoose Formation

Oligocene (23.7 to 36.6 million years):
    Pittsburg Bluff Formation

Eocene (36.6 to 57.8 million years):

187

Keasey Formation
Goble Volcanics
Cowlitz Formation
Yamhill Formation
Tillamook Volcanics
Siletz Volcanics

The most important player in this "Case of the Nehalem Loop" is certainly the Keasey Formation, consisting of easily eroded mudstone and shale, with supporting players being the underlying resistant lavas of the Goble and Tillamook Volcanics, and the overlying Pittsburg Bluff sandstones, with possibly the Yakima Basalt also entering into the plot.

Faulting appears not to have significantly interrupted the contacts of the formations or affected the course of the Nehalem. The relatively straight 25-mile-long, generally east-west course of the Salmonberry and upper Nehalem might suggest this, but such a fracture has not yet been mapped.

Conclusions

A much simplified history of the main structural feature involving the above formations, as first suggested by Warren, et al. (1945) and later presented on the state geologic map (Wells and Peck, 1961), indicates that, beginning perhaps in late Miocene time, the formations named above began to be arched up into a north-northeast plunging geanticline.

Millions of years of slow erosion then beveled off this giant fold, reducing it to a surface of low relief with streams meandering near sea level. Eocene volcanics were exposed in the core of the fold, and outcrops of the later sedimentary formations formed arcuate belts around the plunging north end of the fold. Pliocene and later uplift eventually rejuvenated the streams and incised their meanders into the rising lowlands, etching out valleys in the weaker Keasey Formation.

One resulting deduction (hypothesis #3, modified) is that during this second period of uplift and resulting orographically increased rainfall, the Nehalem River captured all the streams occupying the arcuate belt of Keasey Shale during the rapid clockwise headward erosion of most of the upper part of its valley.

For the 45 miles from Timber to Jewell Junction, the Nehalem River

188

follows this Keasey belt, with the exception of a ten-mile stretch north of Vernonia where its meanders have cut less than a mile into the Pittsburg Bluff Formation. The lower 40 miles of the valley, from Jewell Junction to Nehalem Bay, is mostly carved in resistant Tillamook Volcanics. The river originally meandered across a surface of low relief, now uplifted to 800-1,000 feet, upon which the major drainage pattern was established as the range began to rise.

The lower course of the river became fixed within the underlying volcanic rocks, but the upper course migrated down-dip on the slip-off contact at the base of the Keasey Shale, moving the Coast Range drainage divide 10 to 15 miles to the north and east.

Still another possible deduction (hypothesis #4) proposes that a Middle Miocene Nehalem River, originally flowing east across a topography of low relief, was diverted north and west by flows of Yakima basalt which filled a former broad valley of the Columbia River, then located 10 to 20 miles west and south of its present course. Today, numerous erosional remnants of basalt lie less than ten miles from the Nehalem River along most of its course.

Whichever hypothesis is finally chosen (and the main purpose of this discussion is to spur further investigation), the Nehalem River remains the longest river within the Oregon Coast Range, and the only one with 305 degrees of counterclockwise course.

References

Allen, J. E., 1975, The Wallowa ice cap of northeastern Oregon, an exercise in the interpretation of glacial landforms: *The Ore Bin*, V. 37, n. 12, p. 189-202.

_____, 1989a, Ice-age glaciers and lakes south of the Columbia River Gorge: *Oregon Geology*, v. 51, n. 1, p. 12-14.

_____, 1989b, Northwest topographic maps: *Geol. Soc. Oregon Country Newsletter*, v. 55, n. 11, p. 153-156.

Baldwin, Ewart M., 1981, *Geology of Oregon*: Kendall/Hunt, Dubuque, Iowa, 170 p.

Lund, Ernest, 1971 to 1975, a series of eight short articles on landforms along the Oregon coast, in *The Ore Bin*, v. 33 to 37.

Warren, W.C., Norbisrath, Hans, and Grivetti, R.M., 1945, *Geology of northwestern Oregon west of the Willamette River and north of latitude*

45 degrees, 15': U.S. Geological Survey, Oil and Gas Inv. Prelim. Map 42.

Wells, Francis G., and Peck, Dallas L, 1961, *Geologic map of Oregon west of the 121st meridian*: U.S. Geological Survey, Misc. Geol. Inv. Map I-325.

Concentrate 18c

Remembrances of Personal Medical History 1908-1993

An essay on sickness and health may seem a bit weird, but I have never been accused of hypochondria. Perhaps I am writing it to see how much I can remember, since one usually finds it difficult to recall unpleasant occurrences.

Actually, I have always been interested in medicine and might have gone into it professionally except for poor health during grade school and part of high school, plus the grim tales I began to hear about overworked medical students. I have always found doctors to be highly compatible, perhaps because they use the same method of multiple working hypotheses for their diagnostic work that geologists do in the field and laboratory.

My attitude towards sickness treatments and health activities, as well as about most other things, is encompassed by the phrase "moderation in all things." All my life I have tried to take as few aspirin, sleeping, or any other kind of pill as possible. That is getting harder to do as age creeps on; *now* I take five different pills a day, plus three kinds of inhalant two times a day and one four times a day. And in the past I found that for me, jogging and other forms of extended daily exercises (except for a 20-minute regimen that I will describe later), were utterly boring and unnecessary.

My earliest medical recollection comes from an occurrence in Seattle at the age of two that included sitting up in bed most of the night trying to breath. This asthma was thought to have been brought on by a bout with pneumonia which resulted from eating Gold Dust soap powder. Asthma kept me out of the first, second, fifth and sixth grades of school in Eugene. The only treatment I remember consisted

190

of hovering over a pan of hot mentholated water, breathing the fumes. This was before the days of adrenaline.

Fortunately, University High School in 1920 included sixth and seventh grades, so students could begin to regularly use the university swimming pool at an early age. Swimming developed my endurance and taught me strong breathing methods. I missed making my fourth letter in college swimming due to the measles I came down with just before a major meet in California.

Although I was a pretty healthy character during college, health problems began to show up at Berkeley in 1934 when I began to suffer from terrific headaches while studying for the five Ph.D. written exams. After a series of spot tests that showed that I was allergic to almost everything, Peggy fed me on soybean and rice flour concoctions until I passed the exams and the headaches went away.

While trying to learn to ski near Baker in 1938, I did an "eggbeater" and threw out a knee. This made me hobble around for several months. I decided not to learn to ski since, as a field geologist, my legs were my livelihood. Dr. Roger Biswell became a great friend—going with me on several field trips—but fortunately needed to do little for my health.

As we were leaving Baker a year later, I ruptured a lumbar disk in my back while trying to load a trailer. This has been a recurrent problem ever since, although it didn't become serious until 15 years later in Socorro when I loaded the car for a trip to Santa Barbara. I drove all the way with pain pills supplied by Dr. John Aiken, who had been treating my back, and arrived in pain at Santa Barbara, where I taught for six weeks on crutches. Fortunately the doctor there did not believe in fusion and treated me with hydrotherapy (long hot-water bathtub soaks).

During the last three years of field work in New Mexico I drove a Jeep, and wore a leather and metal "H" belt to protect my back, which I still have and use now and then. Over the years, several bursitis attacks have affected both my shoulders and elbows, but a really traumatic bursitis flared up in my hip in 1953. I passed out from the pain and had to be driven 70 miles to Albuquerque for an operation, after which they dosed me with so much penicillin that I swelled up like a spotted pup and had to be revived with adrenaline. I have had a red star for penicillin on my medical records ever since.

When I came back to Portland in 1956, our doctor was Arthur Jones who regularly stretched my back with a machine that tilted up

191

and then jerked. He told me then that a disc like mine could get better with the years, and it has, although until 20 years ago I needed physical therapy (heat and stretching treatments) every six months or so.

Every morning for the last 30 years I have taken a 20-minute series of exercises which were codified and expanded for me by Jack Arnoux, physical therapist. They consist of pelvic tilt, camel-cat back-bending, neck twists with the hands behind the back and with a towel around the neck, and several others. If I omit them for even one day, I can feel the difference!

Long before retirement in 1974, my internist, Dr. Duane Iverson, had treated most of my ailments and referred me to excellent specialists when necessary. For instance, lower abdomen pains turned out to be caused by multiple polyps; they ended when 13 polyps were excised. My recent lack of further intestinal problems is probably because Iverson finally persuaded me to quit smoking my pipe, and reduce alcohol to one or two glasses of wine a week (lost my daily scotch on the rocks!). I've recently discovered that nonalcoholic beer is just as tasty as the real thing!

I have had three prostate sessions with Dr. Arthur Strandberg, beginning with a stretching at least 20 years ago, followed by a second one in 1980, and then, late in August, 1992, when the cancer test was positive, a complete excision of prostrate and testicles. There has been no hint of recurrence in my semi-annual PSA tests.

Perhaps the most daunting ailment that ever attacked me appeared early in February 1991, when recurrent asthma attacks began and gradually got worse until I wound up early in June in the hospital for a week with oxygen and steroid injections administered every four hours. Apparently not much is known about asthma. My internist tried out a new drug on every visit, and finally I was referred to a lung specialist early in July. Improvement so far seemed to be minuscule, but with the help of drugs Alupent (for emergencies) and Vanceril (every five hours), inhalants, Proventil nebulizer (once or twice a day), and Prednazone pills, I keep going. To try to control the asthma, during 1992, I tried diet, acupuncture, and naturopathic pills from Dr. Sheila Moran and Dr. Jared Zeff with no perceptible benefits.

On January 2, 1993, I suddenly passed out and fell on Peggy, who was trying to get me to a chair. I ended up at the Good Samaritan hospital, wearing an oxygen tube and a radio blood pressure monitor. For three days they tested me by ultrasound and radioscans, but three

192

specialists could come to no diagnosis, so I was sent home and got along pretty well for three months.

During a check-up visit April 6 of that year, Iverson found that my blood pressure was too low and my heart was acting up, and he sent me back to Good Sam. This time the same tests showed that my problems with lungs and heart were due to a large blood clot in my leg! After ten days of treatment to thin my blood and dissolve the clot, I had so completely lost the strength in my legs that I couldn't get around without a walker, which went home with me. We had to install special braces in the bathrooms, so I could get up off the seats and out of the tub!

Since then, besides Deltazone (Prednazone) and four kinds of inhalants to keep my asthma in check, I am taking Coumadin to control my blood clotting, Lanoxin for congestive heart failure, and Lasix (furosemide) for dewatering.

For a couple of weeks after I came home from the hospital, different home-visit nurses came every day or so to give me therapy, take my blood pressure, and take blood samples to see how the blood-thinning medicine was working. One doll of a nurse, Heidi Moore, visited us once a week for several months. As I began to get my strength and balance back I graduated to a cane, which I still use as an emergency stick when walking outside our apartment building. Next to the asthma, the loss of much of my sense of balance is my most difficult handicap.

Concentrate 18d

Meditations on Nearing Age 85

Last night for some reason my mind was more hyperactive than it has been for months, mostly on the subject of how difficult old age was becoming. 1993 was the year of our 60th wedding anniversary (July 26), my 85th birthday (August 12), and the 20th anniversary of my third career, writing.

During the second decade of this third career, there have been four dates of traumatic events that have emphasized the steps of decline engendered by old age. On May 19, 1985, I got a cracked head and lost much of my hearing in an auto accident; on April 29, 1991, my

193

childhood asthma returned in full force; on August 26, 1992, I underwent surgery for a malignant prostate; and on January 2, 1993, I passed out suddenly for the first time in my life, with what my doctor thinks might have been an angina attack.

During that difficult night, and on most other nights when increasingly aching muscles awoke me every hour or so, my mind rehearsed these step-by-step deprivations occasioned by old age, and it occurred to me that I had never read essays on the subject by well-known writers who reached old age (and I might comment that a "ripe old age" can also be rotten). Where are they?

Essayists La Rochfoucauld (1613-1680), Voltaire (1694-1778), and Charles Lamb (1775-1834) come to mind. Do they comment on old age? George Bernard Shaw, who lived to be the oldest of all (1856-1950), wrote a fascinating play *Back to Methuselah* on a somewhat related subject, where a few people learned how to live for 300 years, and later on for 30,000 years. I don't remember any statements of the problems of old age.

As usual, Shakespeare (1564-1616) said it first and perhaps best:

> And so he plays his part. The sixth age shifts
> Into the lean and slipper'd pantaloon,
> With spectacles on nose and pouch on side;
> His youthful hose, well saved, a world too wide
> For his shrunk shank; and his big manly voice,
> Turning again towards childish treble, pipes
> And whistles in his sound. Last scene of all,
> That ends this strange eventful history,
> Is second childishness and mere oblivion,
> Sans teeth, sans eyes, sans taste, sans everything.
> —*As You Like It. Act II, Sc. 7*

Recently I have lost several close friends. One, only two years older than I, has deteriorated into helplessness. One died three days after his 100th birthday, still in fine mental fettle, but unhappy because he could no longer read and was restricted to one room. A third died suddenly last week, leaving a distraught wife.

I still have one longtime friend in the Ione, however, that I admire and try to emulate because he gives me such a boost—he is ten years older than I, but as sharp as a tack and still active and driving his car!

During 1992, we went to seven funerals and came to the decision not to have services for ourselves. First, there are only a few people who would feel they should attend; second, it is a big chore for older people to attend funeral services; and third, so many of the services were either too impersonal or too long.

The medical profession must bear the onus of two things: first, that their ministrations, given with all good will, are directly responsible for the population explosion that could, within a few decades, make this earth uninhabitable. Second, as a by-product, they have extended life expectancy far beyond what is usually bearable, and this in turn has caused the health care crisis among developed nations.

I have three dreads which do not often disturb me, but they do occasionally pop up in the back of my mind. One, of course, is losing my wife of 60 years before I go; another is having to move out of the Ione and into a health care facility after nearly 30 years; another dread, of course, is the horrible possibility of Alzheimer's for either of us.

Mentally, we both still seem to be in pretty good shape. Yes, it takes a little longer to remember names, and we are perhaps a little more forgetful than the usual absent-minded professor and his wife. A reason older people take up crossword puzzles (as I have) is that if you are good at them, it gives you a temporary euphoria when you realize that your old computer can still come up with the required word in only a few seconds. So long as I can do the daily puzzle in ten minutes, and those labelled "hard" or "expert" in 15 or 20 minutes, I feel great.

Physically, my greatest challenge is overcoming the sense of instability (and since my blackout, an occasional aura of scary dizziness) which requires me to use a cane and walk very carefully.

Second, is the fact that as long as I sit still, either at the home or office, I get along fine, but the least amount of exercise, either physical or mental (talking in a crowd) starts me gasping for breath. In order to keep my muscles from aching all the time, I take 15 minutes of exercise in bed before I get up six or seven times a week and then have to hurry to take Ventolin and Azmacort to get my breath back.

A third disturbing debility is my impaired hearing which means that I cannot enjoy most musical events or other entertainment, and I can be driven nuts in a big crowd! The fourth is my step-by-step (or should I say tooth-by-tooth?) loss of dentition. Next week I go from a one-half to a three-fourths upper plate, and I only have nine teeth left in my lower jaw!

Until recently my eyesight had declined very little (I still wear a prescription made in 1963), and my appetite is better than ever, although according to doctor's orders I drink no (well, almost no) alcohol, no caffeine in coffee or tea, no salt, no aspirin, and gave up my beloved pipe (with my charisma) six years ago.

After rereading the above, I think I now understand why older writers have *not* tackled the job of describing the effects of old age! It just isn't possible to make it a pleasant, amusing or even interesting subject of discussion, and it also tends to look too much like bewailing one's fate. Few people can feel comfortable in doing that.

Concentrate 18e

One Hobby at a Time

Webster defines a hobby as "a pursuit outside of one's occupation engaged in for recreation." As far back as I can remember, I had hobbies, but most of them follow one after another, *in sequitur.* Although all my hobbies fascinated me for a while, only a few of them lasted for more than ten years. When I learn as much as I care to know about a hobby, I usually give away or sell the collected artifacts and move on to a new project.

The Boy Scout program during my high school days enabled me to earn 36 merit badges on my way to Eagle Scout and acquainted me with a great variety of interests, many of which later led to hobbies.

Although most hobbies involve collections, I enjoy reading science fiction, detective stories, and magazines of all sorts. Other recreations include accumulating clothes (especially hats, sweaters, neck and bolo ties), and driving a succession of twenty cars of seven varieties (Tailings C). The following list of eleven hobbies or groups of similar hobbies is more or less chronological. They occupied some of my spare time during the last eight decades.

1. Postage stamps. In about 1918, my father gave me his stamp collection; later I bought a large Scott's Stamp Album. For nearly ten years I tried to fill in at least some of the blank spaces for more than 40 countries and probably had at least 1,000 stamps when I became otherwise occupied and sold the collection for $50. My geographic background surely profited from the studying of stamps published by numerous obscure nations.

2. Radio. In about 1922, when a radio station began to broadcast in Eugene, I built a receiver out of a galena crystal, a tickler, an oatmeal box wound with wire for tuning, and earphones. No batteries. Later I built a more expensive (and elaborate) heterodyne set with several now-forgotten parts and dials that operated them.

3. Reading. Because I was read to at an early age, I could read to myself long before I started school. Fortunately, reading has been a lifelong hobby and I still subscribe to probably too many magazines and usually read one book a week. My reading hobbies come under three categories:

A. *Science fiction:* I probably began with "Dr. Hackensaw's Secrets" in Hugo Gernsback's *Science & Invention* magazine; followed by Jules Verne's *20,000 Leagues Under the Sea* and *To the Center of the Earth*; Rudyard Kipling's "With the ABC," "The Village that Voted the Earth Was Flat," "The Ship that Found Herself," and several others; H.G. Wells' "Time Machine" and others; Isaac Asimov's "Foundation" and many others. For many years I subscribed to *Amazing Stories* and later to *Astounding Stories* magazines.

B. *Other magazines:* I probably started with *Boy's Life* and *Popular Mechanics*, followed by *National Geographic, Life, Time, Ellery Queen, Scientific American, American Scientist, Smithsonian, Natural History, Discovery* and many others.

C. *Rudyard Kipling:* Starting with the *Just So Stories* and *The Jungle Books*, followed by *Kim* and *Puck of Pook's Hill*, and then all of a 20-volume set that we inherited from Peggy's father. I read everything I could find of Kipling—one of the most unappreciated authors of this century.

4. Clothes. I have never been really hung up on clothes, but I have collected quite a large number of three parts of my costume:

A. *Sweaters:* After my "Order of the O" sweater, I cherish one that I inherited from my father and later accumulated a variety of more than 20 slipovers, cardigans, turtlenecks, and vests.

B. *Hats and caps:* My earliest cap was knitted for me by my grandmother in about 1918, followed by my Boy Scout balaclava, and my Park Service "Smoky Bear." I bought my first beret in Paris in 1964, followed by felt fedoras and lately many Irish tweed tams, caps, and hats.

C. *Neckties and bolo ties:* Ever since living in New Mexico in the early 1950s, I have been collecting bolo ties with silver, turquoise, ivory scrimshaw, elk horn with abalone, and numerous or interesting colorful minerals or rocks. I also have more than a hundred neckties to fall back on, kept in four boxes for predominantly red, blue, brown & green, and light colors.

5. Carpentry. In high school I was fortunate to have an excellent manual training class that enabled me to tackle most small carpentry jobs, and I accumulated quite a collection of tools. I built several ditty boxes for scout camps, and in 1937, some sectional bookshelves that could be stacked in several ways. I still have them!

6. Photography. I first considered this a convenience and entertainment, then later a professional necessity. Since I bought a box camera sometime in the 1920s, I have taken thousands of pictures with at least seven cameras: a 4 x 6 inch folding Kodak, a 2 x 3 inch folding Kodak, a same-size film pack camera, and a 35 mm reflex. In Japan, I bought a 35 mm Pentax reflex with two lenses, 50 and 200 mm telescopic; I later got a Pentax with 28 to 150 mm zoom lens. I gave the older cameras to the Historical Society and the rest to my grandchildren.

7. Hi-Fi. (1952-55) In Socorro I put together a 65 RPM recorder and built a corner box to house two loudspeakers, a woofer and a tweeter. Lost interest very soon.

8. Coins. In the fifties I filled out penny, nickel, and dime boards which I still have. On our trip to and from Pakistan and during our stay there, we saved the extra coins left over from each country we visited. In Peshawar and Lahore I also bought several silver and copper coins dating back to the time of Alexander (Menander, 163-150 B.C., Antialcides, 125-199 B.C., Vasudeva, 202-230 A.D.). Later, each time we went abroad, we added to the collection.

9. Rugs, etc. It was also in Pakistan that we bought the first two of Peggy's now substantial collection of oriental rugs which cover most of our floors, chair backs, and sofa. We also collected small brass cups, bowls, and trays. Peggy has long collected tiny porcelain pitchers and owls. And she also has a menagerie of furry and plushy baby animal toys, which started with Teddy bears but now includes at least one of the following each: seal, panda, rabbit, dog, raccoon, lion, tiger, meercat.

10. Art. My early tutors taught me to draw from nature (leaves, grasshoppers); I learned to sketch on the blackboard with colored chalk from both William Morris Davis and E.T. Hodge; I took up oils for a year or so, painting two scenes at Emminisky and Socorro. We collect many wall pictures in oil, collage, water color, and Apache sand paintings.

11. Weapons. Any boy is fascinated with weapons, and I have pursued different parts of this hobby for different lengths of time:

A. *Guns (1920-1945):* I have owned only seven guns, most of them I used for only a few years. I sold my last one in 1964 and now wonder whether I should have kept it! My earliest memory is of a BB air rifle, used only for plinking and target practice. Later I had a BB air pistol, and then a single shot .22 caliber target pistol and a tiny one shot .22 derringer. My last early gun was a single shot .22 rifle with which I earned the Sharpshooter Merit Badge in 1924.

In 1935, when I worked in the wilds of Curry County prospecting for chromite, my father gave me the .40 caliber Colt six-shooter that he had used while herding horses north from La Junta, Colorado, in the 1890s. In 1957 I joined the NRA and bought for $12 an army surplus 30-06 rifle still in the original cosmoline. For a year I worked on this in my basement workshop at our house in Portland, restocking it and painting it with six coats of lacquer, and then spent five or six weekend days at a shooting range near Tualatin renewing my shooting eye. When we moved to the Ione Plaza Apartments in 1964, I sold it for $150.

B. *Swords (1965-1975):* After a visit to the Wallace Collection in London in 1964, I began collecting swords, including an 1810 Japanese samurai (cost $50, sold for $900), a sword cane, Chinese ornamental sword, saber, kriis, machete, bolo, etc. They took up too much room, so I got rid of them.

199

C: *Knives (1963-1994)*: I carried an all-purpose scout knife as well as
a Catteraugus hunting knife for most of my 20 years as field
geologist. I first started collecting Ghurka kuhkri knives in
Pakistan. I still have three kukhris, two Japanese, a Persian
hunting knife, Scottish dirk, African knife with a three-metal
scabbard, French, Danish and a Bowie knife carried by Margaret's
father when he was a Texas Ranger. I have a box full of more
than 20 pocket knives, including pen, Boy Scout, whittling,
Swiss, etc.

12. Old geology books. (1952-1994) While at Santa Barbara, I
bought several 1830-1900 texts and continued to add to the collection
for several years.

Concentrate 18f

The Evolution of Tools

During my third career of writing, I have become increasingly
interested in the words applied to things. My hobbies (knives,
swords, and anthropology) encouraged this, and I try here to organize and classify some words that have intrigued me.

As a scientist, during the collection of data on any problem that I
am studying, my first almost inescapable urge is to try to classify!
Classification, in this case of tools, can unexpectedly and frequently
demonstrate significant relationships between groups of data that
have previously been hidden among the many facts.

Ever since our ancestors came down out of the trees and stood up
on their hind legs, thus freeing their hands (i.e. *Homo habilis* or
"handy man"), they have used those very "handy" tree-climbing-
specialized paws to make and use *tools*.

Important breakthrough discoveries or inventions are italicized:

I. **Classification by Need**
A.   **Procuring and preparing food**: 1. By land: hunting (spears,
     arrows, nets, lassos, bolos); gathering (sticks, spades, shov-
     els); *agriculture* (same as gathering tools, plus all the mecha-
     nized instruments of today). 2. By water: fishing (hooks, nets,
     poles), seines, nylon nets, weirs, harpoons (whaling).

B. **Comfort and shelter:** *Clothing, fire,* cave, tent, yurt, first wooden then stone modern houses.

C. **Transportation:** 1. By land: sleds, *wheels,* chariots, wagons, assads, skis, carts, *railroads,* bicycles, all kinds of motor vehicles, *automobiles.* 2. On water: paddles and oars, rafts, canoes, kayaks, proas, junks, biremes, triremes, *sailing* (all kinds of sailing and motor boats!), first steam, diesel, oil, and atomic ships, submarines. 3. By air and space: balloons, *airplanes, rockets.*

D. **Communication:** Signs, *language,* papyrus, parchment, paper, *type,* books, telegraph, telephone, radio, computer, modem, Internet.

E. **Recreation:** Competition, *bulls,* sports (see Concentrate 10b), *Olympics,* art, music.

F. **Combat:** Weapons require a major category, due to my hobby of swords and knives.

II. **Classification of Weapons by Function**
A. **To bash (blunt):** 1. Less than 12 inches: club, billy, blackjack, sandbag. 2. More than 12 inches: staff, mace, cudgel, shillelagh, quarter staff, bat, cane, walking stick, bolo, boomerang, lathi.
B. **To pierce (pointed):** 1. Less than 12 inches: dirk, dagger, stilletto, bold, reed, dart. 2. More than 12 inches: épée, foil, spear, javelin, lance, assegai, pike, shaft, arrow, bayonet, sword cane, gaff, harpoon.
C. **To cut (bladed):** 1. Knives, less than 12 inches: dirk, dagger, Bowie knife, khukri, stilletto. 2. Swords, more than 12 inches: cutlass, rapier, claymore, glaive, Toledo, hangar, bilbo, falchion, yataghan, poinyard, skean dhu, kris, pole axe, battle axe, halberd, tomahawk, bill, partisan, tulwar, machete, bayonet, saber, Japanese sword, Roman sword, scimitar.
D. **To protect:** Bearskin, shield, helmet, armor, blockhouse, stockade, fortification, fortress, castle, parapet, moat, trench, acropolis, citadel, barbed wire.

III. **Classification of Tools by Material**
A. **Wood:** Clubs, spears, javelin, lance, canes, staffs, handles for most metallic tools and weapons, ballistas, ladders.

201

B. **Rock (stone, flint, obsidian)**: Mortars and pestles, rocks for throwing, blades for weapons (axe, arrow), awls, razors.
C. **Metal (copper, bronze, iron, steel, carbon steel, alloy, aluminum, magnesium)**: Knives (Bowie, French, paper, pen, Swiss), axe, hatchet, saw, scissors, adze, sickle, scythe, awl, pins, needles, razors, innumerable tools for woodworking, carpentry and metalwork, etc.

Concentrate 18g

Names in My Life

During a long and eventful life, I have been introduced to thousands of people, but probably less than a few hundred made a sufficient impression on me to be remembered. They represent playmates, tutors, teachers, associates, pals and buddies, girlfriends and lovers, helpers, bosses, peers, mentors, and many others that have affected me in many ways; a few of them even changed my life. This essay is a recognition of those significant people, now gone.

The following names are listed chronologically (as well as I can recall) by the *place* where I first met these people, followed by *why* I remember them. I omit relatives and also my most memorable teachers, since they are covered elsewhere. Neither do I mention the 34 localities in 22 towns where we lived, since that is covered in the Tailings. Those I remember *negatively* are marked with an asterisk!

Seattle: Mrs. Pirkle came weekly to help Mother with the laundry and housework.

Eugene: Billy Foster and I discharged a shotgun in his attic, and we both got lickings. Dean Straub gave me a nickel for candy and told me to be sure and study Greek. Goldie Wells tutored me in the fifth and sixth grades, then went to Africa as a missionary.

Hugh Miller and I had a secret club called the BT (Big Tree) and hid things at the base of a giant Douglas fir we found south of town. Our local gang, consisting of Hugh, Elmer Adams, Dalton and Helen Shinn, and Elizabeth Thatcher, played on the teeter-totter and whirly-go-round that Dad built in the big corner yard south of our house at 1968 Alder Street, and built houses out of the piles of mill-ends firewood delivered there each year in the fall. During World War I we played war games in trenches and a dugout we laboriously excavated on the hill east of us.

Castle McAlister's father had a farm near Central Point where I spent one summer milking nine cows and helping with the other farm work. That was when I decided *never* to take up farming!

Jimmy Carr, who had been a captain in World War I, was Scoutmaster of Troop 1 Boy Scouts of America; my Flying Eagle Patrol included Clair Cooley, Carl Muller, Lyle Grimes, Bradford Datson, Wilbur Jones and Howard Stafford. Roy Ford and my younger brother, Bob, were in another patrol. Several of us on weekends would regularly hike into the forest only a mile east of town and camp overnight. During high school, Clair, Roy, Elise Schroeder, and Margaret Hurley were in a dancing class we held weekly in each other's homes

In college, Elinor and then Janet Fitch were flames for several years before I met Margaret Moss.

Bob Goodall used to visit me in the evenings in the room I built onto the garage at 2239 Birch Lane. Bob and I climbed Mt. Hood together. Roy Kilpatrick and I made a 24-hour climb of both the Middle and South Sisters, and the Eugene "Obsidians" named me "Chief Hotfoot."

La Grande: Clair Perkins was my assistant director at Catherine Creek Scout Camp east of La Grande. Dodie Barnes, a flame in La Grande, was one of the reasons I took my *wanderjahr*—during which I first met Ian Campbell at Harvard who later became an important mentor. I also met J Harlan Bretz in Chicago, and 60 years later wrote about his work in my book *Cataclysms on the Columbia*.

Eugene: George Turnbull taught me the basics of newspaper writing. Warren Du Pre Smith inspired me to change my major to geology and was my mentor all his life. E.T. "God" Hodge could draw colored sketches on the blackboard, exceeded only in skill by William Morris Davis who taught two summer session courses at Oregon in 1930. Hodge could also sketch in the geology for miles around an especially good viewpoint.

Berkeley: N.L. Taliaferro* was the committee chairman who turned down my first attempt at a dissertation on chromite, so it took me five more years to finish the San Juan Bautista dissertation. Howell Williams started me in volcanology. I was a teaching assistant for both Norman Ethan Allen Hinds and Ralph Chaney in their 1,000 student classes. George Louderback* taught us stratigraphy by rote.

203

San Juan Bautista: Robert M. Coats was my roommate before I got married and helped me map my quadrangle. I helped him map the Comstock Lode and environs. I was best man at his wedding.

Crater Lake: Frank Swartzlow was chief Ranger/Naturalist, Elmer Applegate was botanist, Carl Dutton and Warren D. Smith (who got me both this and the Agness jobs) were geologists.

Agness: C.E. Tuttle hired me to prospect for chromite and replied to my first long-winded report: "A fine report, but what shall I *do*?" Arthur Dorn* rented his house to us and tried to get me fired. Bob Owens was my foreman, assisted by Arthur Fry who was chief of the local Indian tribe.

Grants Pass: Howard Stafford was chemist, Ralph Mason engineering geologist. Later, Ralph, along with Edward Baldwin were DOGAMI engineers with me at Coos Bay.

Baker: Roger Biswell, Sr., was the wise old doctor who liked to accompany me on my mine-examination trips. Les Motz was assayer at the DOGAMI office.

Portland: Earl Nixon, Director of DOGAMI, hired me and gave me the best advice I ever received: "All your advancement and promotion will depend upon two things—the number of new ideas you come up with, and the amount of unpaid overtime you put in." When F.W. Libbey* succeeded Nixon, all the geologists left within six months.

Wallowa Lake: Warren D. Smith was head, Wayne Lowell and I assistants to a party of nine that mapped the northern Wallowa Mountains.

North Bend: Ewart Baldwin, Ralph Mason, and I remapped the Coos Bay Quadrangle as DOGAMI Bulletin #27.

State College, Pennsylvania: Frank Schwartz* was chairman of geology and strongly disliked my visiting P.D. Krynine, chairman of mineralogy. When I started to map the Bedford Quadrangle, Schwartz assigned two graduate students to map it for their theses. Ian Campbell was a lifelong mentor, who helped me make nearly every major career change.

Socorro, New Mexico: When I arrived at NMIMT, Clay Smith took me on a field trip, and we were stuck in the mud for 12 hours. Frank Kottlowski and Max Willard were my best friends at the NM Bureau of Mines. Jack Workman* was president and fired me after two years. He would never say why. Pat Callaghan, director of the Bureau, immediately rehired me. Workman later asked me if I would take

Callaghan's job! Stewart Jones was on my faculty and helped me map the Capitan Quadrangle. Dick Jahns visited NMIMT every summer, and we got to know that ebullient character very well.

Nakaibito, Navajo Reservation: Robert Balk, John Schilling, and I mapped the Fort Defiance and Tohatchi Quadrangles for the Navajo Nation. This color map was possibly the first one to be published on photo-mosaics. While Balk was carrying the map separations to the printer, the plane he was in crashed into a cliff east of Albuquerque and he was killed.

Santa Barbara: Bob Webb, Chairman of Geology at USCB, asked me to teach summer session, which I did twice. Bob Norris, in whose house we stayed, was a faculty member there.

Portland: Bob Van Atta was the first of the new faculty I hired at PSC. Brandford Millar was president of PSC and a good friend. For a year, Irwin Lange and I shared an office on the third floor of Lincoln Hall. Miriam McKee, whom I had met when I worked with her husband in Socorro, became our first and only female teacher. Philip Hoffman taught me the techniques of committee work.

Honolulu: I was hired by Gordon McDonald, who had been at Berkeley with me, to teach summer session at the U. of Hawaii. We lived in his house, and he took us on several field trips.

Peshawar, Pakistan: Nabi Baksh, a Ghurka and a treasure as our cook/bearer, took great care of us (for $20 a month!) during our eight months in Pakistan. On our return trip, Howard and Lois Anderson (former grad students at Cal) entertained us in Tehran.

Portland: Paul Hammond, Richard Thoms, and possibly most important of all, Eugene Pierson, came to PSU in 1966. For nearly 30 years, Gene has been staff geologist, and did everything but teach. Before and especially since my retirement in 1974, Gene has taken brotherly and untiring care of the old man in many ways.

In 1976, I was accompanied on the International Geological Congress field trips in New Zealand and Australia by Gordon Oakshott, who later became California State Geologist. During my work with the National Association of Geology Teachers, he became a good friend. Father Skehan of Boston University was a mentor during my presidency of NAGT and nominated me for the Niel Miner Award.

Since my retirement in 1974, the department has had numerous faculty. Those that I still saw daily in 1995 were Paul Hammond, Richard Thoms, Marvin Beeson, Ansel Johnson, Curt Peterson, and Scott Burns, who has turned out to be the most dynamic and promis-

ing of all. A new structural geologist, Kenneth Cruikshank, also
suggests great potential. Scott, Ken, and I were all Eagle Scouts!

Concentrate 18h

Lack of Grieving

As you come closer and closer to that cold grey curtain of nothing-
ness, you begin to look inwards as well as backwards, as I have done
in several Concentrates.

Occasionally I am disturbed and puzzled by the awareness of a
peculiar mental quirk that I have not before revealed to anyone. I
have *never* really grieved at deaths! I took the loss of family and close
associates as a normal part of life and went on with scarcely a pang. I
fondly remember my grandmothers, grandfather, father, mother,
sister, brothers, and close friends, but when they went it disturbed me
very little.

What does this unnatural attitude imply as to my mental makeup?
How did I happen to have or get such a lack of normal emotions? I
don't think that I am hard-hearted. I have never hunted or fished
because I just didn't enjoy killing wild animals. I can shed a few tears
after a spat with my wife of 60 years, at a good movie, or even upon
reading an especially sad story. Both my younger brothers were
much more emotional.

As a child and even during the "terrible teens," I don't remember
ever feeling that I was restricted, mistreated, or unfairly disciplined.
My athletic experiences in high school and college were swimming
and track, not one-on-one sports, and I am sure that I never had a
knock-down-and-drag-out fight. Since I was too young for World
War I and too old for World War II, I missed both those traumatic
experiences.

Although I am not about to go to a psychologist to find out, I
would certainly like to hear some hypothesis that could explain this
attitude. The only one I can think of is that my father did scold me
whenever I made an enthusiastic but ill-advised action or proposal.
Using his most serious epithet, he would quietly but emphatically
say, "Confound it, John, you will never amount to anything if you
can't control yourself better than that!" I learned very early to quickly

hide any emotional reaction. Perhaps my emotions still lie deeply buried in my subconscious, but they never seemed to bother me with dreams or anything else except possibly asthma.

Concentrate 18i

Why the Allens Stay at Home

We are frequently asked why we no longer go on long trips or drives to the coast or elsewhere in Oregon or even to local banquets and picnics of the numerous organization to which we belong. We do not even go to their meetings unless they are held on the campus.

If you MUST know, here are some of the reason why!

Age: We are both 88 years old!

Hearing: My hearing has deteriorated so that I no longer go to church because I cannot hear the sermon or join in the singing. In any large group the noise of the talk is impossible to interpret and very tiring. Peggy is also having trouble with hearing, although she does not yet need an aid.

Treatments and Exercise: In order to control my asthma, I take three inhalents at five in the morning and again at five in the afternoon, and a fourth is taken with a nebulizer air pump. After the morning inhalents, I take 25 minutes of a complicated exercise regimen. Both of us are having trouble getting a good night's sleep, and neither of us can walk more than a block or so without tiring and having me quickly lose my breath. My balance is so poor that I must use a cane whenever leaving the apartment. I must visit my internist every two weeks for blood tests to check the needed daily doses of pills. Every second evening before going to bed I take a half hour of hydrotherapy which involves hot packs followed by icy cold packs on my chest.

Food: I am trying to adhere to a restricted and somewhat difficult diet which my naturopath suggests may help my asthma.

Driving: Neither Peggy nor I drive any longer, although until quite recently I drove regularly to my internist and to the local Safeway store and pharmacy for food and medicine. Until my eyesight forced me to give up driving, I felt safe only when driving in low gear, did not like to drive more than a couple of miles at a time, and would not drive at dusk or at night.

Work: I am trying very hard to finish two new books and have weekly appointments with my co-author and with my editor. I've even recently gotten hooked up online on the internet! I spend two to four hours at my office, "tottering" with my cane *every day* the 300 yards across the Park Blocks and back.

Concentrate 18j

Twenty Ways to Count Sheep and Defeat Insomnia

Introduction

As we get older, no longer do we quickly drop off to sleep—sometimes it takes several frustrating hours when counting sheep may no longer be effective. This is probably why so many of us need to take naps during the day! I present various methods I have used that have worked with me.

The main purpose of these exercises is to turn off that busy brain which insists on churning over the events of the past day. One method that can sometimes shut it off is to recite familiar rhymes and verses that we learned in school. Students now seldom rote memorize unless they are in plays or recitals, although such recollections can be valuable. Another method is *counting* sheep or anything else.

I understand that different people remember either through their eyes (visual), ears (aural), or touch (tactile). My sister was tactile, many of my friends are aural, and I am visual. Consequently, as I use the procedures I have found valuable, I try to bring up visual images of each item.

Preliminaries

1) It is very important to have a pencil and note pad by your bed, so that you can turn on the light and write down all the things that are on your mind to do tomorrow.
2) Take a bite before going to bed—a glass of milk and a cookie.
3) Get comfortable in bed—I use three pillows to lift my head.
4) In cold weather, I warm my feet with an electric pad or blanket.
5) Read for a few minutes—I use detective stories, mainly because the

208

paperbacks are light.
6) If I do not doze off after an hour or so, I take a Tylenol to ease my tensions—usually this is only necessary two or three times a week. Maybe once a week, after several hours, I may take a Tylenol-3 (with codeine).

Recitations
7) Repeat favorite memorized pieces: "Twas brillig and the slithy toves..." (Carroll); "On a tree by a river a little bird sat..." (Gilbert); "I met a traveller from an antique land..." (Shelley); "When to the sessions of sweet silent thought..." (Shakespeare); "This is the forest primaeval..." (Longfellow); etc.

Counting Methods
For each item use *one breath* and mentally visualize or pronounce:
Numbers:
8) Count forward from 1 to 100.
9) Count backward from 100 to 1.
10) Count backward and forward by tens— 100 to 91, 10 to 19, 80 to 71, 30 to 39, 60 to 51, 50 to 41, 60 to 69, 30 to 21, 80 to 89, 10 to 0.
11) Count in Roman numerals: I, II, III, IV, V, VI, as far as you can. Then try it backwards!
12) Count in other languages that you know: Ein, zwei, drei, vier, finf...; Une, deux, trois, quatre, cinque...; Uno, dos, tres, cuatro, cinco...

Other Sequences
Visualize or pronounce!
Alphabets:
13) Forward A to Z.
14) Backward Z to A. The easy way is to go by threes: zyx, wvu, tsr, qpo, nml,....
15) Greek: Alpha, Beta, Gamma, Delta, Epsilon, Zeta, Eta,....
16) Days of the week: Forward, then backward.
17) Months of the year: Forward, then backward.
18) Streets in your neighborhood: Northwest Portland's alphabetical streets are easy, south to north, but then try north to south!
19) Toes and fingers: For tactile people. As you count, try to feel or wiggle each digit in turn, 1 to 20 and back.

20) Recite the 20 Ways to Count Sheep!

Concentrate 18k

The Search for Immortality

Introduction

I have read few explanations of why people feel that they could live forever, hence this essay is the result of only one man's feelings, written at age 86, about this perpetual mystery. As a lifelong agnostic, I believe that when I go, that will be all for me. I expect my own immortality will rest only in my offspring, my publications, the things I have accomplished, good or bad, and in the associations with which I have worked.

A book on the subject that I read in my teens was *Back to Methusaleh*, by George Bernard Shaw, which traces for thousands of years the development of increasing old age, until immortality is finally achieved. As I remember it, the "Old Ones" eventually became so bored that after about 30,000 years they took final action in suicide. Recent biological research has suggested that the only really immortal living particles are the "selfish genes" within the cells that combine to give each organism its unique character. Some of these genes reproduce each generation, have lived for eons, and are truly immortal. Combinations and permutations of thousands of human genes in every individual give mankind an extraordinary diversity which results in a fantastic array of beliefs and cultures.

Religion

Almost every culture seems to include some kind of belief in an afterlife. The oldest archeological records of *Homo sapiens* strongly suggest that religions became important very soon after man learned to talk. Belief in an afterlife is suggested by the artifacts accompanying many burials; Mayan and Egyptian tombs are only two outstanding examples. Evidence for the worldwide prevalence of religion throughout historic time lies in fourteen pages of terms in *Roget's Thesaurus*. A 1993 almanac divides today's world population of 5,385,330,333 souls into the following modern belief groups:

210

Religion	Million	Percent
Christian	1,804	33%
Roman Catholic	(1,010)	(56%)
Protestant	(368)	(21%)
Orthodox	(169)	(9%)
Anglican	(74)	(4%)
Other Christian	(183)	(10%)
Islam	951	18%
Nonreligious	884	16%
Hindu	719	13%
Buddhist	309	6%
Atheist	237	4%
Chinese folk religions	184	3%
"New" religions	141	3%
Tribal religions	94	2%
Sikh	18	
Hebrew	18	
Shaman	10	
Confucian	6	
Baha'i	5	
Jain	4	
Shinto	3	
Other	18	<1%

Protestants are again divided into numerous churches: Baptist, Methodist, United Reformed, Episcopal, Brethren, Pentecostal, Friends, Unitarians, Seventh Day Adventist, Jehovah's Witness, Christian Scientist, Latter Day Saints, etc.

My purpose in listing all these religions is: first, to show that most humans always have had, and still do need, a faith that offers an afterlife to help them cope with life; and second, to emphasize that mankind is so diverse that different peoples require different beliefs.

Archaeology

The 304 pages of *National Geographic's* 1994 *Atlas of Archaeology* describes and beautifully illustrates in color more than a hundred explored archaeological sites, most of which represent different cultures. A large proportion of these accounts yield suggestions of beliefs in immortality. By copying down the dates that bracket these

60 cultures I gave myself quite a lesson in geography, prehistory and history:

1,800,000 to 10,000 B. C.: Prehistoric
9000 to 4000 B.C.	Early Settlements
9000 to 4000 B.C.	Jericho
7000 to 5600 B.C.	Catal Hüyük

4000 to 30 B.C.: Cities and Civilizations
3500 to 1950 B.C.	Sumerians
2000 to 700 B.C.	Hittites
1792 to 539 B.C.	Babylonians
1500 to 612 B.C.	Assyrians
1200 to 146 B.C.	Phoenicians
702 to 330 B.C.	Medes & Persians
3050 to 30 B.C.	Egyptians

2000 B.C. to 476 A.D.: The Classical World
2000 to 1450 B.C.	Minoans
1550 to 1100 B.C.	Mycenaeans
800 to 30 B.C.	Greeks
800 to 200 B.C.	Etruscans
753 B.C. to 476 A.D.	Romans

2000 B.C. to 750 A.D.: Crossroads of Faith
2000 to 900 B.C.	Canaanites
900 B.C. to 135 A.D.	Israelites
1 to 400 A.D.	Birth of Christianity
600 to 750 A.D.	Moslems

6000 B.C. to 1100 A.D.: Europe—Into the North
4700 to 1500 B.C.	Megalith-Builders
800 to 50 B.C.	Celts
500 B.C. to 650 A.D.	Germanic Peoples
790 to 1100 A.D.	Vikings

1050 B.C. to 1650 A.D.: Ancient African Kingdoms
1050 B.C. to 350 A.D.	Kush
1000 B.C. to 1200 A.D.	Aksum and Lalibela
500 B.C. to 1650 A.D.	West African Kingdoms
240 B.C. to 1400 A.D.	Jenne-jeno
1200 to 1500 A.D.	Great Zimbabwe

6000 B.C. to 1500 A.D.: The Indian Subcontinent

2400 to 1500 B.C.	Indus Valley
550 B.C. to 1000 A.D.	Buddhist
600 to 1300 A.D.	Hindu Revival
250 B.C. to 1300 A.D.	Sri Lanka

5000 B.C. to 1500 A.D.: Southeast Asia

802 to 1432 A.D.	Angkor
1057 to 1287 A.D.	Pagan
1240 to 1500 A.D.	Sukhothai and Ayutthaya
760 to 1050 A.D.	Borobudur and Prambanam
5000 B.C. to 800 A.D.	China
3000 B.C. to 900 A.D.	Korea

700 B.C. to 1400 A.D.: Central and North Asia

700 to 100 B.C.	Scythians
500 to 300 B.C.	Pazyryk
100 B.C. to 100 A.D.	Kushan
1100 to 1400 A.D.	Mongols

50,000 to 1800 A.D.: Pacific Islands

40,000 B.C. to 1800 A.D.	Australia
100 to 1600 A.D.	Nan Madol
400 to 1800 A.D.	Easter Island
1000 to 1800 A.D.	New Zealand

12,500 B.C. to 1500 A.D.: North America

4000 B.C. to 1500 A.D.	Nomads of the North
500 to 1500 A.D.	Ozette
2000 B.C. to 1450 A.D.	Desert Dwellers
900 to 1300 A.D.	Anasazi
1000 B.C. to 1500 A.D.	Builders of the Eastern Mounds

7000 B.C. to 1697 A.D.: Meso America

1200 to 400 B.C.	Olmec
200 B.C. to 750 A.D.	Teotihuacan
1200 B.C. to 1697 A.D.	Maya
1200 to 1521 A.D.	Aztec

500 B.C. to 1630 A.D.: South America

500 B.C. to 1200 A.D.	San Agustin
800 to 1630 A.D.	Tairona
200 to 700 A.D.	Nazca

100 to 800 A.D.	Moche
800 to 1470 A.D.	Chimu
1200 to 1532 A.D.	Inca

Posterity

For 5,000 years, royalty was concerned with the immortality of their line of succession to the throne. Little of that remains, but genealogical study still fascinates thousands. The great Mormon catalog kept by the Latter Day Saints in Salt Lake City is an example of the importance to many people of tracing the immortality of their own name and line.

Most undeveloped countries have families with numerous offspring to carry on the family name and take care of their elders. The result, of course, is the population explosion that threatens to devastate the earth.

Art, Architecture, and Literature

Surely the creative urge is fueled by an unconscious desire for some sort of immortality. Why else do people carve statues, paint pictures, design buildings and write books? Michaelangelo, Rembrandt and Shakespeare are immortal because of their accomplishments.

The very first paintings, created 25,000 years ago in caves located in what is now France, may have had religious functions. Possibly the very early sculptures, such as the little clay Venus figures, were representations of fertility.

After Gutenberg (and the Chinese) invented moveable type, writers could perpetuate (immortalize?) in print the ideas and beliefs that previously had to be memorized and passed by word of mouth from generation to generation.

I suspect that my own delight in a third career of writing during the last 20 years of retirement has been in great part fueled by a not-always-unconscious urge to perpetuate my own ideas.

Organizations

The glue that holds cultures of diverse peoples together consists in large part of the thousands of "organizations" which allow people of similar beliefs, professions, needs, intents, and interests to get together. They can then agree on mutual rules of politeness (*Robert's Rules of Order*) and procedures (constitutions or by-laws) that enable them to peacefully and happily mingle and do things together that

214

they could not do alone.

Organizations (see Concentrate 10a) are among the longest-lived cultural phenomena. Members can often feel that they are a part of a relatively immortal group, persistent for hundreds or even thousands of years. Religions, especially, have endured: Hinduism, Buddhism, Christianity, and Islam are all ancient. Masons and Rosicrucians claim old age. Dozens of American institutions have celebrated their hundredth anniversaries. *Roget's Thesaurus* lists a remarkable number of organizational terms, although not as many as the 14 pages of religious terms:

Family: gens, kin, relation, clan, caste, race, tribe, sept

Education: school, academy, lyceum, seminary, college, institute, university, fraternity, sorority

Fraternal: club, coterie, circle, Freemason, Knights Templar, Odd Fellows, Knights of Pythias, PEO, Greeks

Government: legislature, senate, house of representatives, party, faction, forum, bar, court, bench, class, confederacy, agency, coalition, junta, cabal, clique, league, Communist, Bolshevist, IWW, Luddite, Tammany

Commerce: guild, company, firm, corporation, union, store, market, emporium, mall, fair, bazaar, exchange, bourse, bank, curb

---

Concentrate 18l

The Eightfold Consortium of Vertebrate Organisms

A geologist writing about anatomy? I took college courses in biology, psychology, and paleontology, and as I grew older my reading began to reflect a growing interest in living organisms. Lately, another interest has developed: writing capsule descriptions of geological localities. This concentrate is a capsule derived from a layman's elementary knowledge of vertebrate anatomical systems, which may entertain biological professionals with its different points of view.

All vertebrate bodies are composed of and operated by incredibly complicated anatomical systems consisting of myriads of mutually cooperating microscopic cells that have a fantastic diversity of specialized duties. Cells that were originally simple differentiated and adapted during billions of years and joined up to make up the complicated systems we now have.

The eight cell systems I recognize reflect a lifelong use of the scientific procedure which, after collecting information, systematizes and classifies it. These systems are described by functions, organs and processes.

1. **Sensory system.** The brain and nerves receive and processe information from the five senses—sight (eyes), hearing (ears), touch (skin), taste (nose and mouth), smell (nose)—and gives orders to the muscles and glands. I don't remember the eight kinds of nerves that I once learned, but I do remember the pneumonic phrase I used to learn them: "On Old Olympus' Towering Top a Finn and German Vie." The superior development of communication by this system differentiates man from all other forms of life.

2. **Structural system.** The skeleton supports the posture and movements of the organism. It protects the brain in the head, organs in the rib cage. Strong, jointed, hollow bones contain internal marrow which produces blood cells.

3. **Motive system—Muscles and Tendons.** These are contracting and relaxing groups of cells which operate the skeletal elements for locomotion. Tendons tie the muscles and skeletal parts together.

4. **Vascular system—Blood and Lymph.** The heart pumps the nourishment, oxygen & waste products in the blood to all parts of the body. Plasma carries red corpuscles, which carry oxygen, and white corpuscles, which attack intruders.

   Lymph and blood transmit chemical orders from glands by way of secretions. Glands probably could make up a ninth "system," consisting mainly of the liver (secretes bile), kidneys (secretes urine), and pancreas (acts on food); there are many other glands (spleen, adrenal, salivary, etc.).

5. **Respiratory system.** The trachia and lungs transmit oxygen from air to the blood, get rid of carbon dioxide, and allow speech through the larynx and trachia.

6. **Alimentary system—Mouth, Esophagus, Stomach & Intestines.** Processes food for the blood to distribute, gets rid of waste by

216

excretion and through liver and kidneys.

7.   **Dermal system—Skin, Nails, and Hair, etc.** Packages the organism, protects it with scales (fish, reptiles); shell (turtles, armadillo); a flexible protective skin, hair, claws and nails (mammals); feathers, beaks, scales, and claws (birds).

8.   **Reproductive system—Ovary, Womb, and Testicles.** Reproduces the entire organism. The reproductory cells (sperm and egg) are the most incredible and miraculous of all, since this pair of cells carry and transmit to each new generation, selected characteristics from the multitude of diversified cells supplied by both parents.

Concentrate 18m

A Tribute to My Mother

For my 86th birthday, my English professor daughter gave me Gail E. Christianson's biography of Loren Eiseley, *Fox at the Wood's Edge* (Henry Holt, 1991), and I have been reading it for a couple of hours a day ever since.

It fascinates me, since Eiseley was born only one year before I was, and like me, he took more than four years to graduate from college and nearly ten years to get his Ph.D. As he climbed up the academic ladder and moved from Pennsylvania to Kansas to Oberlin to Palo Alto and then back to Pennsylvania, he almost continually had problems with administrators and faculties, with co-authors and publishers. He had very few friends, and again and again he relied on mentors to help him with his academic and scientific problems.

In spite of Eiseley's fame as an anthropologist, writer, and poet, his life seems to have been almost constantly unhappy—he never got over the feelings of inadequacy apparently derived from the antagonistic relationship with a mother that he eventually came to hate. She was, using an expressive term I found in William Least Heat Moon's *PrairieErth*, "half a bubble out of plumb." She screamed at and abused her son whenever they met. All his life, Eiseley, like Christopher Robin's donkey "Eeyore" in A.A. Milne's *Winnie the Pooh*, looked on the dark side. During his later years, his biographer reports that Eiseley began to lose his capabilities and could no longer attend to his

217

responsibilities.

Last night I picked up the summer edition of the *American Scholar*, and first read, as I always do, the lead article by Aristides, which turned out to be a essay about his mother. For eight pages he tenderly analyzes this remarkable Jewish woman, the way in which she raised her family, and her effect upon his own life.

That got me to thinking about my own remarkable mother, Sally (Ida) Elliott Allen. I don't think I have ever tried to write about her, or even thought much about her, and now I find that I remember only a very little about her! I know I couldn't write a long essay like that of Aristides, but it might be interesting to try.

My mother's father, Charles Florian Elliott, was a Unitarian minister whom I remember as having a parish in Keokuck, Iowa. Besides his daughter Ida, Elliott had two sons: Ralph, whom I never knew, and Louis. His first wife died before I was born, and he married the companion known to us as "Granny" who helped raise the family and cared for him during the years of his first wife's illness (which may have been mental).

My mom and dad raised the four children in my family; I was born in 1908, my brother Bob in 1910, and my sister Betty in 1912. I remember almost nothing of them, but a little more of brother Eric, Junior, born eight years later in 1920. I suppose the sparsity of my childhood memories is partly a result of my early bout with pneumonia, followed by the asthma which allowed me to attend school for only the third and fourth grades.

I do have a good memory for places (which is probably why I was a successful field geologist), and retain fairly vivid pictures of the three houses and neighborhoods along the length of Alder Street in Eugene and the one on Birch Lane in which we lived. But my memories of people have always been pretty skimpy. My wife is the "people person" in our family.

From what I do remember, my mother was an elegant lady who never lost her temper, never shouted at me, never hassled me to do this or do that. As far as I knew, she was the one that ran the household; my father never spent much time at home with his children, although he did take us on camping trips and built swings and teeter-totters for us.

Mother assigned errands and chores for me to do around the house, and I did them without any feelings of being imposed upon. If I did something really bad (like abusing my brother Bob or building a

218

fire against the side of the house!), my mother quietly but effectively switched my legs, and that was that. She must have read to me as a child, because I very early learned to read to myself and I knew Mother Goose, A.A. Milne, Lewis Carroll, Grimms Tales, and others.

Mother was an activist, not a homebody, which may be another reason why I remember so little about her. For many years we had a housekeeper, Mrs. Moore, who also prepared some of the meals each day. Mother was thus able, as the wife of the head of the Department of Journalism and later the head of the School of Journalism, to entertain faculty, students and visiting firemen in our home and be involved in numerous other campus activities. She was advisor to her sorority, Kappa Kappa Gamma, active in Phi Beta Kappa, and founded the woman's writers group, "Pot and Quill."

For years, each morning between the hours of nine and noon her study was off limits, as she wrote on her book *Not Hers Alone*, and on plays, some of which were presented by the "Very Little Theater," in which she was also very active.

Addenda:
(Father's family)
William Judge Allen *m.* Josephine Plympton Smith =
Eric, Chester, Hugh, Reeder, Amy, Carolyn, Marjorie.

(Mother's family)
Charles Florian Elliott *m.* (Ellen Douglas Arquitt, stepmother) =
Ida, Louis, (Ralph, died as a child).

Eric William Allen *m.* Ida Elliott =
John Eliot, Robert Kimball, Elizabeth, Eric William, Jr.

John Eliot Allen m. Margaret Moss =
Margaret Anne "Sally."

My 50-Year-Long Affair with Lady Nicotine

Tobacco is a filthy weed: I like it!
It fulfills no earthly need: I like it!
It makes you long and lank and lean: I like it!
It takes the hair right off your bean: I like it!
It's the worst darn stuff I've ever seen: I like it!
—Graham Lee Heminger

I have enjoyed half a century of romance with this seductive dame, and only because of my lifelong policy of "moderation in all things" do I have no regrets from my explorations of her multiple attractions. I was surprised at their number, when, during the waking hours of a white night, I began to list the different kinds of tobaccos and accessories that I had tried out during five decades. Perhaps you may enjoy my recollections of enticing *Nicotiana tabacum*!

Pipe Tobacco:
Edgeworth cut plug came in small flat blue tin cans (similar in size to "Altoid" peppermint drop boxes). The thin slices could be crumbled and put in your pipe or chewed. It was too strong for my taste.

Prince Albert pipe tobacco came in bright red tin cans less than an inch thick, and 4 x 5 inches wide and tall. It was popular with prospectors, who put claim notices in the empty cans and nailed them to the location post. Prince Albert was milder than Edgeworth, but I never used it very much.

Union Leader: My father smoked a pipe, which was probably the reason I took up smoking after I had graduated from the University of Oregon and no longer had to train for the swimming team. Dad always smoked Union Leader, and this light, pure (and inexpensive) Burley tobacco eventually became my favorite. For 40 years I bought the red one-pound cans, which originally cost only 87 cents but escalated to more than $3 by the time I quit in 1982. I usually used about one can (16 ounces) per month. If I smoked half an ounce a day

220

for 40 years, the 480 pounds probably cost me less than $600!

Burley and Latakia and others: Latakia was a strong black Turkish blend. Besides these pipe tobaccos, there were a host of other kinds used in mixtures that I tried out and abandoned after a few cans. My father showed me how to make Indian tobacco"from the dried leaves of the Rocky Mountain shrub *Kinnikinic*.

Chewing Tobacco:

Star plug chewing tobacco I remember only because I needed to chew tobacco during the three months I worked on a Union Pacific bridge-building gang in Eastern Oregon. If it was hot outside your "quid" kept your mouth moist when you couldn't go traipsing off to the water bag every few minutes.

Snuff: Copenhagan was the snuff of choice in those days. Tuck a pinch under your lip, and spit a lot. I tried it, but it was too strong for me, and if I happened to swallow, it made me sick. I never did try to snuff it up my nose the classical way.

Cigars:

Robert Burns Cigarillos were mild, slim and short; on special occasions I rather liked them, but they cost a lot more than a pipe.

Havana cigars were strong, thick, long and costly. I really only smoked expensive cigars when given to me, and I didn't enjoy them all that much.

Stogies were strong, thin, long, black, and crooked. They were fun to smoke, but they were pretty strong, and I never got in the habit. Cheroot is a thin cigar cut off at both ends.

Cigarettes:

Bull Durham cigarette tobacco was pale, flaky, and came in small cloth sacks. During field work I carried a bag as a valuable social tool. The ritual was, when you sat down to talk with a stranger, you offered him your sack and pad of cigarette papers, so that he could roll his own. I used this to great advantage with prospectors, miners, and especially among the Navajo Indians I worked with for two summers on their reservation. I was able to gain their trust and in return receive valuable information from them.

Camels and Lucky Strikes were perhaps the best advertised cigarettes, and although I smoked a few when they were offered me, I doubt whether I ever bought more than five or six packs during those

50 years, and I am sure I never bought a carton.

Marlboroughs, as now, were elite cigarettes, slim and long with a filter. I tried out a few other brands, but never smoked any cigarettes for more than a pack.

"Coffin Nails" was the term frequently and not so facetiously used for cigarettes during the thirties. After 60 years, the medical profession has finally proven the correctness of this name.

Cigarette holders of all kinds were supposed to moderate the ill effects of smoking cigarettes (they were part of Franklin Roosevelt's image). They enclosed a variety of replaceable filters and came in many sizes and materials.

Pipes:

Corncob pipes were cheap and fun to use, but they took a long time to break in and could not be easily cleaned.

Clay pipes were inexpensive but exceedingly fragile, and the clay stem was uncomfortable in the mouth.

Meerschaums are the aristocrats of pipedom. They are very expensive, yet fairly light and fragile. The bowls are frequently carved in artistic or bizarre shapes. The chief characteristic of meerschaum, a pure white clay mineral known as *sepiolite*, is that it absorbs the juices from the burning tobacco and with long use gradually turns to a beautiful deep brown color. Such a pipe can therefore become a cherished possession. I had one once, but was careless and broke it.

Briar: The bowls and part of the stems of briar pipes are carved from briar burl. The mouthpiece and part of the stem is usually plastic, although I have seen them made of tortoise shell or even amber. One can choose among a multitude of shapes, for example:

- Heavy or light bowl
- Short stem, short mouthpiece
- Short stem, long mouthpiece
- Long stem, short mouthpiece
- Heavy bowl, curved stem
- "Sherlock Holmes"
- Light bowl, thin stem and mouthpiece

I tried out a great variety of briars, but finally chose "light bowl, long briar stem, short mouthpiece." I found them to be light (to carry in the pocket), easy to break in, easy to clean, and the long briar stem seemed to give a milder smoke. I also found them quite hard to find. When I gave up smoking in 1982, I gave away two dozen pipes!

Disadvantages:

Most new pipes take several days or even weeks to break in before they yield a mild smoke. Until the carbon cake that encrusts the interior of the bowl builds up, the smoke is harsh. One must always be prepared to knock out the ash from a pipe (or snuff out a cigarette, tap the ash off the end of a cigar). If you can't find an ashtray, you use the cuff on your pants. I became known as a pipe smoker at City Club meetings from the noise made by tapping out my pipe on the glass ashtray.

One must frequently use pipe cleaners (wires twisted with fluffy cotton) to remove excess moisture. There are many kinds of special tools: long blunt ones for tamping the fresh tobacco load to proper density before lighting, or pointed or bladed ones for scraping out excess cake.

One must always carry a multitude of matches for the pipe or a lighter for cigarettes. The "Zippo" lighter became famous during World War I. One must expect that an occasional ember will burn a hole in your suit!

Advantages:

I cited the social value of Bull Durham cigarettes, and I found that my pipe gave me time to think (while I refilled or relighted) before answering a question. My pipe was soothing, and gave something to hold in my mouth, an adult pacifier! Over the years, it became an identifying attribute, part of Allen's "charisma." After more than 12 years I still miss it. Now I suck a piece of hard candy when I want a break. Probably because I almost never inhaled, I had no respiratory problems before 1980.

Envoi:

For fifty years I enjoyed pipe smoking and the "charisma" my pipe gave the geologist and old professor. I had no problem with abruptly and permanently quitting when my internist gently suggested in 1982 that it was now time to give up the habit. This was probably because every year or so I stopped smoking "cold turkey" for a month, just to see whether I still *could* stop. Few apparent harmful results came from smoking my pipe, except perhaps recurrence of asthma or an occasional cough or sore throat during the last few years.

Rules to Live By

Every day we make hundreds of decisions about our activities, attitudes and plans. Some of them can have a major effect upon our lives (Robert Frost, "The Road Not Taken"); most of them are tiny instantaneous two-way options, taken with little or no thought.

Each decision made is a result of rules that comes from the advice or examples set by our parents, friends, teachers, peers, and mentors, or from what we see in movies or TV or have read. Could it be worthwhile to try to classify and get down on paper some of the decision-making rules developed from my own background?

What affects my decisions? I am sure that my years in the Boy Scouts of America were a very important element, resulting in part from the memorization and constant repetition of the Oath, Laws, Motto, and Slogan. (We also learned the description for each law, the motto, and the slogan.)

The SCOUT OATH is:
On my honor I will do my best
To do my duty to God and my country
and to obey the Scout Law;
To help other people at all times;
To keep myself physically strong, mentally awake,
and morally straight.

The twelve SCOUT LAWS are:

A Scout is Trustworthy	A Scout is Loyal
A Scout is Helpful	A Scout is Friendly
A Scout is Courteous	A Scout is Kind
A Scout is Obedient	A Scout is Cheerful
A Scout is Thrifty	A Scout is Brave
A Scout is Clean	A Scout is Reverent.

The Scout Motto is BE PREPARED.

The Scout Slogan is DO A GOOD TURN DAILY.

224

Some Fields of Decision-Making:

General: *Moderation in all things.* That includes moderation in working, eating, drinking, exercising, taking medicines, shopping, walking, driving, etc. This means that in politics, for instance, you can expect to be attacked from each end of the liberal-conservative spectrum!

Attitudes: *Always assume that everyone you meet is honest*—until they prove themselves otherwise. That means that you don't have to worry about them! When, in the rare case you do get stuck, you can change your mind then and thereafter beware.

Personal relationships: *Never go to bed without resolving an argument.* Always tell your wife you love her—at least a dozen times a day! And give her a kiss and a hug when she doesn't expect it. If you have to sleep in twin beds, spend a little time nightly in her bed for a good snuggle and spooning.

Administrative: *Keep your staff informed weekly about what is going on.* Never separate offices far from a central location where workers can quickly reach each other.

Financial: *Never make a loan unless you can regard it as a gift.* Then you don't have to worry about getting it back, and if you do, it comes as a pleasant surprise.

Health: *Regularly take moderate exercise,* at least four times a week, for at least half an hour. *See your dentist and internist* at least every two years until you retire, then see him at least every six months. *Take as few medicines as possible* (aspirin, antacids, inhalents, et al.), and never without consulting your internist. If you are troubled with obesity, *never go on an extreme diet.* The best diet is to push oneself away from the table three times a day! *Drink red wines rather than hard liquors,* and not more than two drinks a day. *Don't smoke,* but if you must, use a pipe.

Hobbies: *Hobbies are great for recreation,* and I have always had one or two going, but never more than that at any one time. Have hobbies

225

in sequitur, so that when you have exhausted your interest in learning about stamps, coins, hi-fi, knives and swords, photography, etc., you can get rid of the collection and try a new hobby. In this way "things" do not pile up so as to become a real burden. (However, if it does become a problem, the best way to get rid of such tyranny is to move frequently!)

Concentrate 18p

A Fourth Career

Since my retirement in 1974, I have been telling people that I have had three careers. The first, beginning in 1928 when I abandoned journalism, was twenty years of learning geology and working as an economic and field geologist. This consisted of examining and mapping hundreds of mines and mineral deposits and making or helping to make seven geologic quadrangle maps: Columbia River Gorge, San Juan Bautista, Northern Wallowa Mountains, Butte Falls, Ochocos, Coos Bay, and Capitan, New Mexico.

The second career, which began in 1948 when I decided that people were more interesting than rocks, consisted of 25 years of teaching at seven different universities: Pennsylvania State College, New Mexico Institute of Mining and Geology, University of California at Santa Barbara, Portland State College/University, University of Hawaii, University of Peshawar in West Pakistan, and Whitman College.

The third career, after 1974, has been 20 years of writing, consisting of the over 200 items in my bibliography printed in 120 publications! Only four of these were more than 100 pages: *Bin Rock and Dump Rock* first edition (1986 autobiography), *The Magnificent Gateway* (geology of the Columbia River Gorge), *Cataclysms on the Columbia* (the catastrophic floods that swept Oregon at the end of the Ice Age), and *Time Travel in Oregon* (about 200 essays on Oregon geology published from 1983 to 1987 in the weekly science section of the *Oregonian* newspaper). A fifth one in the works is *Time Trax*, a hiking guide of Oregon describing the geology along the way.

I am now beginning a fourth career, which began in 1986 after an automobile accident and a series of other medical problems began to develop. This career involves trying to overcome as much as possible the growing restrictions imposed by increasing age and physical and medical inadequacies. It consists in developing a daily regimen that promotes *survival* after age 88 while still allowing some writing and pleasant activities. I am fortunate in having as a model Charley Hayward, a dear friend living in our apartment house, who is 99 years old and still meets weekly with us for dinner.

As usual, I have tried to categorize my present activities in order of relative importance to my survival under four main heads: Goodies, Recreation, Baddies, Procedures.

I. **Goodies (that make my life worthwhile):**
1. The TLC of my loving wife Margaret; the intermittent presence and stable affection of my daughter, her husband, and their children; and the skillful attention to my medical problems by Duane Iverson, my internist.
2. The use of my obsolete Kaypro PC for writing, aided by the emeritus privileges and faculty help at my PSU office as well as the use of the Xerox machine.
3. My so far never-failing appetite (especially for salmon!), with a demi-tasse of decaf coffee after meals and one glass of wine a day.
4. Our dear friends in the Ione and on campus.
5. The fine appurtenances of our apartment and its great view.
6. My daily post-prandial nap.

II. **Recreation (activities that keep me going):**
1. Time for reading
   a. Books: mostly detective and mystery, some science fiction, some books like *Walden* and *Machiavelli's Prince* that I had never read (mostly boring!).
   b. Magazines: I count seven professional and nine non-geological magazines that we still take. A sample: *GSA Bulletin, Geotimes, American Scholar, Popular Mechanics, Smithsonian.*
   c. Other: I skim the daily newspaper and do the daily cross words (which boost one's ego). When I read the monthly catalog *Common Reader*, I greatly regret seeing so many books that I would like to read, but never have.
2. The students that call or drop in; the callers for information or for an autograph in my books.
3. Time for four hours of TV a day, especially the PBS, Discovery

227

and Learning networks. I pass up most news programs which are now dedicated to war, crime, and punishment.
4. Social and educational events *on the PSU campus*. (GSOC, Ferdinand, REPPS, Retired Associates, etc.)
5. My current hobbies: collections of blades, knives, hats, neckties, and books and videos on archeology.

III. Baddies (which I try to pay little or no attention to):
1. Constant precarious and tottery balance, requiring cane.
2. Memory loss of names especially, but also little things in daily procedures, so that I have to write things down if I am to get them done; night ideas require a pad and pencil at my bed, though I recently bought one of those nifty digital voice activated memo machines. I think of so many things before sleep that two to three times a week I need a Tylenol before I can get to sleep at midnight or one.
3. Shortness of breath after slight activity.
4. Loss of hearing (impossible in crowds).
5. Loss of sight by double vision so that I no longer drive.
6. Impaired speech, due to recurrent thick phlegm in my throat.
7. Several petty annoyances, such as cold feet, artificial teeth, dead battery in hearing aid, poor elimination, and as a side effect of one of my medications, I get blood bruises whenever I bump a limb.

IV. Procedures (regimen to promote *survival*):
1. Anticipation and planning for coming events and personal accomplishments.
2. Early morning regimen of inhalants for asthma, 20-25 minutes of exercise, walking to my office.
3. Medication: Pills to help heart, blood clotting, and urination.
4. Miscellaneous: Dinner at one, soup or sandwich for supper, Konsyl, hot baths, hot-cold on chest.
5. Tried but abandoned naturopathic diet, medicines, and acupuncture.

Concentrate 18q

The Next One Hundred Years

Facts:
- Population growth
- Birth rates and death rates
- Climatic changes—a warming planet? Or cooling?

Natural Problems:
- Malthus' prediction, the population explosion, overcrowding, and the slums
- The aging of humanity
- Polyvinyl chlorides, the ozone hole
- Volcanic eruptions: Pinatubo, Krakatoa, etc.
- Carbon dioxide increasing—automobiles?
- Sulphur dioxides—factories?

Human Problems:
- Deforestation of ancient forests in Brazil, Pacific Northwest
- Salinization of irrigated valleys: Indus, San Joachin
- Chemical fertilizers—the green revolution?
- Overgrazing, overfishing
- Over reliance on one subspecies: corn, wheat, rice. Blights?
- Endangered species, extinction of buffalo and other large mammals, big cats, elephants, rhinos
- Political problems: nationalism and wars, religious differences

Possible Partial Solutions:
- Reforestation
- Exhaustion of oil reserves prompting solar and wind power
- Cataclysms or catastrophes: asteroids, quakes, or volcanoes
- Plague: AIDS only an example
- Organic instead of chemical fertilizers (Chinese)
- Wars and genocides: hydrogen bomb

229

Tailings

Where We Lived

Eighteen moves in the first fifteen years of our married lives! A geologist's wife as well as his life can be highly itinerant. Here is a list and a comment about those 35 addresses in 20 towns or locations at which Peggy and I lived for at least two months. In Portland we lived at seven and in Berkeley at four addresses. At times, the dates overlap because we would keep our main residence while on various assignments (such as Hawaii, Walla Walla, Reno, etc.)

#-Date	Town	Address	Time
1-1933	Berkeley, CA	Euclid Ave	4 months

Peggy and I were married on July 26th, and after a two-week honeymoon camping out on Jack Creek near the Metolius River in central Oregon, I left for Berkeley. I had been living on Euclid with Bob Coats, and when Peggy arrived in December, we rented a second-floor apartment across the street, less than a block east of the campus. It was here that Peggy had to devise strict diets for my allergies, cooking bread from rice flour, etc.

2-1934	Berkeley, CA	Haste Ave	4 months

The second semester, we moved into an apartment on the second floor of a house on Haste, a block or so south of the campus and west of Telegraph, where we stayed until the end of the school year.

3-1934	Berkeley, CA	Benvenue Ave	18 months

Next fall we rented half of a charming (and tiny) duplex. It was a vine-covered garden cottage in the back yard of the mayor's house on Benvenue south of the campus, a block or so east of Telegraph. What I remember best about it is the fact that the walls were very thin, and the neighbor's noises all came through.

232

4-1935	Crater Lake, OR	Rim Village	4 months

When we arrived at Crater Lake in June, we came to the rim through ten-foot high banks of snow. Tents had been set up on platforms for the Ranger-Naturalists, each of whom had two facing tents, one for a kitchen-living room, and opposite that, one for the bedroom. The washroom (including showers), toilet, and water tap were 100 yards downhill.

We did have electricity so Peggy could iron my uniform shirts. Bears checked out our garbage can each night at nine. Golden-mantled ground squirrels and Canada jays grabbed for any scraps we left out and would even come into the tent if we raised up the canvas. We left for Agness in late October after the first snow.

5-1935	Agness, OR	Dorn Cottage	12 months

The Dorn log cabin was located 35 miles up the Rogue River from Gold Beach on a narrow bench 50 feet above the Illinois River, half a mile above its junction with the Rogue. During the flood of 1930, the cabin had floated away and had been towed back into place and tied down. It was reached by a narrow half-mile-long riverside trail from a bar at the mouth of the river where we, and our weekly orders of groceries from Gold Beach, were dumped out on the gravel by the mail boat. The Dorns lived in a new cabin they had built 500 feet above us on a prairie, and they rented the lower cabin to us for $40 a month.

Dorn was a criminal (we heard in more ways than one) lawyer, retired (disbarred?) from a practice in San Diego, and married to a gal with a tongue you wouldn't believe. But she took care of the crooked old man, who was delving into the mysteries of Hindu religion.

The log cabin was about 40 by 25 feet, with a porch across the front and a small lean-to on the back which contained a tiny cast-iron cookstove. A water pipe came to the cabin from a box 200 feet up the creek which passed by the cabin and was crossed by a narrow river-trail bridge. During the winter, a heavy storm washed out our water system, and the river rose to within 15 feet of the cabin.

The cabin was heated by a small airtight stove. Both stoves were fed with splits from a four-foot diameter Douglas fir which had been felled behind the cabin and sawed into 16-inch lengths. Each week-end I split one of the rounds and cut it to stove size before going into the field.

233

Skunks and mice occasionally invaded the cabin and created a diversion, but it was pretty cozy on the whole, even with a few inches of snow outside. The tiny cookstove wasn't all that great, but we didn't starve. The airtight heating stove would get red hot and puff like a steam engine when it was fired up.

6-1936	Grants Pass, OR	Motel	2 months

When Rustless expanded the scope of the chrome investigation to all of the West Coast, we moved to Grants Pass. For a few weeks we stayed in a motel near the north end of town, but finding that it was socially unacceptable, we moved as soon as possible.

7-1936	Grants Pass, OR	M St (Skunk Creek)	6 months

This small house was located on the bluff above the Rogue River on M Street just west of Skunk Creek. I was away so much of the time that I really don't remember much about it except that it had our first backyard and lawn to be mowed, and that just across Skunk Creek to the east was the home of Ed and Hazel McKinstry, who became lifelong friends. It was also in Grants Pass that Howard Stafford joined the team as chemist and Ralph Mason joined as engineer.

8-1937	Morro Bay, CA		3 months

The longest spell away from Grants Pass was the expedition to southern California to examine the chromite deposits north of San Luis Obispo. We lived in a tiny cabin on the shore of Morro Bay; our main room had a six-foot wide view window which, during the winter storms, would bend in nearly an inch! It was here that we first got well-acquainted with Ralph Mason, the engineer in charge of logistics, mine mapping, and areal magnetic and resistivity surveys.

9-1938	Baker, OR		13 months

When I left Rustless in May to go with DOGAMI as the field geologist at the Baker office, we moved into a small apartment on the second floor of a house a block north of the main east-west street. I remember that a narrow stairway came up from the outside, near the back of the old house, and that the walls of the apartment sloped with the gable roof. During this year I visited more than 350 mines and prospects and wrote reports that were included in the first volume of the *Mines Handbook*.

We made many wonderful friends during that year in Baker: the Roger Biswells, Forrest Hubbards, the Stockmans, all became lifelong friends.

10-1939	Portland, OR	Haight Ave	3 months

Upon our move to Portland in September, we found an apartment on the second floor of an old house in north Portland. The landlady pinched pennies so hard that she objected if we both took baths the same day, and she made us put new light globes in when we left.

11-1940	Portland, OR	42 NE 45th Street	9 months

We soon found a bungalow in Laurelhurst just north of Burnside. Sally was born while we were there; I remember fixing up her cot in her room. Our landlady (who we believed had a business that consisted of another kind of "house") was very kind in getting us new mattresses and other furniture when we asked for them.

12-1941	Portland, OR	10125 NE Prescott	12 months

After Sally arrived, the bungalow seemed pretty small, and when Lyle Grimes (a friend from Eagle Scout days in Eugene) left for war, he offered to rent us his new home in Parkrose. This was really the first modern home we occupied, and we enjoyed it until his wife decided that she wanted to come back to it. About this time DOGAMI planned the Coos Bay Coal project, and we left for North Bend.

13-1942	North Bend, OR		2 years

We found a livable house on the top of the hill south of downtown North Bend, less than a mile from my office. One vividly remembered event was when Sally fell off the back porch and had a concussion. Another was her pet turtle "Bubbles." Ewart Baldwin joined me and Ralph Mason to form the crew which mapped several of the coal mine areas, drilled out some shallow coals, and refined some of Diller's geology of the 30-minute Coos Bay quadrangle. A two-year project, all for $40,000.

14-1944	Milwaukee, OR	1942 Munroe St	2 months

When we moved back to Portland, we stayed for a while with Peggy's mother in her house in Milwaukee while we hunted for a house of our own.

15-1944	Portland, OR	3925 NE Couch	3 years

Judge Hewitt's house was the first house we bought (for $6,400), and was possibly our favorite of all those we have lived in. It is still in good shape. It had space for a shop in the basement, and Peggy's mother had a room upstairs when she came to live with us. Our nextdoor neighbors were the Theron Fitches; their children, Roger and Carolyn, still visit us when they come to Portland.

16-1945	Berkeley, CA	Telegraph Ave	6 months

Upon completion of the writing of the Coos Bay report, I took leave to finish my Ph.D. and stayed at a boarding house about three blocks south of Sather Gate. When Peggy was visiting me there, we had the first local earthquake (5.5?) that Berkeley had ever been able to record.

17-1947	State College, PA	Shingletown Gap	6 months

After Nixon left DOGAMI, all geologists but me left within six months. I finally left in September for a teaching job at PSC. In December I was followed by my three girls. We first moved into a summer cottage rented to us by Dr. Bonine, the man I was replacing.

The cottage was ten miles from the campus, poorly insulated and hard to keep warm, and the first winter was a rough one on all of us. We repeatedly had more than a foot of snow, and I had to shovel out for several tens of yards in order to get the car out to the main road. Sally was bused four miles to a school in Boalsberg, where the students sat on benches made from crates with boards for desks.

18-1948	State College, PA	West Park Ave	18 months

As soon as we could find one, we moved into a much better house in town, directly across the road from the college stadium. It had a large back yard where Peggy's mother planted and gardened. It had a terribly inconvenient and old-fashioned kitchen with four doors (to back porch, to cellar, to dining room, to front hall!). I best remember my struggles with the coal-fired furnace, which easily went out and was immensely difficult to clean and restart.

19-1948-9	Stone Valley, PA	PSC Summer Camp	2 mo. /yr.

For two summers we spent eight weeks at the Penn State Summer

236

WHERE WE LIVED

Camp lodge in Stone Valley. The main building housed the kitchen,
dining room, and some laboratory and office space. The sleeping
quarters consisted of a row of at least ten screened cabins (the camp
served about 60 students) with bunk beds for six in each.

20-1949	Socorro, NM	525 Mines Road	6 years

This cinder block and stucco house, located halfway between town
and gown, was new when we bought it. About 2,000 square feet, with
a full front porch and separate garage. Two bedrooms, living room,
kitchen and bathroom. The yard was originally gravel, but we had a
cinder block wall built around it after a flash flood came through.

We then planted the front yard with grass, set at least five inches
below the side and entry walks, since the dust storms over a period of
about two or three years would raise the lawn up to grade. Then the
turf would have to be lifted, the land reclowered, and the turf relayed.
Before we left, I even installed sprinklers. Margaret's mother planted
beds of iris and tried to raise other plants. The thing I remember most
was the constant battle with goats heads, a pernicious weed that
spread out over the gravel part of the yard in a mat that had to be
peeled off periodically.

21-1951	Santa Barbara, CA	Webb's house	2 months

Bob Webb, then head of the Department of Geology at UCSB, let us
occupy his house, located on the hill above downtown Santa Barbara,
not far from the then site of the University. I arrived there in pretty
bad shape, since I had wrenched my back in packing the car in
Socorro and had driven the entire distance with painful spasms from
a ruptured disk. I taught for several weeks from crutches. It was here
that I first taught my class in "Minerals and World Affairs."

22-1952	Navajo Reservation	Nakaibito, NM	4 months

The small bungalow that we lived in had been vacated by an
Indian Service employee who just threw furniture and a Navajo rug
out on the dump pile so he could order a new one for his next station.
We rescued some of it and still have the rug! It was here that we got
acquainted with a beautiful young tribal princess and medicine
woman.

23-1952	Navajo Reservation	Tohatchi, NM	4 months
24-1952			

Here we lived, for part of the time, in a large trailer which had been converted into an apartment, and for the rest of the time in a small apartment.

25-1956-63	Portland, OR	1162 SE 58th Ave	7 years

The last Portland house we lived in was located on the lower west slope of Mount Tabor, on the SE corner of 58th and Salmon. A full basement gave plenty of room for storage and a workshop for me. The west-facing entrance opened into a small hall, with glass-paned sliding doors leading to the dining room on the right and to the living room on the left. A closet and stairway occupied the center.

Between the kitchen and the living room at the back of the house was a small study which became our TV room. Upstairs there were one small and two large bedrooms with ample walk-in closets and a front study room. A porch occupied the north side of the house, and there was a paved patio on the east. Behind the kitchen there was a tiny back porch and attached washroom. The garage lay to the south.

26-1961	Santa Barbara, CA	Norris House	2 months

The best thing about Bob Norris' house were the avocado trees and berry vines which kept us amply supplied with fruit. Other than the big garden which had to be regularly watered, that is about all I remember.

27-1963-4	Peshawar, Pakistan	University Village	8 months

Our home in Peshawar was a one-story stuccoed adobe house consisting of three rooms across the front, dining room on the left, living room with fireplace in the middle, and bedroom on the right. The bathroom (shower and toilet) was behind the bedroom, and a tiny kitchen and storeroom were behind the dining room. A backyard as big as the house was enclosed by an eight-foot wall, and behind that was the servants' quarters (Nabi Basch and family).

We rented furniture and bought mattresses and coarse cotton bedding. The fireplace used up several cords of wood over the season to take the winter morning chill off the main room. The windows were screened, but mosquitoes did get in, and we welcomed the numerous geckos that climbed the walls and ate the bugs. Water could be heated on a small electric stove, but there was also a sun heated roof tank that more or less warmed the shower. We filled a gallon thermos with hot water each night so we would have hot water for washing the next morning.

28-1964	Portland, OR	1717 SW Park, #610	6 years

Upon our return from Pakistan, we decided to sell the Mount Tabor house and move into the Ione Plaza apartment building, which is only 100 yards from my office in Cramer Hall on the PSU Campus. It is one of the oldest high-rises (14 stories) in Portland (built in the 1950s), and when we moved in, the tab was less than $200 per month.

The Ione block then included a parking garage, a drug store, a grocery, a bank, a restaurant, a beauty shop, and a service station. Pretty convenient, and the prices until recently had been several hundred dollars less than other newer apartment houses in the area.

I am sure that this move has added at least ten years to my life, since it did away with the daily hassle of driving to work in traffic and hunting for a parking space. Furthermore, an absent-minded professor who forgets some vital notes can run back and get them in five minutes.

29-1965	Santa Barbara, CA	Campus Village	2 months

During our second term at Santa Barbara, we were in a student housing unit north of the campus. We got away from it as often as possible.

30-1966	Hawaii	Kailua, Oahu	2 months

The Gordon McDonalds let us use their home on the north side of the island, a half-hour drive through the tunnel to the campus in Honolulu. A prolific papaya tree and a neighbor with a mango tree kept us in fruit. We were about four blocks from the beach, and the weather was in the high 80s during the day but got down to a brisk 75 before dawn!

31-1970-93	Portland OR	1717 SW Park #507	23 years

We moved into this apartment from #610 to get more space. After a quarter of a century of living in this apartment, though, it got pretty shabby. With its small balcony which opened up to a view of the Park

239

Blocks, and the north side situation of the building, it kept us from getting too hot from the sun.

In 1983, we also rented the adjacent studio apartment #506, which we used for storing our extra clothes, entertaining, and putting up family and occasional VIP visitors. As of 1989, the rental of both apartments including parking, electricity, and hot water was $760.

In 1987, the radiator in the bedroom burst and flooded the entire apartment. In 1989 we got a new refrigerator and davenport, and the stove we brought from Socorro still is in use, although it is now supplemented with a microwave and toaster oven. In hot weather, rigging the small bedroom air conditioner with an extra fan kept most of the apartment cool.

| 32-1974 | Walla Walla, WA | Motel | 5 months |

Our motel was only five blocks from my office on the campus and across the street from a Safeway store, so we got along very well.

| 33-1975 | Reno, NV | Motel | 6 months |

We lived in an undistinguished but fairly comfortable motel only three or four blocks south of the main business district and the very good town library.

| 34-1977 | Socorro, NM | New house | 4 months |

Our dear friends, the Kottlowskis and the Smiths helped us find and furnish a just-finished house a few blocks northeast of the campus. We camped out there very satisfactorily for the four-month period.

| 35-1993 | Portland, OR | 1717 SW Park, #1402 | to date |

After a serious bout with my health, we gave up apartments #506 and #507 and moved into #1402, which has two bedrooms, two baths, and a magnificent view.

Jobs and Payment

Years	Job/Description	Length	Pay
1920-26	Putting in 14 cords of wood	every fall	20¢/hr
	Grocery delivery truck	Saturdays	$2/day
	Paper delivery route–60 to 80 papers		
(bought bike for $70 in eight mo.)			$8/mo
	McAlister farm (milking nine cows)	6 wks	
	Chase Gardens (budding slips)	6 wks	$90
	Hop yards (stripping hop vines)	6 wks	$90
1925	Junior Camp Director, Siuslaw Forest		
	fire fighting on Knowles Creek		Expenses
1926-27	Asst. Camp Director, Camp Lucky Boy		
	Corres. to the Eugene *Register-Guard*;		
	lifesaving instructor		Expenses
1926-27	*Oregon Emerald* (reporter and ad-man)		
1928	Red Cross instructor, La Grande	2 weeks	$60
	Camp Phy, Catherine Creek, 40 scouts	6 weeks	$160
	Carpenter's asst.,Union Pacific		
	Railroad bridge-building gang	8 weeks	
	($4/day less $1.25 for food)		$120
	Cement finisher, Denver	1 day	$5
	Potato harvest, Greeley	3 wks@ $3/day	$45
	Kuner-Empson sauerkraut		
	cannery	5 wks@ $3/day	$60
1929	Milwaukee County Emergency		
	Hospital receiving-room orderly		
	12-on-12-off	4 mo@ $35 mo	$140
	Camp Phy, Catherine Creek	6 weeks	$160

	Chase Gardens Delivery, Eugene	1 month	$80
1930	Topo mapping, central Oregon	6 weeks	Expenses
1931	Field mapping Gorge	June 6 to Sept. 15	Expenses

Years	Job/Description	Length	Month	Total
1931-2	TA at U of Oregon	9 mo	$ 36	$325
32-35	TA at U of California	3 yrs	700	2,100
35	RN at Crater Lake	4 mo	150	600
35-38	FG for Rustless I & S	32 mo	150	4,800
	"Plus all expenses"		> $100	3,200
38-39	FG for DOGAMI, Baker	12 mos	175	2,100
39-40	FG for DOGAMI, Portland		220	2,640
40-41			250	3,000
41-42			271	3,250
42-43			312	3,750
43-44			333	4,000
44-45			354	4,250
45-46			396	4,750
46-47			417	5,000
38-47	**Total DOGAMI**	**9 yrs**		**$32,740**
47-49	Assoc. Prof. Penn S C	2 yrs	354	8,500
49-51	Prof & Head NMSM	2 yrs	500	12,000
51-52	Sr. Geologist NMBMMI	2 yrs	583	7,000
53			625	7,500
54			708	8,500
55			750	9,000
56			800	9,600
49-56	**Total NMIMT**	**7 yrs**		**$53,600**
56-57	Head, Geology at PSU		666	8,000
57-58				
9,000				
58-62			5 yrs@$9,000/yr	45,000
63-64	(Sabbatical in Pakistan)		est.	14,000
65-66				15,000
66-67				16,000

67-68				17,500
68-70		2 yrs		36,000
70-72		? yrs		38,000
72-73				21,000
73-74				21,600
56-74	**Total PSU**	**18 yrs**	**est.**	**$241,100**
74-75	Whitman College	6 mo	1,666	10,000
75-76	Reno	6 mo	1,666	10,000
77-78	Socorro	5 mo	1,666	8,333
83-87	Time Travel	~200 columns at $50/ea		10,000

Cars That I Have Owned and Driven

# Year	Make	Model	Col	Year	Cost	State	Driven
1. 1928	Ford	T	bl	1925	$50	Used	1 year

I learned to drive in the 1920s on another Model T owned by Castle McAlister. I had driven my grandfather's Maxwell and my father's Chevy, but this was the first car I owned. I drove it in to La Grande on weekends from the Scout camp on Catherine Creek, and after my job with the UPRR ended in October, I took off for my *wanderjahr* and got as far as Milwaukee, Wisconsin, before it gave up the ghost and I sold it for $25. It had all the weird and wonderful idiosyncrasies of the Model T; many of these are described in Concentrate 5a.

# Year	Make	Model	Col	Year	Cost	State	Driven
2. 1933	Dodge	Coupe	bl	1925	$45	Used	4 years

We named this black coupe "Epaminondas" and called it "Eppy." It faithfully served us on numerous trips between Berkeley and Eugene, and in the field for two summers at San Juan Bautista, as well as for trips to Virginia City and Crater Lake. During the wet season in Berkeley it grew mushrooms in the leather upholstery above the windshield. I never drove it much over 45 mph, but it would climb any hill and never got stuck—except once at San Juan Bautista when I tried to turn around on a too narrow mountain road and one end dropped off the grade. Took me three hours to jack it up and get it back on the road.

# Year	Make	Model	Col	Year	Cost	State	Driven
3. 1937	Dodge	sdn	blue	1935	$600	Used	2 years
4. 1939	Dodge	sdn	br	1939	$800	New	2 years

I remember very little about these cars, except that these Dodges didn't have enough radiator to keep from boiling on long steep grades. I didn't drive them very much since I had a company car with Rustless (a Ford Model A coupe), with DOGAMI in Baker (a red Dodge pickup truck), and a dark blue Chevrolet panel delivery wagon when working out of Portland.

5. 1941	Olds	sdn	blue	1941	$1,200	New	10 years

This was our beloved "stratosphere blue" sedan that got us through World War II in fine shape. It took us to Coos Bay and then to San Juan Bautista and back, then on to Pennsylvania and finally back to Socorro where it was used in the field during the mapping of the Capitan quadrangle. It was almost the first automatic gearshift car made, and I never had any serious trouble during the ten years and nearly 100,000 miles I drove it.

6. 1951	Chevy	sdn	blue	1951	$1,200	New	2 years

This was my first real lemon. It had the new turbo gearshift, which was slow and indefinite, and the steering wasn't all that accurate. I soon got fed up with it and decided to get an exotic.

7. 1952	Jaguar	MkII		1949	$3,200	Used	2 years

It was a lovely car and would do 100 mph if necessary. But don't ever get a secondhand foreign car—I had to drive the 75 miles to Albuquerque every time it needed servicing. It blew its head gasket on a trip to Zia Scout Camp, and I turned it in on a new Chevy. Too expensive to maintain for my pocketbook at that time.

8. 1954	Chevy	sdn	brn	1954	$1,800	New	7 years

Although it was bought in an emergency, this was one of my best buys and served us without trouble for two years in New Mexico and for five years back in Portland. It was the first of the cars to do away with fins and chrome and return to a basic small sedan.

9. 1961	VW	Bug	red	1961	$2,100	New	2 years

This bright red bug started my 12-year-long love affair with Volkswagen. The only reason I sold it after two years was that we went to Pakistan!

10.1963	VW	Bug	wh	1963	$1,400	Used	5 years

In Peshawar we were able for four months to get along with a bicycle to get to school and a tonga to get to town until the father of an Air Force man stationed in Peshawar bought a VW Bug in Ger-

245

many and drove it to Pakistan. He didn't want to drive it back, so, although it was illegal to buy and sell cars there, I arranged to give him a down payment and then a final payment after I brought it back to Oregon. So I had a car for five months until we left in May, and SEATO paid for the shipment back to the States! It served us faithfully until we decided that we needed a little more room.

| 11. 1968 | VW | SqB | red | 1968 | $2,800 | New | 5 years |

We also enjoyed this bright red VW squareback and drove it on a trip through Mexico to Durango, Mazatlan, and return, over pretty bad roads. But it became a little too rugged as we got older, and we decided to upgrade to a vehicle with more comfort.

| 12. 1973 | Volvo | SW | grn | 1972 | $4,200 | Used | 10 years |

This was a great car which for ten years took us and all our luggage all over the country (Walla Walla, Reno, Socorro). It got pretty well beat-up before we decided to bring it up to date with another (and ill-fated) Volvo station wagon.

| 13. 1983 | Volvo | SW | tan | 1982 | $11,200 | Used | 3 years |

We probably would still be driving this station wagon if I hadn't totaled it in May, 1986. Luckily, the insurance was able to pay for another Volvo which we decided could be a sedan, as we wouldn't be making further long trips.

| 14. 1986 | Volvo | Sdn | sil | 1984 | $11,200 | Used | 10+ |

We like our sedan and have no plans to replace it. It has all the things we could want for a car. Numbered in order of frequency of use and convenience:
1. One key operates all the door locks from the driver's door.
2. Car keys are double sided; you don't have to worry about which side is up. Trunk can be opened from button in glove compartment.
3. Motorized window controls.
4. Remarkably efficient brakes (disc all-round).
5. Remarkably short (35 feet) turning radius. Can turn within an ordinary paved street.
6. Overdrive button allows braking on gentle downhills, second gear on steep downhills.

246

7. In spite of only four cylinders, acceleration possible for passing under nearly all conditions. Tachometer guards against excessive revs.
8. Excellent air conditioner and ventilation facilities, including sun-roof.
9. Handy safety belt and steel beam surround—which probably saved my life when I totaled Volvo No. 2.

I don't think I ever bought a car on time. For eight of the 14 cars we owned, I was able to find ones with just a few thousand miles on the odometer and several thousand dollars off the new price. Total initial cost of the 14 cars was $41,795. That's only $697 per year, or an average cost of $2,985 per car. I wish I had kept the logbooks that I maintained of expenses for each car; they would have given some interesting statistics! For instance, I am sure I spent more on the Jag than on any other car! As for total time driven for each manufacturer during these 60+ years, I drove a Ford for one year; a Jaguar for two years; a Dodge for eight years; a Chevrolet for nine years; an Oldsmobile for ten years, a Volkswagen for 12 years; and a Volvo for 21 years, so far.

Résumé

JOHN ELIOT ALLEN
Emeritus Professor of Geology
Department of Geology
Portland State University
P. O. Box 751
Portland, OR 97207

Born:
August 12, 1908, Seattle, Washington.

Education:
Eugene, Oregon, Public Schools, 1917-20.
University High School, 1920-26.
University of Oregon, (Journalism) 1926-28, (Geology) 1929-32, B.A. 1931, M.A. 1932, Geology of the Columbia River Gorge.
University of California, Berkeley, 1932-35, 1943-44, Ph.D., Geology of the San Juan Bautista quadrangle, California.

Professional Experience:
Junior Camp Director, Boy Scouts at Mapleton, Oregon, 1925.
Assistant Camp Director, Boy Scouts at Blue River, Oregon, 1926, 1927.
Camp Director, Boy Scouts at Catherine Creek, Union County, Oregon, 1928, 1929.
Red Cross Swimming and Life Saving Instructor, 1928, 1929.
Ranger Naturalist, Crater Lake National Park, summer 1935.
Field Geologist, Rustless Iron and Steel Corporation, 1935-38.
    "   "   , Ore. Dept. of Geology & Mineral Industries, 1938-40, *Senior Geologist,* 1940-1947.
Associate Professor and *Director of Summer Field Camp,* Pennsylvania State College, 1947-49.
Professor and Head, Department of Geology, New Mexico School of Mines, 1949-51.
Visiting Professor, University of California, Santa Barbara, summer session, 1951.

248

Senior Geologist, New Mexico Bureau of Mines and Mineral Industries, and *Faculty Associate*, New Mexico Institute of Mining and Technology, 1951-56.
Professor and Head, Department of Geology, Portland State University, 1956-74.
Visiting Professor, University of California-Santa Barbara, summer sessions, 1961, 1965.
Professor and Head, Department of Geology, for Southeast Asia Treaty Organization (SEATO), University of Peshawar, West Pakistan, 1963-64.
Visiting Professor, University of Hawaii, summer session, 1966.
Emeritus Professor of Geology, Department of Geology, Portland State University, 1974 - present.
Visiting Professor, Whitman College, Walla Walla, Washington, Nov. 1974 - June 1975.
Visiting Scientist, Nevada Bureau of Mines, Reno, Nevada, Sept. 1975 to March 1976.
Visiting Scientist, New Mexico Bureau of Mines and Mineral Industries, Jan. to May 1977.

Professional organizations:
Geological Society of America, 1944 - present. Fellow, 1957 - present.
Society of Economic Geologists, 1957-1972.
National Association of Geology Teachers, 1943 - present. Secretary-Treasurer, 1948; Vice President, 1966; President, 1967; Neil Miner Award, 1972.
American Institute of Met. & Mining Engineers, 1943-61. Chairman, Oregon Section, 1946.
American Association of Petroleum Geologists, 1946-66
Oregon Academy of Science, 1956 - present.
American Association of Professional Geologists (#925), 1965-1980.
Registered Geologist, State of Oregon, 1978-1985.

Honorary organizations and awards:
Phi Beta Kappa, 1931. Sigma Xi, 1932. Order of the "O", 1931.
Spaulding Cup, 1931.
Silver Beaver Award, BSA, 1955.
Who's Who in Science, since 1955.
Who's Who in America, since 1960.
Neil Miner Award, National Association of Geology Teachers, 1972.

Citation by Oregon Academy of Science, 1975.

Fraternal organizations:
Sigma Pi Tau, 1926-1931; Delta Upsilon, 1932. Theta Tau (Epsilon), 1933.

Community and public service:
Boy Scouts of America, Eagle Scout, 1924; Wood Badge Award, 1954; Leadership Training Chairman, Kit Carson Council, 1955. Assistant Leadership Training Director, Philmont National Scout Camp, 1955.
Geological Society of the Oregon Country, 1938 - present. Editor, *Geological Newsletter*, 1941; President, 1946; Fellow, 1947.
City Club of Portland, 1945-47, 1956 - 1989.
Oregon Museum of Science of Science and Industry, 1945-47, 1956 - present. Trustee, 1958-68; Life member, 1970.
The Nature Conservancy, 1970 - present. Governing Board, Oregon Section, 1980 - 1989.

Consulting:
1966 Evaluation of geology departments at Michigan State University, University of Wisconsin, Beloit College and Antioch College; for the American Geological Institute, three weeks, 1966.
1970 Evaluation of the Department of Geology, Eastern Washington College, Cheney, Washington, one week.

Major publications: (from a total of over 220)
1932 *Contributions to the structure, stratigraphy and petrology of the Lower Columbia River Gorge, Oregon and Washington*, University of Oregon, M.A. Thesis, 145 p. and map.
1938 *Chromite deposits of Oregon*: Oregon Department of Geology & Mineral Industries, Bull. 9, 71 p., 11 figs., 2 pl.
1939 (and others)*Oregon Metal Mines Handbook, northeastern Oregon, east half*: Oregon Department of Geology & Mineral Industries, Bull. 14-A, 125 p.
1941 *Geological investigations of the chromite deposits of California: California Journal of Mines & Geology*, Rept. 37, p. 101-167, 31 figs.
1941 (and Smith, W. D.)*Geology and physiography of the northern Wallowa Mountains, Oregon*: Oregon Department of Geology & Mineral Industries, Bull. 12, 64 p., 11 pl. and map.

1941 (and others) *Oregon Metal Mines Handbook, northeastern Oregon, west half:* Oregon Department of Geology & Mineral Industries, Bull. 14-B, 157 p.

1944 (and Baldwin, E. M.) *Geology and coal resources of the Coos Bay quadrangle, Oregon:* Oregon Department of Geology & Mineral Industries, Bull. 27, 157 p., 31 pls., 3 maps.

1946 *Geology of the San Juan Bautista quadrangle, California:* California State Division of Mines, Bull. 133, 112 p., 12 pls., 10 figs, 3 maps.

1954 (and Balk, Robert) *Mineral resources of the Tohatchi and Fort Defiance quadrangles, New Mexico and Arizona:* New Mexico Bureau of Mines & Mineral Resources, Bull. 35, 192 p., 19 tbls., 21 figs., 16 pls. and map.

1955 *Mineral resources of the Navajo Indian Reservation in New Mexico (exclusive of uranium, oil, coal, gas and water):* New Mexico Bureau of Mines & Mineral Resources, Bull. 44, map and text, 2 figs.

1979 *Magnificent Gateway—a layman's guide to the geology of the Columbia River Gorge:* Timber Press, 150 p., 38 pls., 27 figs.

1985 *Time Travel in Oregon—a geology scrapbook* (120 articles on Oregon geology published weekly in the *Oregonian* from Nov. 3, 1983 to Oct. 31, 1985): Portland University Press, 140 p., 50 illustr.

1986 (et al.) *Cataclysms on the Columbia, a layman's guide to the effects of the catastrophic Bretz floods in the Pacific Northwest:* Timber Press, 211 p., 87 illust.

1987 *Time Travel Two in Oregon—a geology scrapbook* (105 articles published weekly in the *Oregonian* from Nov. 7, 1985 to Nov. 6, 1987): Portland University Press, 153 p., 50 illust.

Bibliography

(1908 - 1995)
* More than 10 pages. ** More than 50 pages. *** More than 100 pages.

1931 ** *Contributions to the structure, stratigraphy, and petrography of the lower Columbia River Gorge*: University of Oregon, M.A. thesis, 145 pp. and map.

1935 "Some waterfalls in Crater Lake National Park": Nature Notes, v. 8, n. 1, p. 6-8.

b   "Caves within Crater Lake National Park": (unpublished manuscript in park files). See 1984.

c   "Travels of the 'Old Man of the Lake'—a floating tree stump": (unpublished manuscript in park files). See 1984.

d   "Structures in the dacitic flows at Crater Lake, Oregon": *Journal of Geology* v. 44, n. 6, p. 737-744, 4 figs.

1938 ** *Chromite deposits in Oregon*: Oregon Department of Geology & Mineral Industries, Bulletin 9, 71 pp., 16 figs., 2 pl.

b   "Structures in West Coast chromite deposits" (abstract): *Geological Society of Oregon Country Newsletter*, v. 4, n. 24, p. 277.

1939 * *First aid to fossils, or what to do before the paleontologist comes*: Oregon Department of Geology & Mineral Industries, Bulletin 18, 28 pp., 2 pl.

b   "Geological features of West Coast chromite deposits": (abs.) *Mining and Metallurgy*, v. 20, no. 386, p. 100.

c   *** (and others) *Oregon Metal Mines Handbook, northeastern Oregon - east half*: Oregon Department of Geology &

Mineral Industries, Bulletin 14-A, 125 pp.
d   "Pretty pebble" (a poem): *Geological Society of Oregon Country Newsletter*, v. 5, n. 10, p. 90-91.

1940 "Chromite in Oregon" (abstract): *Geological Society of America Bulletin* v. 51, n. 12, pt. 2, p. 2015.
b   "Chromite in Oregon": *Geological Society of Oregon Country Newsletter*, v. 6, n. 16, pp. 132-133.
c   "Tectonics of the northern Wallowa Mountains, Oregon" (abstract): *Geological Society of America Bulletin*, v. 51, n. 12, pt. 2, p. 2015.
d   "Tectonics of the northern Wallowa Mountains, Oregon": *Geological Society of Oregon Country Newsletter*, v.6, n. 16, p.133.

1941 ** "Geological investigations of the chromite deposits of California": *California Journal of Mines & Geology*, Report XXXVII, pp. 101-163, 31 figs.
b   ** (and Smith, W.D.) *Geology and physiography of the northern Wallowa Mountains, Oregon*: Oregon Department of Geology & Mineral Industries, Bulletin 12, 64 pp., 4 figs., 11 pls. and map.
c   "Indian mounds on the Nestucca River": *Geological Society of Oregon Country Newsletter*, v. 7, n. 4, p. 36.
d   "The occurrence of hisingerite in Oregon": *Geological Society of Oregon Country Newsletter*, v.7, n. 17, p. 155.
e   ** (and others) *Oregon Metal Mines Handbook, northeastern Oregon - west half*: Oregon Department of Geology & Mineral Industries, Bulletin 14-B, 157 pp.
f   "Where is Oswego iron mine?": *Geological Society of Oregon Country Newsletter*, v. 7, n. 20, p. 183-184.

1942 "Chromite—an immediate national need": Oregon Department of Geology and Mineral Industries, Ore-bin, v. 4, n. 1, p. 1-8.
b   "Chromite deposits of Oregon": (in) *Ore deposits as related to structural features*, edited by W.H. Newhouse, Princeton Univ. Press, p. 116.
c   "Igneous features of Juniper Ridge, Oregon" (abstract): *Geological Society of America Bulletin* v. 53, n. 12, pt. 2,

253

p. 1815.

d   "Lava River Caves State Park": *National Speleological Society Bulletin*, n. 3, p. 14-15.

e   ** (and Harrison, Harold) "An investigation of the reported occurrence of tin at Juniper Ridge, Oregon": Oregon Department of Geology & Mineral Industries, Bulletin 23, 54 pp., 5 pls.

f   ** (and others) *Manganese in Oregon*: Oregon Department of Geology & Mineral Industries, Bulletin 17, 78 pp., 3 pls.

g   "Phantom Montevilla volcano": *Geological Society of Oregon Country Newsletter*, v. 8, n. 21, p. 169.

h   "The Portland earthquake of Dec. 24, 1941": *Geological Society of Oregon Country Newsletter*, v. 8, n. 1, p. 2.

i   "The spot-test method of semi-micro chemical analysis in mineralogy": *Geological Society of Oregon Country Newsletter*, v. 8, n. 1, p. 16.

1943 "Humphrey's spiral gravity concentrator treats Oregon black sands": Oregon Department of Geology & Mineral Industries, *Ore-Bin*, v.5, n. 10, p. 61-63.

b   "Snow snails": *Geological Society of Oregon Country Newsletter*, v. 9, n. 5, p. 31.

c   "Tall tales from Oregon's Red River country": *Geological Society of Oregon Country Newsletter*, v. 9, ns. 1, 3, 4, pp. 6, 16, 25.

1944 "Coos Bay coal, Oregon's forgotten resource": *Geological Society of Oregon Country Newsletter*, v. 10, ns. 2, 3, 4, pp. 9, 15, 22.

b   *** (and Baldwin, E. M.) *Geology and coal resources of the Coos Bay Quadrangle, Oregon*: Oregon Department of Geology & Mineral Industries, Bulletin 27, 157 pp., 31 pls. and 3 maps.

c   "To be investigated": *Geological Society of Oregon Country Newsletter*, v. 10, n. 15, p. 95.

d   "War minerals in Oregon": *Geological Society of Oregon Country Newsletter*, v. 10, n. 19, p. 117.

1945 "A vanadium-bearing black sand deposit of middle

Mesozoic age in central Curry County, Oregon":
Geological Society of Oregon Country Newsletter, v. 11, n.
4, p. 21.

b   "From a field geologist's notebook": *Geological Society of
Oregon Country Newsletter*, v. 11, ns. 1, 3, 7, 13, pp. 6,
15-16, 39-40, 81-82.

c   "Oregon's volcanic history": *Geological Society of Oregon
Country Newsletter*, v. 11, ns. 17, 18, pp. 113-115, 121-
123.

1946 "The geological yardstick": *Geological Society of Oregon
Country Newsletter*, v. 12, n. 2, p. 11-13, time chart.

b   *** *Geology of the San Juan Bautista quadrangle, California*:
California State Division of Mines, Bulletin 133, 112
pp., 12 pls. ten figs. and 3 maps.

c   * *Perlite deposits near the Deschutes River, southern Wasco
County, Oregon*: Oregon Department of Geology &
Mineral Industries, Short Paper, n. 16, 17 pp., 8 plates.

d   * *Reconnaissance geology of limestone deposits in the Willamette
Valley, Oregon*: Oregon Department of Geology &
Mineral Industries, Short Paper, n. 15, 15 pp, 4 pls., 2
tbls.

1947 "Another perlite deposit in Oregon": Oregon Department
of Geology & Mineral Industries, *Ore-Bin*, v. 9, n. 8, p.
60-62.

b   *** *Bibliography of geology and mineral resources of Oregon,
1936-1945*: Oregon Department of Geology & Mineral
Industries, Bulletin 33, 108 pp.

c   (and Baldwin, E. M.) "Physiographic divisions of Oregon":
Geological Society of Oregon Country Newsletter, v. 13, n.
2, p. 11-12.

d   "Status of topographic and geologic mapping in Oregon in
1946" (abstract): *Geological Society of America Bulletin*,
v. 58, n. 12, pt. 2, p. 1245-1246.

1949 (and Lowry, W.D.) "An investigation of the sea-cliff
subsidence of March 30, 1943, at Newport, Oregon"
(abstract): *Oregon Academy of Science Proceedings, 1944
meeting*, v. 1 (1943-1947), p. 31.

b   * (and Mason, Ralph) *Brick and tile industry in Oregon*: Oregon Department of Geology & Mineral Industries, Short Paper, n. 19, 28 pp., 3 figs., 3 tbls.

c   (and Baldwin, E. M.) "Geology and coal resources of the Coos Bay quadrangle": *Oregon Academy of Science Proceedings, 1945 meeting*, v.1 (1943-1947), p. 54-55.

d   "Geology of a perlite deposit on the Deschutes River, Oregon" (abstract): *Oregon Academy of Science Proceedings, 1945 meeting*, v. 1, (1943-1947), p. 78.

e   "The Penn State Polylith": *Mineral Industries*, Pennsylvania State College, v. 18, n. 6, p. 1, 3-4.

f   "Pennsylvania coal through western eyes": *Geological Society of Oregon Country Newsletter*, v. 15, n. 8, 6 pp.

g   "Suggested outline of physiographic divisions of Oregon" (abstract): *Oregon Academy of Science Proceedings, 1947 meeting*, v. 1 (1943-1947), p. 101-102.

h   "A vanadium-bearing black-sand deposit of middle Mesozoic age in central Curry County, Oregon" (abstract): *Oregon Academy of Science Proceedings, 1944 meeting* v. 1, (1943-1947), p. 26-27.

1950 "Why is a geologist?": *Geological Society of Oregon Country Newsletter*, v. 16, n. 4, p. 69-73.

1952 "The seminar as a senior 'polishing course' in geology: *Journal of Geological Education*, v. 1, n. 3, 8 pp.

b   "The Carrizozo malpais, New Mexico" (abstract): *Geological Society of America Bulletin*, v. 63, n. 12, pt. 2, p. 1319.

c   (and Jones, S. M.) "Geology of the Capitan quadrangle, New Mexico" (abstract): *Geological Society of America Bulletin*, v. 63, n. 12, pt. 2, p. 1319.

d   "A Mexican trip in your own backyard": *Geological Society of Oregon Country Newsletter*, v. 18, n. 10, p. 101-103.

1954 "Tohatchi formation of Mesa Verde group, western San Juan Basin, New Mexico": *American Association of Petroleum Geologists Bulletin* v. 37, n. 11, p. 2567-2571.

b   *** (and Robert Balk) *Mineral resources of the Tohatchi and Fort Defiance quadrangles, New Mexico and Arizona*: New Mexico Bureau of Mines and Mineral Resources,

Bulletin 35, 192 pp., 19 tbls., 21 figs., 16 pls. and map.
c   * *Your underground resources*: New Mexico Mining Association and Bureau of Mines & Mineral Resources, 15 pp.

1955 ** *Mineral resources of the Navajo Reservation in New Mexico (exclusive of uranium, coal, oil, gas and water)*: New Mexico Bureau of Mines & Mineral Resources, Bulletin 44, map and text, 2 figs.
b   * *The making of a mine*: New Mexico Bureau of Mines & Mineral Resources, Circular, n. 36, 10 pp., 1 fig.

1956 "The art of geology": *Journal of Geological Education*, v. 4, n.1, p. 1-4.
b   Estimation of percentages in thin-sections—considerations of visual psychology: Journal Sedimentary Petrology, 2 pp., 1 fig.
c   Titaniferous Cretaceous beach placer in McKinley County, New Mexico (abstract): *Geological Society of America Bulletin* 67, n. 12, p. 1789.

1957 "The art of geology": *Geological Society of Oregon Country Newsletter*, v. 23, n. 2, p. 9-11.
b   (and Pray, Lloyd C.) "Outlier of Dakota (?) strata, southeastern New Mexico": *American Association of Petroleum Geologists Bulletin* v. 40, n. 11, p. 2735-2740.
c   (and Sun, M.S.) "Authigenic brookite in Cretaceous Gallup sandstone, Gallup, New Mexico": *Journal of Sedimentary Petrology*, v. 27, n. 3, p. 265-270., 1 fig.

1958 * (and Kottlowski, F.E.) *Scenic trips to the geologic past, Roswell-Capitan-Ruidoso and Bottomless Lakes State Park*: New Mexico Bureau of Mines and Mineral Resources, n. 3, 47 pp. (see also 1967, 1981).
b   * *Guidebook for field trip excursions, Columbia River Gorge*: Geological Society of America, Cordilleran Section, 23 pp., 5 figs.
c   * *Scenic trips to the northwest's geologic past (viewer's guide)*: General Extension Division, Oregon State System of Higher Education, 38 pp.

1959 * (and Wilkinson, W.D.) "Field trip n. 7, Picture Gorge to Portland via Arlington": (in) *Field Guidebook, Geologic trips along Oregon highways*: Oregon Department of Geology and Mineral Industries, Bulletin n. 50, p. 109-135, maps.

1960 (and Crawford, T.C.) "A fusion method for quick determination of certain rare metals": *Journal of Geological Education*, v. 8, n. 1, p. 11-13.
b   "Ideas on the origin of Oregon agate": *Geological Society of Oregon Country Newsletter*, v. 26, n. 7, p. 53-55.

1961 "The High Cascades graben and the 'myth-interpretation' of Mount Multnomah" (abstract): *Oregon Academy of Science Proceedings*, 1 p.

1962 Op. cit.: Oregon Department of Geology & Mineral Industries, *Ore-Bin*, v. 24, n. 2, p. 22.
b   Op. cit. (abstract): *Northwest Science*, v. 36, n. 1, p. 21.
c   "Symbols for mineral deposits and mine workings": American Geological Institute data sheet n. 38, *Geotimes*, v. 7, n. 4, p. 41-42.

1963 * (and Van Atta, R.O.) *Geologic field guide to the northwestern Oregon coast field trip*: Portland State College Press, 20 pp.

1964 (in) *Dani, Ahmed Hassan, Senghao cave excavation, ancient Pakistan*: Department of Archeology, University of Peshawar, Pakistan, Bulletin v. 1, p. 5-11.

1965 "Courses in geology for advanced nonmajors": *Journal of Geological Education*, v. 13, n. 5, p. 145-147.
b   "The Cascade Range volcano-tectonic depression of Oregon": *Lunar Geological Field Conference Transcription*, Bend, Oregon, p. 21-23, 2 figs.

1966 (Book Review) "The wild Cascades, by Harvey Manning, Sierra Club, San Francisco": *Journal of the West*, v. 5, n. 4, p. 544-545.

b   "Some laws of field geology": *Journal of Geological Educa-tion*, v. 14, n. 5, p. 145-147.

1967 "On the transmission of zest": op. cit., v. 15, n. 1, p. 22.
b   "The stainless steel curriculum": op. cit. v. 15, n. 2, p. 95.
c   ** (and Kottlowski, F.E.) *Scenic trips to the geologic past, Roswell-Capitan-Ruidoso and Bottomless Lakes State Park*: New Mexico Bureau Mines & Mineral Resources. n. 3, 50 pp. (second edition).

1968 "What I have learned": *Journal of Geological Education*, v. 16, n. 1, p. 7-8.

1970 "Mount Rainier—our only glacial volcanic park": *Science and Children*, v. 7, n. 6, p. 12-14.
b   "Art and geology": *Geotimes*, v. 15, n. 4, p. 16-17.
c   "Artists scan rocks for inspiration and credit": *Dateline in Science*, v. 5, n. 15, p. 6.

1971 (and Roberts, Miriam) "The Oregon Department of Geol-ogy and Mineral Industries": (in) Origin and develop-ment of the state geological surveys, *Journal of the West*, v. 10, n. 1, p. 154-158.
b   "One man's bout with TV": (in) *Teaching introductory geology by television, Council on Education in Geological Sciences, Program Publication* n. 6, p. 35-36.
c   "Mount Rainier - our only glacial volcanic national park": (in) *Helping Children learn Earth Science*, National Science Teachers Assn., p. 89-91.
d   *Memorial to Edwin Thomas Hodge*: Geological Society of America, Spec. Pub., 8 pp.
e   (Book Review) "Undergraduate geology—a strategy for design of curricula, by Frank H. T. Rhodes and others": Council on Education in the Geological Sciences, Program Pub. n. 8, American Geology Inst.: *Geotimes*, v. 17, n. 2, p. 34-37.
f   "Geology and the Oregon Country": *Geological Society of Oregon Country Newsletter*, v. 38, n. 4, p. 26-28.

1973 (Book Review) "Earth and universe, by Benjamin F.

Howell, Jr., Charles E. Merrill (1972)": *Journal of Geological Education*, v. 21, n. 1, p. 37-38.

b (Book Review) "The bone hunters, by Earl Lanham, Columbia Univ. Press (1973)": *Oregon Historical Society Quarterly*, v. 75, n. 1, p. 78-79.

c "Art and the earth sciences": *Geological Society of Oregon Country Newsletter*, v. 39, n. 8, p. 68-69.

1974 (Book Review) "The evolving earth, by Fredrich J. Sawkins, and others, Macmillan, (1974)": *Geotimes*, v. 19, n. 8, p. 36-37.

b (Book Review) "The channeled scablands of eastern Washington, by Paul L. Weis and William L. Newman, U. S. Geology Survey, (1973)": *Pacific Search*, v. 8, n. 10, p. 31.

c "Tales of Hathaway Jones": *Oregon Outdoors*, August, p. 39.

d "Past president names railroad station": *Geological Society of Oregon Country Newsletter*, v. 40, n. 9, p. 57-58.

e "The Catlin-Gabel lava tubes": Oregon Department of Geology and Mineral Industries, *Ore-Bin*, v. 36, n. 9, p. 149-166; also in National Speleological Society, Oregon grotto, *The Speliograph*, v. 10, n. 12, p. 162-166.

f "Lolo Pass field trip": *Geological Society of Oregon Country Newsletter*, v. 41, n.11, p. 75-76.

1975 * "Volcanoes of the Portland area, Oregon": Oregon Department of Geology and Mineral Industries, *Ore-Bin*, v. 37, n. 9, p. 145-157.

b * "The Wallowa ice cap of northeastern Oregon—an exercise in the interpretation of glacial landforms": Oregon Department of Geology and Mineral Industries, *Ore-Bin*, v. 37, n. 12, p. 189-202.

c "How to collect cliffs": *Geological Society of Oregon Country Newsletter*, v. 41, n. 12, p. 89-90.

1976 "Acceptance of the Neil Miner Award": *Journal of Geological Education*, v. 23, n. 5, p. 147.

b * *Index to Bulletin 72, Correlations of Great Basin stratigraphic units:* Nevada Bureau of Mines & Geology Bulletin n.

72-A, p. 1-19.

c   * *Index to Isochron/West*: New Mexico Bureau of Mines & Mineral Resources, n. 17, 25 pp.

d   "How to collect cliffs": *Journal of Geological Education*, v. 24, n. 4, p. 123-124.

e   * (and Beaulieu, John D.) "Plate tectonic structures in Oregon": Oregon Department of Geology and Mineral Industries, *Ore-Bin*, v. 38, n. 6, p. 87-99.

1979 "Speculations on Oregon calderas, known and unknown": Oregon Department of Geology and Mineral Industries, *Oregon Geology* (formerly *Ore-Bin*), v. 41, n. 2, p. 31-32.

b   "Waterfall alcoves in the Columbia River Gorge": op. cit., p. 33-34.

c   *** *The magnificent gateway: A layman's guide to the geology of the Columbia River Gorge*: Timber Press, Beaverton, Oregon, 144 pp., 59 illus.

d   "A century of popular geology in Oregon": *Oregon Outdoors*, v. 13, n. 9, p. 30-31.

1980 *** (editor) *Portland State University - the first 25 years*: Portland State University Press, 144 pp.

b   "Department of Earth Sciences": (in) op.cit., p. 52-54.

c   * "Geology at Portland State University: 1950-1980": unpublished manuscript, 35 pp.

d   "A note on diastrophic rates in Oregon" (abstract): *Oregon Academy of Science Proceedings*, v. 16, p. 21.

e   "Early geologists in the Columbia River Gorge" (abstract): *Geological Society of America, Cordilleran Section, Abstracts with Programs*, v. 12, n. 3, p. 93.

1981 "Why do volcanoes erupt?æ: *Geological Society of Oregon Country Newsletter*, v. 47, n. 6, p. 72-73.

b   "The volcanic story of the Columbia River Gorge": op. cit., v. 47, n. 5, p. 57-60.

c   *** (and Kottlowski, F.E.) *Scenic trips to the geologic past, Roswell\Ruidoso\Valley of Fire and Bottomless Lakes State Park*: New Mexico Bureau of Mines & Geology, n. 3, 96 pp. (third edition).

d   "The volcanic story of the Columbia River Gorge": *Journal of Geological Education*, v. 30, n. 3, p. 156-161.

e   "The isogyre" (a poem): *International Stop Continental Drift Society Newsletter*, v. 4, p. 1.

f   "Scientific access to Mt. St. Helens 1980" (abstract): (In) *Proceedings of Mt. St. Helens: one year later*, Eastern Washington University Press, p. 235.

1982 "Speculations on Oregon calderas – II": *Geological Society of Oregon Country Newsletter*, v. 48, n. 9, p. 211-213.

1983 "One man's shadow": *Journal of Geological Education*, v. 31, n. 1, p. 22-25.

b   "Geology of Camassia Preserve": *Geological Society of Oregon Country Newsletter*, v. 49, n. 7, p. 58.

c   "Geology of Governor Tom McCall Preserve": *Geological Society of Oregon Country Newsletter*, v.49, n.8, p. 64-65.

d   "Oregon Museum of Science and Industry": *Journal of Geological Education*, v. 31, no. 11, p. 406.

1984 "The Caves of Crater Lake National Park": Oregon Department of Geology & Mineral Industries, *Oregon Geology*, v. 46, n. 1, p. 3-6; also in *The Speleograph*, v. 20, no. 3 & 4, p. 13-17.

b   "A note on some remarkable concretions from the Yamhill Formation, Oregon": Oregon Department of Geology & Mineral Industries, *Oregon Geology*, v. 46, n. 2, p. 19.

c   "Geology of the Sandy River preserve": *Geological Society of Oregon Country Newsletter*, v. 50, n.1, p. 7.

d   The capes and headlands of the northern Oregon coast: *Geological Society of Oregon Country Newsletter*, v. 50, n. 2, p. 11-13.

e   "Geology of Pelican Lake preserve": *Geological Society of Oregon Country Newsletter*, v. 50, n. 3, p. 21-22.

f   "Washington Park Zoo": *Journal of Geological Education*, v. 32, n. 3, p. 193-194.

g   "An unusual thunder egg from central Oregon" (a cover photo): Oregon Deptartment Geology & Mineral Industries, *Oregon Geology*, v. 46, n. 5, p. 50.

h   "Pseudokarst in Portland, Oregon": *Geo 2*, National

BIBLIOGRAPHY

Speleological Society., section on cave geol. and
geography, v. 11, n. 2, p. 24-25, 4 illustr.

i * "Geology of the Gorge": (in) *The Columbia Gorge, a unique
American treasure,* compiled by Michael S. Spranger:
Washington State University Cooperative Extension
and U. S. Department of Agriculture, p. 20-30.

j "Oregon lakes and their origin": Oregon Department of
Geology & Mineral Industries, *Oregon Geology,* v. 46,
n. 12, p. 143-146, 6 plates.

k "Remarkable thunder egg permits deduction of six episodes in its formation" (a colored cover photo): *Journal
of Geological Education,* v. 33, n. 1, p. 2.

1985 *** *Time travel in Oregon - a geology scrapbook* (120 articles on
Oregon Geology published in the *Oregonian* from
November 3, 1983 to October 31, 1985): Portland State
University Press, 140 p., 50 illustr. (See also 1987-b)

b "Allen's laws of field geology": *Oregon Geology,* v. 47, n. 10,
p. 121.

c *** *Bin rock and dump rock: recollections of a geologist*: Pri-
vately printed, 112 p.

d (Book Review) "A field manual for the amateur geologist,
by Alan Cvancara": *Geological Societyiety of Oregon
Country Newsletter,* v. 51, n. 10, p. 63-64.

e (Book Review) "Rivers of the west – a guide to the geology
and history, by Elizabeth and William Orr": op. cit., p.
64.

1986 (and Pugh, Richard N.) "Origin of Willamette meteorite –
an alternate hypothesis": Oregon Department of
Geology & Mineral Industries, *Oregon Geology,* v. 48,
n. 7, p. 79-80, 85.

b (Book Review) "The story of earth, by P. Cattermole and P.
Moore": *Paleogography, Paleoclimatology, Paleoecology,*
Elsevier Science Publishers, v. 55, p. 100-101.

c "Tsunami – a coastal hazard": *Geological Society of Oregon
Country Newsletter,* v. 52, n. 9, p. 46-48.

d *** *Cataclysms on the Columbia – a layman's guide to the
features produced by the catastrophic Bretz floods in the
Pacific Northwest*: Timber Press, Portland, Oregon, 211

p., 87 illus.

1987 "Glimpses of DOGAMI history": Oregon Department of Geology & Mineral Industries, *Oregon Geology*, v. 49, n. 4, p. 49.

b   *** *Time travel two in Oregon – a geology scrapbook* (105 articles published in the *Oregonian* from November 7, 1985 to November 6, 1987): Portland State University Press, 140 p, 50 illustr., (See also 1985a).

c   "Countdown to the present – the geologic story of the Hood River Valley": (In) *History of Hood River County, Vol. II*, Hood River County Historical Society, p. 8-11.

1988 * "A passage through time": (in) *Columbia River Gorge*, by Holloway, Siddall, Kelly and Allen: Graphic Arts Publishing Company, p. 29-34.

b   "Makah cultural and research center": *Journal of Geological Education*, v. 36, n. 2, p. 131.

c   "Monterey Bay aquarium": op. cit., p. 131-132.

d   "The geomorphology and geology of the Willamette Valley as seen from I-5, Portland to Eugene, Part I, Geomorphology": *Geological Society of Oregon Country Newsletter*, v. 54, n. 3, p. 10-11.

e   Op. cit., "Part II, Geology": v. 54, n. 6, p. 29-30.

f   * "Volcanic hazards from High Cascade peaks": Oregon Department of Geology & Mineral Industries, *Oregon Geology*, v. 50, n. 5/6, p. 56-63.

g   "Outrageous hypotheses": *Geological Society of Oregon Country Newsletter*, v. 54. n. 12, p. 68-69.

h   "Everyone has a stake in 1851 survey that cut NW into identifiable slices": *Coos Genealogical Forum Bulletin*, Fall v. 23, n. 2, p. 5-8.

1989 "Ice Age glaciers and lakes south of the Columbia River Gorge": Oregon Department of Geology & Mineral Industries, *Oregon Geology*, v. 51, n. 1, p. 12-14.

b   "Catastrophic floods sculptured Newberg landscape": (in) *A Century to Remember, Newberg 1889-1989*, Newberg Graphic, Centennial Issue, p. 6-7.

c   "Mapping the geology of the Gorge and Mount Hood in

264

1931": *Friends of the Columbia River Gorge, Spring Newsletter*, p. 8-9.

d "New road guides for geology buffs": *Geological Society of Oregon Country Newsletter*, v. 55, n. 6, p. 113-114.

e "Geology of the Sandy River": *Geological Society of Oregon Country Newsletter*, v. 55, n. 7, p. 119-123.

f "Some joints around Portland": op. cit. v. 55, n. 8, p. 127-128.

g *The geologic history of the Columbia River Gorge*: U. S. Army Engineers, Portland District, 2-page handout at Bonneville Dam Information Center. Also in *Geological Society of Oregon Country Newsletter*, v. 55, n. 12, p. 163-164.

h "Columbia River Gorge geologic history provides many possibilities for exploration": *Explorations*, Columbia Gorge Interpretive Center, Skamania County Historical Society, p. 2-3.

i "Geologists refine explorations into time and space": *Geological Society of Oregon Country Newsletter*, v. 55, n. 9, p. 135-137.

j (Obituary) "Viola LeGasse Oberson, 1909 -1989": op. cit., v. 55, n. 9, p. 132-133.

k "Northwest topographic maps": op. cit. v. 55, n. 11, p. 153-156.

l *A passage through time (in the) Columbia Gorge*, by Holloway, Siddall, Kelley and Allen (second edition): Graphic Arts Center Publishing Company, Portland, p. 29-34.

m "The geologic story of the Portland Basin": (in) *History and folklore of the David Douglas Community*, Howard and Grace Horner, editors: David Douglas Historical Society, p. 14-15.

1990 "Boring lava field": *Geological Society of Oregon Country Newsletter*, v. 56, n. 1, p. 7.

b (Book Review) "Wy'east, the mountain (1930), McNeil's Mount Hood Revisited (1990), by Joe Stein": op. cit., v. 56, n. 2, p. 13-14.

c (Book Review) "The odyssey of Thomas Condon, Irish Immigrant, Frontier Missionary, Oregon Geologist, by Robert D. Clark": *Journal of Geological Education*, v. 38,

n. 1, p. 65-70 Also in *Geological Society of Oregon
Country Newsletter*, v. 56, n. 1, p. 5-6.

d   (Book Review) "Volcanoes, by Cliff Ollier": op. cit., v. 56,
n. 1, p. 8.

e   "Some meditations on earthquakes": op. cit., v. 56, n. 2, p.
11-13, *Journal of Geological Education*, v. 40, n. 4, p. 343.

f   "Scouting as prelude to geology": *Journal of Geological
Education*, v. 38, n. 2, p. 158.

g   "The case of the counterclockwise river": Oregon Department of Geology & Mineral Industries, *Oregon Geology*, v. 52, n. 3, p. 67-69.

h   "Revisiting Crater Lake": *Geological Society of Oregon
Country Newsletter*, v. 56, n. 6. p. 36-37.

i   "Some meditations on earthquakes": *Ohio Department of
Natural Resources, Division of Geology, Geology Newsletter*, Winter, 1990, p. 7.

j   "Capsule geologic history of the Columbia River Gorge":
Journal of Geological Education, v. 38, n. 4, p. 372.

k   (Book Review) "Volcanoes, by Cliff Ollier, Oxford, New
York, Basil Blackwell, Ltd. 1988, 228 p.": op. cit., v. 38,
p. 366.

l   (Book Review) "Mineral resources and the destiny of
nations, by Walter L. Youngquist, 1990, National Book
Company, Portland, Oregon, 280 p.": *Journal of
Geological Education*, v. 38, n. 3, p. 257.

m   "Seven trends in geology, 1970-1990": (in) *University of
Oregon, Department of Geology Science, Alumni Sympo-
sium*, p. 3-5. Truths debated: *Oregon Scientist*, v. 3, no.
3, p. 22.

n   "Crater Lake and chromite": op. cit. v. 38, n. 5, p. 480-81.

1991 "How geologists think – the method of multiple working
hypotheses": op. cit., v. 39, n. 1, p. 67.

b   (Book Review) "Mineral resources and the destinies of
nations, by Walter Youngquist, National Book Co.,
Portland, Oregon, 280 p.": *Geological Society of Oregon
Country Newsletter*, v. 57. n. 2, p. 11-13. (see also 1990-
l)

c   (Book Review) "Volcanoes of North America, United
States and Alaska, edited by Charles A. Wood and

Jurgen Kienle": Cambridge University Press, 354 p., Op. cit., v. 57, n.3, p.18. Also in *Oregon Geology*, v. 53, n. 5, p. 115, and *Journal of Geological Education*, 1992, v. 40, n. 1., p.81.

d   "Royal British Columbia Museum": Museum and Gallery Corner, *Journal of Geological Education*, v. 39, n. 3, p. 261.

e   "Geological introduction": (In) *Geologic history of the Columbia River Gorge, as interpreted from the historic Columbia River Scenic Highway*, by Ira A. Williams, 1923, reprinted by the Oregon Historical Society, p. xvii-xxix, 135 p., colored map and cross-section.

f   (Book Review) "Crystal quest 1., by Marcel Vanek, Geoscience Press, Inc., 93 p.": Oregon Department of Geology & Mineral Industries, *Oregon Geology*, v. 53, n. 4, p. 94. Also in *Journal of Geological Education*, v. 40, n. 1, p. 81.

g   "Exercises in imagineering and writing": *Journal of Geological Education*, v. 39, n. 4, p. 422. Also in *Geological Society of Oregon Country Newsletter*, v. 56, n. 8, p. 48.

h   "The case of the inverted auriferous paleotorrent – exotic quartzite gravels on Wallowa peaks": Oregon Department of Geology & Mineral Industries, *Oregon Geology*, v. 53, n.5, p. 104-107.

i   *** (and Marjorie Burns) *Cataclysms on the Columbia – a layman's guide to the features produced by the catastrophic Bretz floods in the Pacific Northwest*: Timber Press, [second edition], paperback, 211 p

1992 (Book Review:) "Crystal quest 1., by Marcel Vanek, Geoscience Press, Inc., 93 p.": *Journal of Geological Education*. v. 40, n. 1, p. 81. (also see 1991-f).

b   (Book Review:) "The tenth muse, the pursuit of Earth Science, by Ronald B. Parker, Charles Scribner's Sons, 1986, 211 p.": *Geological Society of Oregon Country Newsletter*, v. 58.

c   (Book Review:) "Economic Geology, U. S., edited by Gluskoter, H., J., Rice, D. D., and Taylor, R. B., Volume GNA P-2 of The Geology of North America, 1991, Geological Society of America, 630 p., 9 plates in

slipcase": *Geological Society of Oregon Country Newsletter*, v.58, n. 6, p. 37-8.
d * "Geology": (In) *Columbia River Gorge, a complete guide,* Philip N. Jones, editor: *The Mountaineers,* 270 p., p. 31-43.
e "Some meditations on earthquakes": *Journal of Geological Education,* v. 40, n. 11, p. 343. (See also 1990i)
f "Cataclysmic Columbia, a guide to the spectacular geologic history of the Gorge": *The Columbian,* Vancouver, WA, June 10, 2 p., and June 10, 2 p.
g "Reflections on the ecology of science": *Geological Society of Oregon Country Newsletter,* v. 58, n. 10, p. 60-62.
h (Book Review) "Geology of Oregon (4th edition), by Elizabeth 1. and William N. Orr, 254 p.": *Geological Society of Oregon Country Newsletter,* v. 58, n. 11, p. 69.

1993 "Oregon Museum of Science and Industry (better known as OMSI)": *Oregon Geology,* v. 55, n. 1, p. 21-22.; *Journal of Geological Education,* v. 41, n. x, p. x
b "When is a Richter not a Richter?": Oregon Department of Geology & Mineral Industries, *Oregon Geology,* v. 55, n. 3, p. 57-8.
c "Capsulization": *Journal of Geological Education,* v. 41, no. 2, p. 180-182.
d "Reflections of a field geologist on the ecology of science": op. cit., v. 41, n. 3, p. 275-76

1994 "Incised meanders – neglected clues to Oregon coastal terrace problems": *Geological Society of Oregon Country Newsletter,* v. 60, n. 4, p. 20-24.
b * "Geologic field work in Oregon and other parts of the West since the 1930s": Oregon Department of Geology & Mineral Industries, *Oregon Geology,* v. 56, n. 3, p. 65-69.
c "Is cruise control optional?": *Oregonian,* 3 June, 1/2 p.
d (and Scott Burns) "That important first lecture to the introductory geology class": *Journal of Geological Education,* v. 42, n. 4, p. 313-15

Excerpts from the "Time Travel" series of articles

from the *Oregonian*,1984-1987

Wallowas Stand as Alps of Oregon and Provide Finest Study in Glaciers

The Wallowa Mountains, which contain at least 21 peaks above 9,000 feet in elevation, have been accurately described as the "Alps of Oregon." Nearly all of the Wallowa peaks and the Cascade Mountains were glaciated during the Ice Age from 2 million to 12,000 years ago.

While the highest peaks in Oregon are the Cascades, ranging from Mount Hood's 11,235 feet to the Middle Sister's 10,053 feet, by far most of the mountains between 9,000 and 10,000 feet are in the Wallowas in northeastern Oregon.

In these mountains, some of the glaciers extended many miles down their flanks. In the Cascades, for example, a glacier from Mount Hood came 20 miles down the Sandy River to Cherryville, about six miles east of Sandy, and, a glacier from the Three Sisters probably extended 22 miles down the McKenzie River almost to Blue River.

In the Wallowas, the deeply carved mountain mass occupies nearly 1,500 square miles of Baker, Wallowa and Union counties. The ice covered 337 square miles of the range, with great half-mile-deep glaciers radiating out from Eagle Cap for as many as 22 miles, and filling 11 deeply incised valleys with dozens of tributaries.

There was no "ice cap" since the glaciers did not cover the peaks and ridges above 8,500 feet, even in the center of the range. Ice surfaces of the glaciers sloped down the valleys to a level as low as 3,000 feet elevation on Pine Creek.

Eagle Cap and three other smaller peaks to the west were completely surrounded by ice, thus earning the name of "nunatak," an Eskimo term for an ice-surrounded pinnacle. The total area in which glaciers occurred was about 1,000 square miles, and approximately 100 glaciers covered about a third of this area.

There were nine glaciers more than ten miles long, with the Lostine River glacier's 22 miles being the longest. Other major glaciers were the Imnaha River, 20 miles; the Wallowa River, 13 miles; Hurricane Creek, 13 miles; East Eagle, 13 miles; Eagle Creek, 13 miles; Pine Creek, 12.6 miles; and Bear Creek, 12 miles.

There were seven glaciers between five and nine miles long, eight between two and five miles, and 86 isolated glaciers or "neve fields," less than two miles long.

In terms of the area of each glacier, the Minam River glacier was the

271

largest, covering 67.5 square miles, followed by the Lostine River glacier with 55 square miles. The ten longest glaciers covered 278.7 square miles, or nearly 83 percent of the glaciated valleys.

The student of glacial geomorphology can recognize at least five depositional and six erosional landforms in the Wallowa Mountains. The best viewpoint for the casual visitor is on Mount Howard, above the tramway at the head of Wallowa Lake, from which examples of nearly all of these features can be seen.

Wallowa Lake may be the best preserved and most spectacular morainal lake in the country. It's bounded by terminal, recessional and lateral moraines, composed of debris carried by the glacier and dumped at the end and along the sides when the ice melted.

The lateral moraines stand nearly 900 feet above the lake surface, and on the east side there is an array of 10 to 15 recessional moraines, produced by separate slight advances and retreats of the ice. The outwash plain extends outwards to the east, north and northwest for five or six miles beyond the lake.

All of the major glaciers occupied U-shaped valleys, but the outstanding example of this landform is the Lostine River canyon, which is accessible in the summer by car for 16 of its 22-mile length.

Nearly all of the smaller glaciers have their heads in circular, steep-walled amphitheaters known as cirques, and many of these cirques are occupied by tarns, or small rock-bottomed lakes. There are nearly 100 lakes in the Wallowa Mountains, and a large percentage of them are tarns. There are 20 lakes, varying in size from a few yards to half a mile long, in and around the Lakes Basin, just north of Eagle Cap at the head of the Lostine River, Hurricane Creek and Wallowa River glaciers.

The high, triangular peaks along many of the ridges, carved by intersecting cirques, are known as "matterhorns." Switzerland's Matterhorn itself is not a typical example; Sawtooth Peak, Pete's Point or Glacier Mountain would be better examples.

The jagged ridges between the glaciated valleys are known as "aretes." The Hurwal and Hurricane Divides are splendid examples. The low sags in these divides, caused by two intersecting cirques, are known as "cols."

272

Wallowa Reef Once in Austria

An ancient reef in Oregon's Wallowa Mountains was once part of a giant coral reef whose other parts now lie in Austria, according to two scientists studying the Wallowas.

This graphic illustration of how the earth's crust moves over millions of years is detailed by George Stanley, a University of Montana paleontologist, and Baba Senowbari-Daryan of Erlanger-Nurnberg University in the November, 1987, issue of Natural History magazine.

They gave new information on the massive and richly fossiliferous 200 million-year-old coral reef limestone in the Wallowa Mountains of northeastern Oregon known as the Martin Bridge Formation.

The two say that the Wallowa reef is identical in fossil content to, and hence was once part of, a giant reef known as the "Dachstein Reef Limestone" of Austria. In addition to the fossils, rock characteristics such as color, bedding, cavities, cements, and in-filling by reddish reef sediment are strikingly alike between Dachstein and Martin Bridge.

Secondly, Stanley believes that the Martin Bridge does not belong to the terrane known as "Wrangellia," as was formerly thought.

I must note that Stanley began his article with, "In 1985, a colleague from West Germany and I excavated the first fossils from a huge limestone outcrop in the Wallowa Mountains." This shocked me, since in 1938 I helped collect an extensive group of fossils from the Martin Bridge. This field work resulted in Bulletin 14, and the first colored geologic map of the Wallowas, published by the Oregon Department of Geology and Mineral Industries. But that is another story, and I have written him about it.

Stanley has now helped write another chapter in the increasingly complicated story of "suspect, "displaced" or "accreted" terranes, which are now thought by many geologists to make up much if not most of the older rocks in North America west of the Rocky Mountains.

Continental plates rafted

The hypothesis proposes that numerous scraps of continental plates, which are composed of rocks that are lighter that the basaltic oceanic plates, have been rafted for thousands of miles north and east across the Pacific Ocean. Although they move only a few inches a year, 200 million years of such movements have plastered or "accreted" these pieces to the North American Plate.

For instance, the Klamath Mountains are now thought to be made up of at least 16 accreted terranes. I suspect that it will be decades before we get all these terranes sorted out and their origins pinned down.

Stanley believes that he has located in Austria the exact place from which the Wallowa sliver of coral reef came. He gives it a new name the "Wallowa-Seven Devils Terrane," separating it from its former identity as part of "Wrangellia." (That is a group of continental scraps with similar fossils and rock types that have variously docked in southern Alaska, the Queen Charlotte Islands, southern British Columbia including Vancouver Island, and in Eastern Oregon.)

As of now, the Wallowa-Seven Devils' accreted terrane is thought to have grown, along with the Dachstein Reef coral reef, in the Tethys Sea. During the Triassic about 225 million years ago, this sea separated the continent of Eurasia from Gondwanaland (Africa, India, Antarctica and Australia.)

Atolls built by coral

On a shallow offshore volcanic platform, atolls were built by 20 or so different coral species, along with sponges, algae and a multitude of other invertebrates, eventually to form a thick reef complex in the Tethys sea. During an 8-million-year interval between 218 million and 210 million years ago, limestone piled up to a thickness of more than 4,000 feet.

Plate movements then broke up the Tethys reefs, and fragments were carried across the entire former Pacific Ocean as they rode eastward on the conveyor-belt of the ancient oceanic plate.

During their travels, between 166 million and 159 million years ago, Wallowa collided with another volcanic island terrane, situated to the east. These were subsequently welded together but did not dock with North America until about 100 million years ago. This gave plenty of time for Wallowa to move the 5,000 miles across the Pacific at the very conservative rate of three inches per year.

274

Hells Canyon Lays Bare Rocky History of Region

(1 of 3)

Hells Canyon is exceeded in length only by the Grand Canyon of the Colorado River. It is both the narrowest and the deepest gash on the North American continent.

For nearly 150 miles, its amber cliffs expose multiple packed flows of basaltic lava, and granite and metamorphic rocks beneath the basalt. The 190 mile round trip up the Snake River from Lewiston, Idaho, to Johnson Bar (a vertical ascent of more than 60 feet) and back is one of the great river boat rides of a lifetime.

The upper part of the canyon is accessible from Baker City by 70 miles of Oregon 86 to Oxbow Dam. From there, paved roads run north along the east side of the river for the 15 miles to Hells Canyon Dam and south along the west side of the river 12 miles to Brownlee Dam, connecting via Idaho 71 with US 95.

The bottom of the canyon is extremely hot and dry in the summer, and in consequence it has desert vegetation of sagebrush and prickly cactus, with a few scattered western yellow pines and stunted hackberries. Occasional cottonwoods and aspen may grow near the river. Where irrigation is possible, small orchards can produce superb fruit. The upper slopes far above the gorge are used for grazing.

For 40 miles between the Seven Devils Mountains of Idaho and the Wallowa Mountains of Oregon, the Grand Canyon of the Snake River averages 5,500 feet in depth. From the summit of He Devil Peak, seven miles east of the river, the depth to the edge of the river is 7,900 feet; from Hat Point in Oregon, three miles west of the river, the depth to the edge of the river is 5,620 feet. The Grand Canyon of the Colorado from Bright Angel Point, seven miles from the river, has a depth of 5,650 feet.

From Huntington to Lewiston, the Snake River descends an average of nine feet to the mile—in some stretches more than 12 feet per mile.

Only the upper part of the canyon is traversed by a road whose course mostly follows an old railroad grade. Below Hells Canyon Dam there is no road for more than 90 miles.

The 1,282 feet of difference in elevation between Huntington (at 2,020 feet) and Lewiston (at 738 feet) has led to the construction of the three hydroelectric dams within a distance of 30 miles.

For almost two thirds of its course, the river has cut completely through the Columbia River basalts, which are up to 6,000 feet thick, and as much as 2,000 feet into the underlying older rocks, which date from the Permian to the Cretaceous period, from 75 million to 250 million years ago.

The older rocks consist mostly of volcanic sediments (volcanoclastics) and lava flows, with lesser amounts of conglomerate, limestone and shale. All of them have been sheared and broken, in places into a "melange" of giant isolated blocks in a matrix of ground-up rock.

The volcanic rocks have metamorphosed into greenstones and the limestones into marble. These altered sediments and lavas comprise a 4- to 6-mile thick sequence of Permian to upper Jurassic age that was deposited in the ocean that covered Oregon during that period.

The episodes of mountain-making that folded, faulted and intruded the older rocks during the Jurassic and Cretaceous periods (160 million to 75 million years ago) were followed by a 60 million-year-long period of erosion during the lower Tertiary.

During the late Jurassic, several batholiths of gabbo, diorite and granite were intruded. Eighty million years later in the late Cretaceous, the sediments were again intruded by granites of the same age as the Idaho batholith.

The 60 million-year-long period of quiescence was long enough to reduce the relief of the mountains to less than 1,000 feet and to expose 11 originally deep-seated granite intrusions, before the area was inundated by the basalt floods in the middle Miocene times, about 16 million years ago. The river has now exposed the tops of these ancient mountains.

Earlier Wanderings of Snake River Lost Amid Basalt Floods

(2 of 3)

About 18 million years ago, basalt floods from long north-south trending fissures near the present Snake River and in the Wallowa Mountains began to cover the plateau near the river.

These Imnaha basalts of the middle Miocene were followed, a million years later, by the Picture Gorge basalts that covered an area in the center of Oregon in the present drainage of the John Day River.

Finally, about 16 million years ago, the Yakima basalts, the greatest flood of all, began to pour out by thousands of cubic miles, eventually to inundate much of eastern Oregon and Washington and western Idaho, covering the older rocks to a depth of several thousand feet, across 50,000 square miles, and finally reaching the ocean along the northern Oregon coast.

The floods of Imnaha basalt were fed from miles-long vertical north-south trending fissures and cooled to form "dikes," up to more than 50 feet thick, that now stand out as long narrow ridges, cutting across the slopes.

In the canyon, they are not easy to spot, but in the Wallowa Mountains where they cut through white granite, many of them can be seen running across the ridges for up to three miles. When I was mapping the Wallowas in the late 1930s, I mapped 82 such dikes and noted 42 more. The total length of those mapped was more than 50 miles.

Before the basalt floods, the Snake River had a much different but still unknown course. Remnants of river gravels resting on granite beneath the lava flows are found high in the Wallowa Mountains. Beneath the basalt cap of Lookout Mountain at 8,800-feet elevation, a 50-foot thick bed of gravel contains giant rounded boulders of quartzite, which could only have come from far to the east in the Rockies.

Ancient river gravels also have been found 60 miles west of the present Snake River at 6,000-feet elevation near Greenhorn, 30 miles west of Baker City in the Elkhorn Mountains. They contained the petrified fossil stumps of the tree fern tempskya, of the lower Cretaceous age. The basalt is so extensive that the pre-basalt course of the Snake River may never be determined.

After the basalt floods, the Snake River was dammed by the lavas, forming a great late Tertiary lake called "Lake Payette," in the valley to the south and east of Huntington. In this lava-dammed basin, lake beds up to 3,000 feet thick were laid down, forming the "Payette Formation" that contains numerous remains of the animals and plants which existed during the late Miocene and early Pliocene.

H.E. Wheeler and E.F. Cook proposed, in 1954, that during this period the waters from Lake Payette might have escaped up the Owyhee drainage, south into the Nevada Great Basin, and eventually westward into the Feather River.

Uplift of the Wallowa and Seven Devil Mountains probably began in the late Miocene or early Pliocene, perhaps as much as ten million years ago. If the uplift began ten million years ago, the river would only have to cut down at a rate of .84 inches per 100 years in order to keep up with the rising land.

At the same time, two sets of major faults, one trending a little east of north and the other northwest, began to break the course up into great blocks, some of which dropped down to form the Baker and Grande Ronde valleys. Both these valleys were once occupied by lakes, which have since filled with sediments.

Other blocks, such as the Blue Mountains, Elkhorns, Seven Devils and Wallowas, began to be uplifted, folded and faulted. The great north wall of the Wallowas above Joseph and Enterprise was formed by one such northwest-trending fault, which has uplifted the peaks by nearly two miles.

Snake River Follows Fault Line Along Part of Its Course

3 of 3

In the last two weeks, we have discussed the early history of the Snake River Canyon. Now we will try to explain how the river attained its present course.

Since rivers usually follow lines of weakness in the rocks, the straight course of the Snake River in its gorge now follows fault lines along at least a part of its course. These fault lines are not simple fractures—they frequently are broad zones where rocks have been crushed and broken as the sides of the faults moved against each other.

The Snake River Canyon follows such fault zones, which trend a little east of north over much of its lower course. The courses of much of the Grande Ronde and Imnaha valleys in Oregon and the Salmon River valley in Idaho probably resulted from those rivers following such fault lines.

One hypothesis describing a possible course of the Snake River during the early Pleistocene was suggested by D.C. Livingstone in 1928. He proposed that when Lake Payette in the Idaho basin to the south overflowed, it passed up the Powder River valley, through the Baker and Grande Ronde valleys and down the Grand Ronde River Canyon. Instead of spilling over through a low gap to immediately form its present course, the ancestral Snake River wound through these basins and across the plateau in a series of meanders now preserved in the incised bends of the lower Grande Ronde River.

The Snake River above the mouth of the Grande Ronde was a tributary, which rapidly ate its way headward through a low point north of the Oxbow and eventually captured the main drainage at the mouth of the Powder River, draining the upper Miocene-lower Pliocene Lake Payette.

Wheeler and Cook disagreed with this hypothesis in 1954. They pointed out that the sediments of the Payette Formation are separated from the later thinner sediments of the Idaho Formation, and used the term "Lake Idaho" for this later lake. They believe that Lake Idaho spilled through the gap a few miles below the Oxbow at about 3,300 feet elevation into a tributary of the Salmon River.

This means that the lower 1,600 feet of the gorge was cut during the last two million years or so, at a rate of about one inch per hundred years. This is a little more than the rate of erosion for the gorge as a whole, but we know that during the ice age, the rivers in the Northwest were larger than before or after. The catastrophic Bonneville Flood of 15,000 years ago must have done a lot of work, too.

As the Snake River Canyon approached its present depth, there were several periods when the river reached a temporary base level and had to expend its energy in widening rather than deepening the valley. Each time it widened the valley, it deposited gravels and sands that now form terraces, some of which contain fine flour gold.

There are a series of at least three terraces, one above another, along the banks of the upper part of the canyon. Perhaps terracing occurred in part when the valley, far to the north in Washington, was filled with intracanyon lava, raising the base level.

During one of these terracing periods, the river formed a broad meander at the Oxbow. When the downstream obstruction was removed, the river began to cut down and preserve the unique incised meander now found there.

I mapped these terraces during the late 1930s, and discovered that they had been raised and arched by folding, which must have continued well into the Pleistocene. The higher terraces were arched more than the low ones.

Summer thunderstorms occasionally produce flash floods that come down the side canyons and spread out their debris to form alluvial fans, which in a few places extend out into the river to form temporary partial dams and later rapids in the river.

The hamlet of Homestead was built on one such fan, and it was devastated by a flash flood in the 1930s. Old-timers know that alluvial fans, although they can furnish relatively level ground and fresh water from shallow wells, are not good places to build a house.

There are at least 11 groups of mining claims in the older rocks around Homestead and copperfield, but the only one that produced significantly was the Iron Dyke Mine at Homestead three miles north of Oxbow.

The Iron Dyke was discovered in 1897 and had several tunnels. The lower tunnel was 1,300 feet long and rich copper ore was mined there from a body 140 feet wide and 210 feet long which was encountered at 800 feet. As late as 1980, it was being explored for possible unmined reserves.

Two miles north of Homestead the famous Kleinschmidt Grade climbs for ten miles up the east wall of the canyon in a series of hair-raising bends to Cuprum, 4,000 feet above the river, where the Red Ledge Mine operated many years ago. The first seven miles of road climbs 3,500 feet, or 500 feet per mile.

Wallowa Batholith Covers 324 Square Miles

The Wallowa Mountains are made up of a massive, granite-like rock formation that is twice the size of the next largest similar formation in Oregon (Bald Mountain, northeast of Baker City).

The formation, called a batholith, is a body of granitic, igneous rock that is exposed over an area greater than 40 square miles and that cooled so slowly deep beneath the surface, that its crystals grew to a size where they can be seen by a hand lens. Since they cooled at depths of at least a mile, they must have later been exposed by long-continued uplift and erosion.

Most batholiths are at least five million to ten million years old; those in Oregon are nearly 100 million years old. Oregon's batholiths are not true granite; they are "granodiorite," which means that unlike granite, they contain no quartz, and the potassium found in granite is in large part replaced by sodium and calcium.

There are eight batholiths in Oregon, and many bodies of granodiorite covering less than 40 square miles. The smaller bodies are called "stocks" or "plutons." Six of the eight batholiths are found in the Klamath and Siskiyou mountains of Southern Oregon, the one at Grants Pass being the largest, with an exposed area covering 102 square miles.

The Ashland and Persall Peak batholiths cover 96 square miles each; one southeast of Roseburg covers 90 square miles, and one near Wilmer just makes the grade with 40 square miles.

Northeastern Oregon has only two batholiths, but they are both larger by far than those in the southwest part of the state. The Bald Mountains batholith, which lies northwest of Baker City in the Elkhorn Range, covers 144 square miles, and the largest of all, the Wallowa batholith, is exposed over 324 square miles.

The northeastern Oregon batholiths are both between 90 million and 150 million years, according to the few potassium argon radioactive datings available. This means that they came up from below the lower Cretaceous, when the ancestral Blue Mountains were first folded up and intruded, at about the same time that the Rocky Mountains were first formed.

Both mountain ranges were deeply eroded and the batholiths exposed during the ensuing 50 million years, and then only recently (during the last 15 million years) uplifted to their present heights.

In fact, the worn-down remnants of the ancestral Wallowa Mountains were covered by the Columbia River Basalt Floods between 17 million and 13 million years ago. The floods came up through vertical, north-south trending cracks in the granodiorite and the older rocks, some of which were from one to two miles in length.

More than 100 great black lava dikes can easily be seen coursing across the white granodiorite.

An ancestral Snake River must have crossed the present site of the range before the basalt filled its valley. Proof of this is found in a bed of river gravel up to 30 feet thick that was found lying upon the grandiorite at an elevation of 8,800 feet beneath the capping of Columbia River basalts that forms the summit of Lookout Mountain, 13 miles southwest of Enterprise.

This early Tertiary gravel contains round boulders of water-worn and polished quartzite, aplite (from white granitic dikes) and other igneous and metamorphic rocks up to three feet in diameter. The quartzite boulders are nearly all scarred with crescentic "chatter marks," and make up more than 20 percent of the bed.

Quartzite is a metamorphic rock, derived from sandstone that has been so deeply buried and recrystallized that the original sand grains have been cemented together by silica to form one of the hardest and most resistant rocks known.

These boulders must have traveled long distances in a large turbulent river to have become so well-rounded. The chatter marks are signs that the boulders bounced along the riverbed and were scarred by heavy impacts.

In the western part of the Wallowa quadrangle, 16 other peaks above 8,000 feet in elevation have small cappings of basalt lying upon the granodiorite. Many of these cappings lie along the crest of the ridge west of the Lostine River.

Any study of the elevations of the base of the basalt in the Wallowa Mountains shows that the granitic surface over which the basalt flowed had a relief of from 500 to perhaps as much as 1,500 feet.

The ridge west of the Lostine River may have been in the valley of the Snake River 17 million to 50 million years ago, another example of reversed topography like the Table Rocks north of Medford, where the ancient Rogue River was filled with a lava flow that now stands high above the valley.

The great north escarpment of the Wallowa Mountains that trends northwesterly for at least 15 miles was formed during the last ten million years by a major fault.

The base of the Columbia River basalts southwest of the fault lies at above 8,000 feet in the Wallowas, and the top of the basalt northeast of the fault lies at about 5,000 feet or less, beneath Joseph and Enterprise.